everyone

has

a

story

to

tell

HEAD *ON*
STORIES OF
ALOPECIA

Deeann Callis Graham

Head-On, Stories of Alopecia
Photos & Text Coordinated by Deeann Callis Graham

Published 2015 by Head-On Publishing
Sedro-Woolley, WA 98284
www.headonpublishing.com

Publisher: Head-On Publishing
Project Coordinator/Author: Deeann Callis Graham
Layout & Design: Kristan Lloyd
Foreword: Margaret H. Baker

Library of Congress Control Number: 2015906873

ISBN: 978-0-9962444-1-1

First Edition
10 9 8 7 6 5 4 3 2 1

Printed in the United States of America

To order additional copies and for more information about this book, please visit us online at www.headonpublishing.com

Dedicated to Kyla and Lyric who are wonderful, unique, and beautiful children with qualities to match their firm convictions about how the world should behave.

Table of Contents

Foreword

Houghton Mifflin defines identity as, "the awareness that an individual or group has of being a distinct, persisting entity." But what is identity really? And can it exist in the absence of stereotypes?

What in life defines you?

In preschool, we have *No biases; No fear of difference; No grouping; Only Sameness.* But as we grow and develop a vocabulary, adjectives begin to play an important role. Labels are created and opinions are formed based on past and present stimuli. We are all guilty of this. It's our primal fight or flight response to potential danger. We formulate stories to assimilate rather than accepting just…What is!

Many favorite childhood games identify sameness through the matching of pictures. But what happens when your picture has no match? How does one feel, when the image staring back at you is strikingly different than it was years, months, weeks, or even days before?

Your life dangles from a delicate thread - as you try to piece together the broken you in an old point of view. It is vulnerable and painful. Raw and Real. We find ourselves naked and exposed, with no way of hiding while hanging onto our authentic selves. A fate we may never fully accept, but adapt to over time because we must. The fear that accompanies loss, forces us to shed our old skins, beliefs, and thoughts for anew. And once we are able to let go, abundance flows.

The men and women featured in this book remind us that when you accept yourself, you become the magician in your own life, making the impossible eminently possible. As Nelson Mandela once said, "It always seems impossible until it's done." We have a tendency to compare our journeys in life. But we are all in this together. Our individual lives are tributaries leading to the same great body of water called life. Everyone will identify with this book. No journey is greater than the last and none shall surpass those to come. When we accept that we are part of something larger than ourselves, we begin to breathe.

As I write this, I wear no cover. I am the primed canvas of the life that's chosen me. My bald body is my purple heart, my badge of courage. I bare its crown with pride, now boldly standing beside my siblings sans hair. Over time, I have learned that it's not whether I don scarves, hats, or wigs that matters; as long as I remain authentic and embrace my beautiful bald reality, head on.

Margaret H. Baker has worked in multiple facets of entertainment, striving to create a public platform that celebrates female talent outside of Hollywood's traditional beauty norm. Margaret has traveled the globe, working as an international spokesperson on behalf of the alopecia community. She is co-creator of, Women Behaving Baldly, a major television project currently in development which uncovers the emotional truths of being bald and female today in the land of big hair. Merging her talents as writer, actress, singer, model, and international spokesperson, Margaret's work aims to celebrate the human condition at its deepest core. www.margarethbaker.com

"No one who achieves success does so without acknowledging the help of others. The wise and confident acknowledge this help with gratitude."

Alfred North Whitehead, English Mathematician

Acknowledgements

This book never would have made it to press had it not been for all of the willing storytellers who readily passed their stories over to me, entrusting I would appropriately care for and share them in the way I saw fit. I cannot thank the writers enough for freely sharing, not only their words, but also their vulnerability. They set in motion the possibility to change perception, raise awareness, and continue to take steps toward celebrating their own alopecia.

When I started this project, I wanted intriguing black and white images that would emphasize the message of each writer's story. Some photos were taken by family or friends, but the majority of them were taken by professional photographers who wanted to help give visual life to the book. I am incredibly thankful to all of the photographers who generously offered their time and creativity. The images clearly show how passionate they are about their work.

Things to think about as you read: For those of you who are unfamiliar with alopecia areata, please take note of some of the common misconceptions that surround us in our daily lives.

*Alopecia is not cancer.
    Wherever we are in our journey, we are constantly confronted with questioning looks and inquiries about our "cancer." As you read along, my hope is that when you see someone without hair, you will think "alopecia" just as many times as you do "cancer."

*Alopecia areata and hair loss is not "easier" for men and boys.
    Feeling and looking different is not easy for any of us, especially as children. It is important to understand that comments like, "Well, at least he's a boy. So it's no big deal." or "At least you're a guy. It's totally acceptable for men to be bald" minimize the sense of loss men and boys are experiencing. This double standard is one that clearly needs to be extinguished.

Look at us. See us for who we are. Each of us is a gifted, unique, beautiful, and accomplished individual - just like you.

Introduction

When I started losing my hair again, all I wanted to do was feel better about myself. I wanted to stop feeling inadequate, embarrassed, and devastated by my hair loss. I also felt guilty for comparing my own tiny sense of loss to the much bigger ones around me. My fixation on all of these things was hindering my ability to fully participate in life.

In my thirty years of living with alopecia, I had never met another person with the same condition. I had never seen any photos or read any stories I could personally connect with about my alopecia.

What began as daily journaling soon turned into pages and pages of my story and the realization that there must be others who also had stories to tell. After reaching out and discovering I was not alone, I finally began connecting with those who understood.

I shared my vision for this project, and story submissions started piling up on my desk. Photographers started materializing, seemingly out of nowhere. Everyone was excited about the possibility of making a difference with their photos and stories.

On a personal level, this book is exactly what I would have wanted when I was seven years old and feeling lonely and confused: beautiful photos and the discovery of how to move beyond my experience by sharing, finding value in my own talents, and pushing the limitations of society.

On a much bigger scale, *Head-On, Stories of Alopecia* has the potential to be something more remarkable. I know it's ambitious to think the world's perception of hair, beauty, and worth can be transformed with this book, but I am confident these powerful stories and photos have the ability to alter these perceptions in HUGE ways.

Alopecia 101

Throughout the book, many of the writers refer to alopecia areata, totalis, or universalis simply as "alopecia."

As you read, you'll often see reference to a number of the below listed words. For the sake of simplicity while reading, shortened versions and abbreviations are also listed. Please note the listed resource links for additional information.

Alopecia Areata (AA) - Alopecia areata is considered an autoimmune disease, in which the immune system, which is designed to protect the body from foreign invaders such as viruses and bacteria, mistakenly attacks the hair follicles, the structures from which hairs grow. This can lead to hair loss on the scalp and elsewhere. In most cases, hair falls out in small, round patches about the size of a quarter. In many cases, the disease does not extend beyond a few bare patches. In some people, hair loss is more extensive. www.niams.nih.gov/Health_Info/Alopecia_Areata

Alopecia Totalis (AT) - Total loss of hair on the scalp.

Alopecia Universalis (AU) - Complete loss of hair on the scalp, face, and body.

Cicatricial Alopecia (Scarring Alopecia) - The cause of cicatricial alopecia is not well understood. Redness, heat, pain, or swelling occurs at the upper part of the hair follicle. That is where stem cells and sebaceous (oil) glands are located. Stem cells are cells that can develop into different kinds of cells. If the stem cells and oil glands are destroyed, the hair follicle cannot regrow, and hair is permanently lost. www.niams.nih.gov/health_info/Cicatricial_Alopecia

Androgenic Alopecia (AGA) - Women who have androgenetic alopecia usually have increased thinning or diffuse hair loss all over. It is most noticeable at the part line and top area just behind the bangs, while often maintaining the front hairline. Androgenetic alopecia causes a woman's hair follicles to become more sensitive to hormones, or androgens that already exist within the body. Inside these follicles are androgen receptors. The androgens (hormones) tell the androgen receptors to produce less hair. Consequently, the individual hair growth cycle is shortened while hair becomes thinner and finer. Even though the follicle itself is still intact, it becomes "miniaturized" and eventually will not produce new hair. www.herhairlosshelp.com/2015/03/treatment-for-androgenetic-alopecia-in-women

Although androgenic alopecia is not considered an autoimmune disease, resulting hair loss and the emotional effects are identical. AGA also affects men, and is commonly referred to as "male pattern baldness."

National Alopecia Areata Foundation (NAAF), also referred to as "conference"

Canadian Alopecia Areata Foundation (CANAAF)

Children's Alopecia Project (CAP)

Australia Alopecia Areata Foundation (AAAF)

Although a cure is not imminent, researchers are making headway toward a better understanding of the disease. This increased understanding will likely lead the way to better treatments for alopecia areata and eventually a way to cure it or even prevent it. Studying hair follicle development, understanding stem cell biology, finding genes (and genetic variations), and developing animal models are some promising areas of research right now. www.niams.nih.gov/Health_Info/Alopecia_Areata/#11

**FACT: 2.1% of the world's population (approximately 146 million people)
have had, do have, or will experience alopecia areata in their lifetime.**

While research has been ongoing for decades, answers are still relatively challenging and difficult to find.

Everyone's triggers are different, with no substantial common thread. Although most of us don't know exactly what our trigger was/is, many of us have a suspicion of cause. We have all been told something by our doctor, and the most common diagnosis is "stress."

"Stress" is such a loaded word. It somehow implies we are incapable of handling any slight difficulty in our lives. Inadequacies surface as we question our ability to deal with the things others seem completely adept at handling. How is it possible that our young child could be losing their hair because of stress? Is there something wrong with them, or is there something wrong with me that this would be the result? Doubts and questions are endless.

Whether they are educated guesses or actual medical diagnoses, the list below gives an idea of the many potential triggers/stressors I documented while collecting stories over the last several years. There will always be more to add:

Stress - Diet - Vitamin Deficiency - Stress - Gluten Intolerance - Divorce - Virus - Fungal Infection
Vaccines - Change in Your Environment - Tight Rubberbands - We Don't Really Know - Hair Dye
Leaky Gut - Tight Ponytails - Your Girlfriend Breaking Up with You - Your Response to a Death - Antibiotics
Anesthesia - Cornrows - Silicone Implants - Poor Nutrition - Having Another Autoimmune Disease
Car Accident - Hair Weaves or Extensions - Hair Relaxer - More Stress - Hormones - Genetic Predisposition
Surgery - Tooth Fillings - Eating Disorders - Hair Pulling - Giving Birth - Menopause - Frequent Blow Drying
Side Effect to Medication - Pets - Inflammation - Virus - Lyme Disease - Puberty - Gut Inflammation…

It is not just about healthy eating and living or the right spiritual attitude. Olympic athletes, marathon runners, vegetarians, yoga gurus, and even nuns have been diagnosed with alopecia areata. No matter what our religious beliefs, healthy or meditative lifestyles are, there does not seem to be a one-size-fits-all approach or result.

All of the below listed treatments were either prescribed by medical doctors, or suggested by therapists or well-meaning friends and family. The temptation to try all of them, regardless of how foolish they sound, shows how powerful the longing for hair is. It is important to remember what works for one may not work for another, and what worked once, oftentimes does not work again:

Anthralin - Minoxidil (Rogaine) - Topical Corticosteroids - Injected Corticosteroids - Topical Immunotherapy
(Diphenylcyclopropenone (DPCP) - Squaric Acid - Praying - Orthomolecular Medicine - Photochemotherapy
Rosemary - Essential Oils - Going Gluten Free - Cow Dung - Onion Juice - Garlic - Coconut Oil
Henna - Hibiscus - Indian Gooseberry - Going to Church - Egg - Iron Supplements - Vitamin D
Elimination Diet - Supplements - Whole Foods Diet - Tar Shampoo - Hot Peppers - Vegan Diet
Burdock - Nettle - Fish Oil - Ginger - Turmeric - Quercitin - Probiotics - Aloe Vera - Diprosone
Anti-Inflammatory Diet - Castor Oil - Acupuncture - Biotin - Aromatherapy - Paleo Diet - Kale Smoothie
Silica and Zinc - Vinegar - Pig Urine - Cayenne Pepper - Sage - Therapy to De-Stress - Yoga - Meditation
Praying More - Beer - Nioxin - Hormone Therapy - Having Another Baby - Getting Rid of Your Pets
Moving Somewhere Warm - Monistat 7 - Kenalog Injections - Coal Tar Shampoo - Multivitamins…

Deeann

This book, this labor of love, started out as a kind of therapy for me when my hair fell completely out for the second time. I wondered why there wasn't something positive and visual to help people cope with hair loss from alopecia areata. I also wanted to educate others who knew nothing about alopecia. Even though I did not know what it would be, I vowed to produce something that could help guide all of us who wrestled with our new identity.

Ten years ago, I found myself losing my hair again. I was caught up in all the emotions that happen when experiencing loss. I felt weak and self-centered for not coping better. Logically, I knew there were so many monumentally worse things that could be happening to me, but I still found myself fully immersed in grief.

So I wrote. I wept. I wailed. And then I wrote some more. I soon discovered I didn't want to write about pain any longer. I knew what I would have wanted when I was first diagnosed. Stories of possibilities:

possibilities of how my life with alopecia might play out; possibilities of how living life without hair could be beautiful; and possibilities of having the pages reveal positive role models who were happily living their lives with alopecia. Soon, I regularly found myself meeting just these types of people. People who were incredibly driven - fashion designers, television hosts, musicians, mothers, nurses, teachers, coaches, and even a Miss America contestant...and they wanted to share their stories.

Discovery - Ask anyone with alopecia, and they will tell you their moment of discovery. It may have been a hairdresser, a friend standing above them, or like me – my mother found it.

I can still remember...

I can still hear her soft intake of breath as she combs my hair after a bedtime bath. I'm only seven years old and although I'm not all that intuitive, I still feel her concern. I turn to look at her and notice she's put her hand to her mouth, trying to quiet her gasp. I ask, "What's wrong?" until she finally gives in and wordlessly and gently places my fingers on a small bald spot toward the right side of my head. We rub the condensation off the mirror, and I awkwardly crane my head to try and see it. Now that I know it's there, it's easy to find. The spot feels clammy and strange, not like the same soft feel of skin on my arm or neck.

My mom tries to reassure me that it's nothing, and I believe her. We quietly get ready for bed, not giving much energy to this new-found "thing." I'm not worried as I drift off to sleep. One of us sleeps well that night. My seven-year-old self is unaware that my parents stay awake, quietly talking long into the night. Their questions go unanswered. There is no internet to tell them what it is. Will it go away? Will it get bigger? There are just too many questions and no immediate answers.

Diagnosis - *The next thing I remember, is being in a doctor's office. He tells us there is a name for it, and it's called, "alopecia areata." "Is there a cure?" my mother asks. He shrugs his shoulders, "No. Not really, but take this cream home and put it on her head several times a day to try and stimulate hair growth."*

I look intently at the doctor as he gives me this bleak diagnosis, and all I remember thinking is, "Wow. This guy is really orange." His complexion is an unnatural shade of orange. The white of his doctor's coat is so stark in contrast to his orange face. "Carrots. Maybe he eats too many carrots." I can't stop staring. "So... orange," keeps repeating over and over in my mind as I look at him.

Little did I know that my earnest curiosity about him was giving me a glimpse of what I would soon experience for the rest of my life. Adults, children, family members, and strangers would stare at me and wonder: Was I contagious? Was I dying? Was I in pain? Did I have cancer?

Coping - In my family, we dealt with things quietly. We didn't give a lot of time or conversation to feeling sorry for ourselves. After all, this wasn't our first time dealing with a challenging diagnosis. I had been diagnosed with Type 1 diabetes after being admitted to the hospital when I was two years old

and dangerously close to going into a coma. Being and feeling different wasn't foreign to me. I already hid the fact that I needed insulin injections to stay alive, and while the other kids played at recess, I sat alone and grudgingly ate my mandatory mid-morning snack. Now, I also felt the need to conceal my hair loss in an effort to blend in as much as possible.

Although we were given the very basic skills to manage diabetes, managing alopecia involved more than the medical community would provide. We were very much on our own emotionally and medically in both situations. As a family, we failingly tried to make our way out of the puzzling maze we were in. Without realizing, we became a product of the system, one that trusted the advice of doctors, didn't ask too many questions, and passively accepted this as our new normal.

You must know by now, the magic cream didn't work. We did not try anything more because nothing else was offered. We moved, and I started at a new school. By the time I began third grade, I was mostly bald. I wore a limited number of hats that had the sole purpose of covering my bald head. After several months of hats, my parents took me to get my first wig. Although I was excited about the possibility of looking and feeling normal again, I also resented having to do it at all.

It's like it was yesterday…

I step out of the car and stare at the sign that reads, "Lynn Gaye Wigs." As we pull the heavy glass door open, all I can look at is the speckled linoleum floor. My parents explain who we are. "I have been waiting for you," she says. I am drawn to her serene voice. When I look up, I am immediately struck by how beautiful she is, especially with her long dark hair. I notice almost identical wigs on Styrofoam display heads behind her and begin to imagine how I will look in one. Will I be just as beautiful as her?

I start feeling hopeful. Lynn Gaye asks permission to take my hat off. My face flushes with embarrassment as I allow

My Story Continues . . .

her to look at me. She places her hand on the smooth skin of my head. Her touch feels motherly and loving, and she knowingly nods at me as if she understands. She spends the next hour measuring my head and talking about what color and length I want my new hair to be.

Many years later, I found out she was bald too and that the hair she wore was not her own. Looking back, the bond we had that moment in the salon was unbreakable. Maybe I was intuitive after all. I'm surprised at what I am experiencing even now as I write this. I am crying, knowing what a world of difference it would have made to know that someone else looked like me and truly understood. Strange as it sounds, it would be almost thirty more years before I would finally meet someone else who had alopecia.

A custom-made wig was ordered for me that day, and at a later date I returned to have it fitted to my head. I soon discovered the wig was oppressive in the California heat, and the sense of freedom I yearned for simply wasn't there. I went back to school the same day and thought I could actually fool people into thinking it had grown back and was my own. I was wrong and was immediately flooded with questions of, "Is that your hair? Is that a wig?"

The Next Step - To make a long story somewhat short, I made the best of it. I spent time learning how to do a cherry drop off the monkey bars with my wig still attached to my head (wig tape didn't exist in those days) and had a huge accomplishment of winning a relay race against my fourth grade nemesis. I wrote an award-winning essay which won me a trip to Disneyland, swam bald in the community pool, went camping with my Girl Scout troop, and had crushes on all the popular boys. My fantastic group of friends stuck up for me when I walked down the hall. They were my protectors from the ever-present hands that tried to yank my wig off. When standing in line for the drinking fountain, I purposely angled my body sideways so the back of my head was never exposed to the crowd. It only took one telltale tug

on the back of my wig, while getting a drink, to learn that lesson. The helpless feeling of my wig slipping out of my not-so-quick grasp and plopping into my small puddle of shame, was enough for my self-preservation instincts to kick in.

I had an older sister who treated me like I was a pest, and a younger one who had concerns of her own with trying to take a full breath of air after her diagnosis of asthma. They never looked at me like I was different, and I was just a "sister" to them. My parents pushed me to "be tough and strong" through it all, rising to the challenge of all the life lessons I was presented with. My faith in a God was one that I often questioned and struggled with. Any doubts I felt about my lot in life, were stifled by my new coping mechanism of "being strong and pushing ahead."

My life went on like this for another seven years. I learned to "deal," and it wasn't so bad. Then, something happened. The summer before eighth grade, my hair made a spontaneous return. It grew back just as quick as it had fallen out. My older sister gave me a retro haircut, and I set about feeling normal after so many years of not feeling anything close to normal. Getting absorbed in my new identity was easy. I was no longer hiding behind a wig and wondering what life would look like from the other side. I was finally there. Boys were paying attention to me. Strangers weren't feeling sorry for me. What more could a fourteen-year-old girl ask for? Life was good! Or so I thought.

For the next few years, my hair had a life of its own. It was like a rebellious teenager who came and went as it pleased. Most of it hung around, but then it started acting "funny" again - a small spot developing here or there. I worked to cover these new spots with eyeshadow that never quite matched. I moved with my family to another state and was ready to start anew, without anyone's knowledge of my days as a bald girl. I succeeded in never telling anyone about it but constantly struggled to hide new spots that developed, grew in, and then showed up somewhere else. I became an adult, moved out on my own, got a job, traveled, had a boyfriend, and when my hair started rapidly falling out again, I decided to see a dermatologist. This one, was the first I'd seen since the "orange" one.

He assured me my hair would regrow quickly with steroid injections. After several appointments and relatively little results, I arrived to what would unbeknownst to me, be my last appointment with him. Right away, I noticed his dominant arm was cradled in a cast and sling. When I doubtfully looked at him, he guaranteed that he absolutely could perform the injections. Against my better judgment, I went ahead and allowed him to do it. He failed miserably. To this day, I still remember the sensation of my fingertips frantically pushing against the pits and mountains he had created by the injections in my once smooth scalp. I was absolutely horrified! Why was I doing this to myself? What was I thinking? That was it! In that moment, I decided to never mistreat my body ever again for the sake of hair.

I tried not to resist what my hair naturally wanted to do, and it held on for a while longer. Life went on. I met a wonderful man, got married, opened a business, and we eventually started a family. During my pregnancy, my hair took a drastic turn for the worse, and the top two thirds of it fell out. I was consumed by my lack of hair while giving birth to our daughter. In the delivery room, I wore a wash cloth on my head to cool me, but it was mostly there to cover the glaringly obvious bald dome of my scalp. I was exposed in so many ways, but the thought of the wash cloth slipping off my head overshadowed one of the most amazing experiences of my life. Talk about not being in the moment! Then, six months later I had a full head of hair. A year later, almost complete loss again, and within another year, I struggled to know what to wear on my head as matron of honor in my friend's wedding.

Being the ever-sensible man, my husband simply suggested, "Just get a wig." I cringed at the idea of wearing a wig after so many years. It represented so many things for me: Loneliness; Hiding; Shame. Would wearing a wig make me feel better? If I got a wig, did that mean I believed my hair was never growing back? I still had a bit of hair at this point and didn't quite feel ready to give in. My options were pretty limited though. I could find a knit hat that would cover the wispy mad scientist hair I had left, or wear a dreaded wig. I reluctantly chose the wig. Buying a wig from a beauty supply store wasn't something I looked forward to. I can still remember the slightly nauseating smell of nail polish as I looked around. When I finally chose a few wigs to try on, the saleswoman helpfully and embarrassingly tugged my hat off while I stood in the middle of the store. I felt the need to escape as quickly as possible, and I hurriedly chose a long dark wig that resembled my hair at its very best. The wig did succeed in helping me feel more confident than I had in ages, but it was supposed to just be temporary hair until my own grew back. This was not to be. My hair continued to fall out until after my son was born three years later.

My husband, who had cautiously been waiting for me to make a decision about the last fragile bits of hair, strongly recommended that I, "Shave it off!" Admitting it wasn't coming back was still very difficult for me. Instead of taking action on my own and saying, "You're done!" and yanking it out, I quietly waited for it to tell me, "I'm all done." So...it stayed, until it didn't.

I was now completely bald, and I can truthfully say I was thankful to be off that crazy roller coaster. I could now finally concentrate on something other than my hair loss. I re-visited the idea of this book, and it slowly began to brew in the back of my mind. I needed more information, and during my research, I soon discovered a place where I thought all things alopecia might be found.

I can still feel my uncertainty…

My Story Continues…

Community - *While packing my suitcase for the trip cross country, I am torn between wearing a wig or a scarf to my first alopecia conference. I decide to wear my wig because that is how I am most comfortable in the world right now.*

I deliberately keep myself isolated by staying at a different hotel, eating alone, and walking ten blocks to get here. As I scrutinize the hotel from across the street, I am pleasantly surprised by what I see. There are just as many wig wearers, as there are bald heads. Although I'm still pre-occupied with the fact that I'm wearing a wig, I now feel like I have the ability to fit in with at least one group. After a few minutes of lingering, I covertly try to enter the building like any other hairy person and head to the registration area.

My fixation on the wig reminds me of why I'm here: information; meeting others with alopecia; the book. Throughout the day, I navigate from one session to another, finally ending up in one called, "Women and Alopecia." I soon find myself sitting next to a young woman, and halfway through the session I clasp her hand in between mine while she sobs and tells the story of her younger years, when all the kids in school tried to hit her wig off during dodgeball. My heart physically hurts as her story triggers memories of my own tortured dodgeball experience. I had never wanted anyone else to feel what I was going through, but in this moment, the realization is clear that I am not alone and I never have been.

At conference, I discover having Kleenex is a necessity. It is a time to sit together and share our experiences, ask for help, and move toward finding solutions. As I look around, I realize most participants are first-timers who need answers, and the others have returned to reconnect with friends they have made in previous years.

That first year, I keep mostly to myself. After an intense day in sessions, I decide to check out the view from the top of the hotel. The lobby is fairly empty, and there are only a few of us getting on the elevator in the middle of the day. It's just me, two children and their mothers. The mothers look shell-shocked. Their nametags reveal this is their first conference too. I can tell we've all reached our capacity for information and just want to step away from it all. The

kids don't know each other, but they don't let that get in the way of conversation. They make faces at each other in the mirrored elevator doors and talk about their day at camp. As the elevator slowly ascends, we smile as we observe their interaction. The mothers' expressions abruptly change from smiles to concern as one child casually asks the other, "Are you a girl or a boy?" Before the mother can apologize, the question has been answered and then asked again by the other child. They each nod, smile, and become buddies for the remaining fourteen floors. I feel young again and decide to embrace this moment. It's bittersweet, to witness what I could have had – the ability to not feel so alone.

The moment passes, and I realize this innocent interaction is so telling of how we are all identified. As I look at the children, I see the nuances that tell them apart. Although they both wear blue basketball shorts and white camp t-shirts, I see the very tiny earrings in the earlobes of one child and can just barely make out the thin pink stripes on the other's light blue tennis shoes. The elevator doors open and with a little wave, each family goes their separate way.

The next day, I go out for lunch. Although I notice a large group of parents and kids who are obviously from conference, I decide to sit alone. I watch them from my booth and after a while decide to try an experiment. I ask my waitress, who is very young and wide-eyed, if she knows what is, "going on with that group of people?" She looks at me and stage whispers in a high pitched and serious tone, "It's some kind of chemo conference." "Oh." I say as my sparse eyebrows arch in disbelief, and I continue to look at my menu. I barely have time to wonder what I will say next, before the words tumble out of my mouth. "Actually, it's not a chemo conference. All of them have an autoimmune condition called alopecia. I also have it." Without responding, she takes my order and proceeds back to the kitchen. This is the first time I admit to a stranger that I have alopecia. My hands are shaking, and I feel the air conditioning cool the sweat that has surfaced on my skin. My waitress returns with a completely unpredictable question, "So...you don't have to shave your legs?" she asks. "Unbelievable! I have just bared my soul and this is what you're asking me?" I think. I can't stop my burst of laughter as I reply, "Umm...No." "That's cool," she says before leaving my table. Next thing I know, the entire kitchen staff leans out the double doors, trying to catch a glimpse of me. I'm not quite sure what they are hoping to see, but my long-held feelings of inadequacy are beginning to thaw, just a little bit. I leave the restaurant, energized to start sharing more with others.

When I return to the conference, closing ceremony is just starting. I watch a slideshow of the weekend as the kids swim in the pool and go on field trips. I notice their first day reluctance as they registered and went off to camp. As the slideshow progresses to the talent show and dance, I clearly see the transformation in them. They look like they have found a new home, and I can tell they are completely comfortable. This time, I have come prepared with my own wad of Kleenex, but I am not prepared for how deeply I am moved by the photographs. The kids. I decide, it's all about the kids. I realize, if I had only known just one other child who had alopecia as I grew up, the deep sense of loneliness I felt may have only been short lived. Instead, it followed me into adulthood.

I left the closing session with more direction of where I wanted to go with this book project. However, motivation and intention don't always result in something right away. The year went by, and I was able to consider living life without being covered up. So much of my life was spent trying to fit in: wearing a wig, hiding under a hat, or saying "thank you" when someone said how lovely my "hair" was, that I was exhausted by the end of each day. Something had to change.

Conference number two was much different. I left my wig at home. I slapped a color coordinated bandana on my head and went to the airport. When I arrived, I looked around, saw someone with alopecia and approached them, asking if they were attending the conference and if they would like to share a cab. It's not my recommendation to just go with anyone who has alopecia, but it worked and we made it safely to the hotel. At registration, I mistakenly got a VIP nametag which was normally meant only for first time attendees. I decided I would take it off after getting settled, but I inadvertently forgot about it as the

hours went by. This decision led to meeting a group of people who were essential in helping me continue on my path to restore my sense of self.

I smile as I remember…

"Hey, you're new!" says a voice behind me. I turn to see a young lady who looks as if she's stepped off the pages of Golf Digest in her polo shirt and checkered shorts. "You're coming with us." And you know what - I did. I find myself talking about alopecia with a group of women who can't be more different from me, but somehow we instantly connect on a profound level. We are an odd mix: one high school student on her way to being a golf pro, a college student working on her psychology degree, a mother and business owner, a successful fashion designer, a legal secretary, a geologist, and a waitress and historian with a unique infatuation with Abraham Lincoln. We leave the hotel to get something to eat. I feel my confidence continue to grow as we form a united front and strut down the street. We don't know where we are going, but it's as if we know, that metaphorically, we will arrive there together.

We're not just a group of people who have alopecia and meet up once a year. Our bonds run deep because of our alopecia connection, but we have also become life-long friends who genuinely care about one another. Over the years, we have traveled together as often as possible, been there in spirit for engagements and weddings, births, and graduations, and continue to support each other through the more difficult times. At one time or another, we've each been the hand that helped the other across the wide expanse of uncertainty that came with our alopecia diagnosis.

"Personal transformation can and does have global effects.
As we go, so goes the world, for the world is us.
The revolution that will save the world is ultimately a personal one."
Marianne Williamson, American Author

Emily Macauley

Corrine

Alopecia is a word unbeknownst by the majority of the population. Yet this disease deeply impacts millions of sufferers who are largely unrecognized around the world. The onset is rarely predicted and is never easy for those involved. I was eight when I started to lose my hair. It was 1976, a world away from a quick online fact check for symptoms, cures, and support. My young mother was in tears, and we were all alone. At that time, alopecia was an enigma, one the medical world tried to solve with the injection of hundreds of unnecessary needles and the application of burning creams on my scalp, none of which ever worked. With the onset of modern science, a cure may finally be close at hand, but women with alopecia still hide in the shadows, afraid to be themselves because society has not come to terms with the meaning of hair.

Throughout my childhood and into my teens, the only other remedy available, besides the painful medications, was to suffer under awkward wigs. I never felt fully safe or secure, and taunting and teasing from neighborhood children forced my parents to move me to a new grade school. Bullies called me Kojak because I wore glasses, and because they knew I was bald beneath my conspicuous wig. In seventh grade, a boy threw a fake spider on my head. Someone innocently tried to swat it off and the wig came with it. I ran into the nurse's office and hid for the rest of the day. Near the end of high school, enough hair grew back so I could part and pull it into some kind of hairstyle that feigned semi-normalcy.

As the years progressed, I toyed with the idea of getting rid of what was left and enjoying a life uninhibited from the worries of covering up. But somehow, that possibility seemed unfathomable

Corrine's Story Continues . . .

in such a hair-oriented society. Girls with luscious heads of hair plastered the covers of almost every magazine, and celebrity haircuts became the center of water cooler talk the next day. My friends obsessed about their hair, while talk shows seemed to feature endless segments on hair styles, hair makeovers, and hair products. Walk into any grocery store, and it's quite noticeable that the section of hair products is just as big as the natural foods or vitamin section. Americans fret more about their hair than their health. However, one day I got angry at never having a choice about my hair, and my notions became reality.

In 2006, I was rear-ended on my way to work. Most of my hair had fallen out again, and at the time I was wearing scarves. The force of the impact was so great that my scarf and glasses went flying. I couldn't find either one, and by the time the police arrived, I was forced to leave the car and stand on the highway, unable to see and with whatever strands of hair I had left just hanging. Instead of feeling upset that my car was totaled, I was embarrassed at the humiliation I felt from being exposed. The next day, I found a razor and took control of my life. I finally felt powerful and had a new confidence! The positive reaction of my friends and family members was invigorating. But almost as quickly as I started to bask in the happiness of being free and at peace with how God wanted me to be, something happened that I hadn't even considered. A little girl pointed at me in public and loudly said, "Mommy. That lady doesn't have any hair!"

The reason women with alopecia do not fit within societal norms is based on the perception of hair throughout recorded history. Cultures and societies have viewed hair differently, and many past ideas still permeate modern society. Shana Alexander, a prominent American journalist, once wrote, "Hair brings one's self-image into focus. It is vanity's proving ground. Hair is terribly personal, a tangle of mysterious prejudices." Hair represents self, the human perception of the world, and the human perception of each other. It can show status, acceptance, power, and virtue. Its social and cultural significance is evident in centuries of art, literature, and folklore. And because it is so easily changeable and magically rejuvenates itself, it has been given an almost mystical distinction.

Hair has been regarded as a fundamental female quality since almost the beginning of recorded history. As far back as ancient Egypt, women used hair extensions and wigs made of real hair or sheep's wool to enhance their beauty. The Greeks viewed hair as a means of self-expression, and hairdressing is mentioned in early works by Homer and Aristophanes. Biblical references in the book of Corinthians call hair the "glory to a woman," and in the 16th century, reformist Martin Luther referenced female hair as the "richest ornament of women." Hair not only reflected a woman's beauty, but was used to signify status or social class. During the Middle Ages, the hair of a single woman was generally worn long and visible. While a married woman would keep her hair up or covered. In 18th century France, no hairstyle was too grand for the aristocratic elite ladies who fought for top status. Lavishness ruled, and hair reached new heights, literally, as they showed off towering styles almost three feet off the wearer's head which actually required engineering tricks.

In the 20th century, women began to experience new political and social changes, particularly after the 19th Amendment to the U.S. Constitution was passed. After World War I, many women began to enter the workforce and enjoyed new freedom. As a result, hairstyles became shorter and more easily managed. During the turbulent '60s, the Afro became fashionable in the United States when more African Americans began to let their hair grow longer and assume its natural shape. For centuries, many African Americans had styled their hair to look like other men and women in the larger predominantly white society. For some, it represented freedom and independence from the older generation, as well as opposition to the attitudes of white America.

If it's true that a woman's hair has been historically associated with beauty and female identity, then it must be assumed that baldness is therefore representative of ugliness and masculinity. The concept of hair thus defines the concept of baldness. As a result, baldness has been used as a punishment geared specifically toward women in an attempt to strip them of their femininity. In some societies, women who committed adultery had their hair shaved off, as was true in India, some ancient Teutonic nations, and ancient Babylon. During the Inquisition in Germany in the 15th century, women accused of witchcraft were shaved and pricked with needles. Even in modern times, women thought to have been Nazi collaborators were publicly shaved and humiliated by the French resistance.

Hair has become so rooted in our minds over time as part of our culture and history, that it is almost impossible to detangle it from our psyche. So, why did that little girl point her finger at me? Because baldness has never been associated historically with women as a positive trait. Hair has played a significant part in women's history by representing beauty, status, and social class, but baldness has not. A bald man can walk down the street or stand in a crowd without drawing attention. Presidents, actors, and male athletes can sport a dome, and nobody will say a word. Yet, when a woman goes out in public without a lock of hair, fingers point and questions are inevitably asked. Why are people so shocked? Because the strong, undeniable link between hair and female identity has still not been broken, and even in our "modern" society, the public perception of female baldness is stuck in the past.

Female baldness still bears these stigmas in today's world. When a woman chooses to shave her head, she is thought to be rebellious or seriously ill. Remember when Britney Spears had a meltdown and was deemed "crazy" for shaving her head? Sinead O'Connor? When she recorded her first album, the label wanted to make her over into a doll-like sex symbol, and she responded by cutting all of her hair off. I am approached on a daily basis by strangers who insist I explain why I am bald. After all, what woman in her right mind would want to be void of her femininity and display it in public to boot?

Until we change our mindset about the importance of hair in our society and realize our history keeps bald women from ever being accepted as a societal norm, those who go free without cover will continually be approached. Why that girl pointed at me is, in essence, all of history repeating itself. Hair equates to beauty, acceptance, and female identity. It is even powerful enough to bond mothers and daughters. After all, what mother doesn't spend time at night brushing her daughter's hair before bed? Girls learn to wield a hairbrush long before they've even learned how to read. If people can understand how these ideas have been perpetuated, perhaps the next little girl in the store won't stop and point, but will quietly just wonder what I do at night before bed with my mommy if I don't have any hair to brush.

Corrine currently lives in the Philadelphia area, where she works as the director of client services for a meeting and consulting services company. When not working, she enjoys studying wines, going to museums, and traveling. She is blessed to have a wonderful family, many friends, a good sense of humor, and faith in God!

Sooner, Rather Than Later

Coming to terms with alopecia tends to happen progressively over time, but I promise you, it still does happen. Although it is never easy, it is more straightforward for some. While these stories appear to be abbreviated alopecia journeys, they are still infused with life lessons and challenges that all of us face.

Many young children often experience this shortened process because they have had alopecia areata all their lives, and dialogue in their family is open and accepting. Others possess a unique capability to quickly maneuver over the hurdles in front of them.

Whether they find it by simply seeing the logic in it, accepting the things they cannot change, or embracing the limitless possibilities, they find their sense of peace . . . sooner, rather than later.

"People come in all shapes, forms and sizes . . ." - **Dave**

"The main point of my story is that alopecia is not limiting." - **Marlina**

"I can do what other people do." - **Deryck**

"We approach alopecia with an "Oh, so what!" attitude." - **Deryck's parents**

"You don't need hair to breathe, move, talk, or eat." - **Franchesca**

"This is how God made me!" - **Lucy**

"So, now I'm the bald science fiction writer with a hat…" - **Rob**

"Whatever hair I have, I have, and what I don't have, I don't have." - **Jannica**

"I get to wear lots of pretty hats and different wigs. I call them my crowns." - **Madison**

"This experience has positively affected us all and made us a stronger family unit." - **Madison's Mom**

"Possibilities are endless when you really want something." - **Marina**

"It felt kind of scary at first to be bald, but then I kind of liked it." - **Dakota**

Dan Eden

Dave

I'd experienced mild effects of alopecia back in 2004, when a patch appeared above my right ear. I could hide it, but I recall worrying far too much about it which probably didn't help it to grow back!

In late 2005, I got glandular fever followed by shingles, and then all my hair fell out over about a week. It was a shock at first. I looked very different, especially once my eyebrows jumped ship. These days, it doesn't bother me at all.

The only people that have ever been unkind about it are exactly that, unkind. I tend to avoid shallow or ignorant folk and shrug off mean spirited comments.

I currently have pretty much no hair on my head at all (aside from a few blonde hairs). I guess this is easier for me than when it tries to grow back sometimes, as it causes me to shave daily to hide the patches. I have grown it out despite it looking rather strange

to some. I must admit, I do feel more comfortable wearing hats, plus it's obviously warmer in winter.

That's one of the funnier sides of alopecia. I've kind of become known for my preference for flat caps, which is a comfortable look for me. I probably have around twenty hats, more than your average bear. I often wear them out until they need to go to the flat cap graveyard.

My advice for anyone experiencing alopecia is to simply accept it and realise that you probably think about it far more than others. If it does "bother" others, then that's their problem! People come in all shapes, forms, and sizes, and if anyone isn't accepting of that, then they don't get what this is all about.

Alopecia isn't the end of the world, and it can be character building. My girlfriend has seen old photos of me and always says she prefers this me!

Dave McPherson is an English singer songwriter from London. Best known for his work as lead singer and principal songwriter in award winning British rock band InMe, he has success as a solo artist in his own right. Dave's recent album, Dreamoirs, was released in June 2014, and can be found at www.davemcpherson.bandcamp.com.

Sarah DeNeui

Marlina

Sharing Beginnings

My alopecia story begins, as I'm sure many do, with clumps of long blonde hair falling through my finger tips and flowing into an Arizona spring breeze. When I remember my hair falling out, I think about that scene from *Forrest Gump*, where the feather gently sways in the wind while the movie score plays in the background. I also picture my hair ending up in the tangle of an ever-gathering tumbleweed along Interstate 10. Much like a rogue tumbleweed or a floating feather, I too have "gone with the wind" and with me as always, is my gift of alopecia.

From Being Comfortable to Being Confident

When I was in high school, I was comfortable with my alopecia. I wore wigs. My close friends knew they were wigs. As I have come to find out, so did everyone else. I tried to hide my alopecia to make life easier—so I could be comfortable. From life experience, I have learned that hiding truths makes life only more difficult.

As I have developed and grown into an adult, I have become truly confident with my alopecia. When someone asks if I got a haircut, I emphatically reply, "I got a new wig! I have alopecia, so I am always wearing new wigs. Do you like this one?" Generally, the conversation evolves into something along the lines of, "That is a great wig! I would have never guessed. My uncle; sister; niece; friend; co-worker . . . has alopecia too." Before you know it, I have developed a tie with another person. That person now knows something personal about me. They feel I have opened up to them, and in turn, they now feel they can open up to me. Being confident with your alopecia develops close, trusting relationships with others.

My Husband is a Hunk

Depending on your experience with alopecia, marriage or intimate relationships may or may not be something you contemplate often. Being a mature eleven-year-old when I was diagnosed with alopecia, I almost immediately committed myself to being alone forever. "How will someone ever love me? That girl has hair, and I do not. Who would choose me?" This was a type of coping mechanism - one that, regrettably, I still utilize today - of picturing the worst-case-scenario.

This year, I got married. My husband is a very handsome man. As my thirteen-year-old sister puts it, "He is a hunk!" To be sure, he is also compassionate and strong in his convictions. He has the type of faith in God that I aspire to. If my eleven-year-old self could see me now, I think she would be shocked.

The main point of my story is that alopecia is not limiting. If anything, alopecia opens doors you may not realize are otherwise there. As I am re-reading my story, I am contemplating whether or not it is "too boring." There is nothing overtly shocking about my life. Alopecia has not limited me. As I think about it, this is the strongest message my eleven-year-old self could have received - and I think I must share it for that reason. Alopecia is not limiting. Alopecia is a gift.

Marlina is on her way to graduating from the University of Tulsa, College of Law in May. She and her husband will be moving to be near their families. Marlina plans on taking the bar exam in July, and her goal is to work in a corporate setting or small law firm. She hopes to also eventually post more regularly on her blog at www.legally-bald.com.

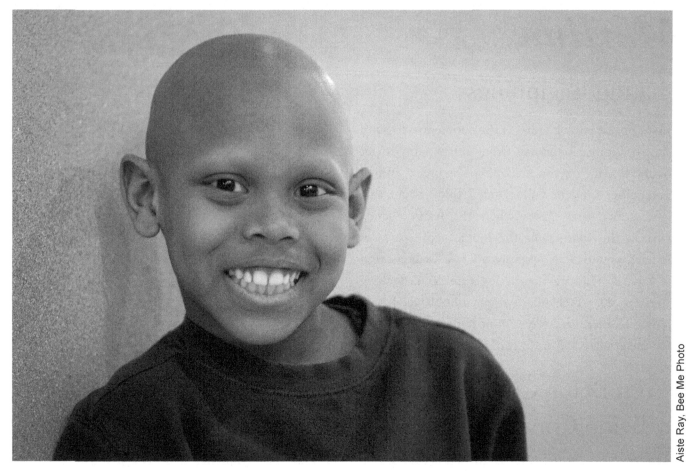

Aiste Ray, Bee Me Photo

Deryck

I feel like anybody else, and I am still like a regular person. I just don't have any hair. I can do what other people do. I can walk or sleep or eat. Other people have it too, and just some people get it. I'm the same as any other boy or girl. Not many people tease me. I have friends, and they are really nice friends. On the first day of school, I went to a party at my friend Nate's house. I have play dates with other friends too. People don't feel bad about me having alopecia. They still play with me, and they don't play tricks on me.

Mosquitos bite my head a lot because I have no hair. There's not that much that I don't like about alopecia. I'm used to it. I don't have to comb my hair as much, and I don't have to go to the barber like other people do.

There are people in my support group with alopecia. Other than that, I don't know anyone else. I don't know anyone in my family with it. My dad shaves his head, but it is not alopecia.

I like to play games like tag, hide-n-seek, and practice catch and baseball with my little sister. I also like to play games and watch movies on my iPad. I love to read mystery books. I also like to ride my bike and scooter.

I want to be a digestive doctor (one that works on stomach problems). I learned a lot about the digestive system in first grade, and I like it. Food goes through the stomach. Then, goes into your small intestines, then back up because first it has to go through the esophagus. I think that is interesting.

"Deryck is a charming child. He is funny and playful. However, it still remains a challenge to get him to choose better foods, as he has a weakness for breads and sweets. Deryck is starting to show much independence and can give a little attitude if he doesn't get his way. Nevertheless, he's still a cutie patootie and everyone's best friend." – Mom

Mom and Dad's Perspective

Deryck is seven years old. He started experiencing hair loss patches at eighteen months old. Doctors could not offer any suggestions as to what caused this so suddenly. Prior to this, we had never heard of alopecia. We were offered steroids, which we did not want to do. There began our search for alternative treatments. By the time Deryck was three years old, he had lost all his hair, including eyebrows and eyelashes. His alopecia was also accompanied by terrible eczema.

We were fortunate to find a holistic pediatrician who explained autoimmune conditions and their relationship to digestive issues. Deryck showed signs of certain food allergies. Today, his eczema has cleared up, with only an occasional flare-up. The doctor believes the hair loss is a symptom of various stresses to his immune system. Deryck has some peach fuzz all over his head, but they never grow, or eventually fall out.

We approach alopecia with an "Oh, so what!" attitude. While we have not given up hope that his hair will grow back, it is not a primary focus. When people say it is only a cosmetic problem, it bothers me. Deryck was born with a head full of hair. Humans have hair on their body for a reason. For example, during the springtime, he experiences issues because he does not have eyelashes to block some of the pollen. The hair loss is telling me that something is not quite right. This is his body's way of alerting us. Without the hair loss, I would not have realized that his immune system was stressed. We try our best to eat healthily and avoid toxins. If this helps Deryck's hair to grow back, then so be it. If his hair never grows back, we are prepared to accept that and enjoy life just the same.

Basically, we are grateful for life and all our many blessings. However, we will continue to learn about alopecia, nutrition, and whatever else can help us better understand this condition. The truth is, so much is unknown, and to say there is no cure is not accurate…we just do not know what it is. The body is remarkable and can heal many conditions, even far worse ones than alopecia. We just have not figured out what our trigger is and how to address it. People should not give up on the best they can be, especially when it comes to health.

34

Franchesca

Who we are isn't defined by the color of our skin, by our weight, or by our eye color or our hair.

Who we are, as humans, is defined by our thoughts and actions to others we know and most importantly, don't know.

Growing up as a child diagnosed with alopecia, I was faced with the thought of humanity before any other child my age. I was forced to think about why the world wasn't the kind place that every child thinks it is, and to be honest, I wouldn't have it any other way.

I realized quickly that humans are humans. How could I be mad at someone for staring at me? How could I be mad at a child for laughing? That is humanity. I looked different, and it was strange to them. I couldn't be upset at people for not having the opportunities given to me as a child. The opportunity to realize everyone is different and to be comfortable and respect something that is out of the ordinary. As a child, I realized that having hair wouldn't make me any happier than not having it. I have lived my life with this thought in my head.

I distinctly remember listening to a speaker talk about her hair loss during cancer. She said that when she lost her hair, she had never been more depressed and never wanted to go anywhere. I listened to her speak, and it brought me such sadness. Hair is an asset, and that's all it ever will be. You don't need hair to breathe, move, talk, or eat. Someone without hair is able to do everything someone with hair can.

One day, I would love for everyone with alopecia to feel exactly the same as someone with hair. I don't want them to wake up every day, look in the mirror and have their hair loss be the first thought to run through their head. I don't want them to label themselves as something different.

I live my entire life this way and can't imagine letting something so small destroy me.

As soon as Franchesca graduated high school, she moved cross country to California to pursue her career as a professional dancer. She is currently signed with Movement Talent Agency and continues to audition and take classes to push herself as a dancer. She recently traveled to Switzerland to dance for Carlos Leal, a Swiss musician. Her plans are to continue auditioning and networking to create a name for herself in Los Angeles.

Lucy

I am five years old. Alopecia? This is just the way my head is. I don't like having alopecia because I want long hair like the other girls. My favorite thing is that I can take a quick bath, and my sister, who has tons of hair, takes forever and cries when you brush it.

I have seen pictures of other kids with alopecia but never met any yet. I met Becky at Taco Mamacita where she was working, and I think she is beautiful. I'm happy when I think about both of us having alopecia.

When I grow up, I can't decide if I want to be a horserider teacher or the person who orders pizza at Pump-It-Up.

"Lucy is a confident, beautiful little angel. She is funny and smart, and enjoys being "class clown" in school. When other kids ask why she doesn't have hair, Lucy responds, 'This is how God made me!'" - Mom

Lucy's Parents

Lucy Elizabeth is our little bald princess. She has a severe amount of attitude and spunk, which I know she will find useful in the future.

She was born with a full head of dark hair and beautiful hazel eyes. When she was about ten months old, all of the hair on her head fell out within the span of three days. My husband and I are both in the medical field. So, we called every medical friend we knew to help figure out the problem. Of course, at first we assumed the worst, that something must be wrong with our baby. She had labs drawn, was seen by every pediatrician in the practice, and finally someone said the thing we didn't want to hear, "We think she has alopecia."

The news was devastating because we knew there was no treatment or cure. The thought of our child being bald was almost too much to cope with.

We found a dermatologist who wanted to try a treatment of SADBE on her scalp. This was a topical solution that causes a "dermatitis" on her scalp in hopes of making hair grow. It actually worked for quite a while. She grew enough hair to hold a small bow. After about six months of treatment, I noticed her eyelashes thinning, and her brows seemed to be disappearing. Then all at once, her hair fell out again. This time, her condition had progressed to alopecia universalis, and everything was gone.

For my husband and I, this loss was more painful than the first. This time, we knew what was happening. We went into panic mode and began increasing the dose of SADBE. At this point, however, it was not working at all. It was as if we were putting water on her scalp - no redness or irritation. We rushed her back to the dermatologist who had no answers for us. Soon after, when Lucy was about two-and-a-half, we decided to completely stop all treatments. This was a life changing time for us. It was a giant load off our shoulders now that we were totally accepting and embracing alopecia.

Our attitude became, "This is the way it is going to be. So, let's make the best of it." Instead of being in constant agony of any new regrowth falling out, we now talk to her about her beautiful bald head and tell her how special she is because of it.

Social networking has had a huge impact on our lives. Lucy loves to look at pictures of her fellow Alopecians, and I can see the joy on her face that she is not alone.

Damian Vines

Rob

Alopecia Areata and Other Imaginary Heavy Metal Bands

As a young man, I wanted to be a rock star. I wanted people to remember me, to recognize me. I envied the manes of big hair like my older brothers and the heavy metal rockers I admired had. But as a high school wrestler, I never had the luxury of letting my "freak flag fly." Every year, I grew it and grew it. Then, wrestling season brought out the shears. I had to settle for a Kevin Bacon Footloose era short haircut, and my skinny tie partly undone. My style was a bizarre blend of new wave and animal print metal.

Along the way, I played in a few bands: Mysterious Traveler, Cut Glass, performing some originals and lots of covers: Petty, Priest, Ozzy, Kiss, and me. I played guitar well enough to write music to go along with my lyrics. I hung out with friends of future famous folk from bands only a few have heard of: The Melvins, Metal Church, Shrapnel and Hall Aflame. At one point, I started a novel about this era of near misses. The working title was, *Horseshoes, Hand Grenades and Slow Dancing*.

I wrote stories and acted in plays. My creative streak was an easy mile wide. After high school, I took the opportunity to grow my hair long. That is, until I was cast to play World War II-era soldier, Roy Selridge, in Biloxi Blues. Getting the buzz cut was quite an event. All the young men playing soldiers in the play went to

the theatre, and one by one we went under the knife, so to speak. Actually, it was an old black electric razor that looked like it might have been around since 1942. My shoulder length hair was the longest and got the most attention.

When the hair lay in clumps on the floor, a problem appeared as plain as the nose on my face. On the back of my head there was a silver-dollar-sized spot of hair that was so white that under theatrical lights it shone bright. Margaret, the hair-stylist, dyed the spot, but it didn't take well; it still glared under the lights.

After the show closed and my hair grew back in, I grew it out for years, all the way down to the bottom of my shoulder-blades. I pursued a degree in theatre: performance and education. For some roles, I used a ponytail, and for others I tucked it under a hat and the stylist cut a false hairline underneath. I turned down roles that required me to cut my hair. The best use of my long hair was when we did cross-dressed scenes. I didn't give that little white spot of hair much thought.

In college, I wrote fiction with the intent to publish. After a few years, I sold a few stories, but I mostly collected rejection notes. I grew rhino skin along the way by receiving 600+ writing, acting, and musical rejections. When I graduated from University, I searched for teaching jobs. More rejections. After a lack of success finding a permanent position, I finally got my hair cut but saved the ponytail. I got a teaching job, though I have no idea if the haircut helped me get it.

Around the same time, the white patch multiplied, and the patches started becoming bare. They migrated around my head, growing back in brittle and white at first and then eventually looking more normal. At the same time, other patches would appear. One stylist I went to cut away some of the darker hair, leaving what he called "jet streaks."

I discovered these patches were alopecia areata, likely an irreversible condition. I didn't realize the impact it would have. The patches moved around, but for the most part they stayed hidden. The strange shiny spots underneath became targets for my distracted fingers. Some people twist their hair, I rubbed the bare spots. One of the pieces of advice I got was to rub the spots to promote blood-flow. Various people suggested "cures," like corticosteroid shots in my scalp, over and over again. No way! I tried Tea Tree Oil Shampoo. It burned my eyes but didn't bring back the hair.

When another bare silver dollar-sized patch showed up above my forehead, I decided to shave it all off. Part of the reason was embarrassment. It looked odd, and one of the students started calling me Patches. Despite my laughing it off on the surface, it still stung. Other students were supportive. I later found out some of the girls in my classes were plotting to shave their heads in support!

A couple years later, I had a young man in class with the condition. He was a rock drummer and had pretty big hair. He said the doctor had told him that when it happened to kids, it usually grew back. Sure enough, by the time he graduated, it was back and full.

Mine did not. The patches got bigger, and the hair grew back less. I bought a buzz-cut razor for $18.88 and haven't had to pay for a haircut since. I took time off from writing and focused on acting. Less rejection, though I think building my tolerance for rejection also built my tolerance for dealing with being the guy with the weird hair. When faced with adversity, one can either make themselves crazy complaining, or accept it and move on. I moved on.

As the years went by, I grew more accustomed to it. One of the strangest things was that as the amount of hair on my head decreased, the patches that returned grew in dark. It was interesting to watch the patterns. My daughter suggested we do Celtic style henna tattoos in the various spots, but we never got around to it. Over the last few years, the hair on my head has gotten light again and is practically non-existent.

One year, I grew it out for the month of October to play a Zombie, with my strange tufts, for Halloween. Then, I continued to let it grow for no-shave November, finally buzzing it off when it became too annoying. I've now lived with a fairly extreme version of the condition for over a dozen years, and it defines me.

Along with the alopecia, I am also defined by the various cheap hats I buy to cover my scalp. I am a bit vain. I don't really want an ugly scarred up head, so I protect it with sunscreen and hats. I buy a lot of hats because I tend to lose them. Though my hair is not very attached to my head, luckily, my head is attached to my shoulders, or I'd likely lose it too.

So, now I'm the bald science fiction writer with a hat who also teaches a broad melange of high school classes, and plays guitar and writes songs on the side. Sometimes, I still even do theatre. I never made it to rock star status, but I'm happy with all the creative endeavors I've attempted. I wouldn't mind if my eyelashes grew in a bit thicker, but the alopecia helps make me memorable. That's what I wanted. That's what I've got. I don't need to be more famous.

Rob's debut young adult, apocalyptic, science fiction novel, "All is Silence," is getting rave reviews, and the sequel, "Straight Into Darkness," will be released summer of 2015. You can learn more about Rob's writing at www.desertedlands.com, or what else he's up to at www.robslater.com.

Abra Klinger

Jannica

"If my hair grows back, I'll cry." Yes, you read correctly, and I'll get to that.

I noticed my first bald spot in August 2013. I then shaved my head in February. It is now October 2014, the month of my birthday and eight month baldie birthday. I can't quite believe that I have had eight months of no hair. Eight months of putting on wigs and not putting on wigs.

A couple of months after the head shave, I also lost my eyebrows and eyelashes. Somehow, that wasn't a big deal. Once you have accepted that your head hair is gone, your identity, then anything else is either a bonus or not a big deal. That is not to say that I haven't had my frustrating moments of learning how to draw amazing looking eyebrows and apply eyeliner without stabbing myself in the eye. It is funny how you adapt to never touching the eyebrow area when eyebrows are on, and the impulse of running my fingers through my hair is, well, also gone.

Let's get back to that weird statement of, "If my hair grows back, I'll cry." First of all, I was not accepting of my alopecia in the beginning. I wouldn't identify myself as someone who had alopecia because I was going to cure it, fight it...whatever non-embracing word you could use. I lost some hair, and then it started growing back. I was winning! I corrected my diet so it wasn't full of inflammatory foods anymore. I looked awesome. My body felt great, and then more hair fell out. And more...and then it started thinning out to the point where it was actually visible. This was by the end of December 2013. I was angry, frustrated, sad, anxious, panicked, and full of suffering.

The turning point came when I embraced it. How do you do that? For me, it was actually getting that this was what was so. The reality was - I'm losing hair. Whatever hair I have, I have, and what I don't have, I don't have. That was the first step to actually being ok.

The second step, once I got over the word "wig" being a nasty one, was going to a wig store with a friend and finding out that I didn't have to spend thousands of dollars on a wig. It didn't even have to be real hair to look great. I tried one on that looked just like my own hair used to look, and I was so moved by seeing ME again. I knew then, that life as a bald woman could be full of exciting possibilities. I could have my "old" hair back and have it detach whenever I wanted to. How cool! I would have the superpower of instant physical transformation! And now I do. I own that.

My hair loss was the access for me to be more than I thought I was. It confronted me with the question - If I have the same thoughts and feelings as I did before... nothing is different on the inside, but physically I'm completely different. That means I'm not my hair, and if I'm not my hair, then I'm not my body. Then who am I?

I got to experience not being attached to what I look like. I do not derive my sense of worth out of my physical appearance. That is pure freedom. And now, I am free to create and be whomever I want. Yes, I can be a brunette, a blonde, a redhead, or a kickass bald chick all in one day, but beyond that, I get to no longer live with the constraints of what I should look like or who I should be in order to be normal, beautiful, and perfect.

Who decides what that is anyway?

Jannica is a Los Angeles based actress. Born and raised in Sweden, she is also the founder of I(a)mperfekt; an internet platform that takes conversations on beauty, perfect, and normal to a new level. Jannica has been rocking the bald look for a little over a year and says that alopecia is a blessing. Why? Having access to instant physical transformation really is a superpower!

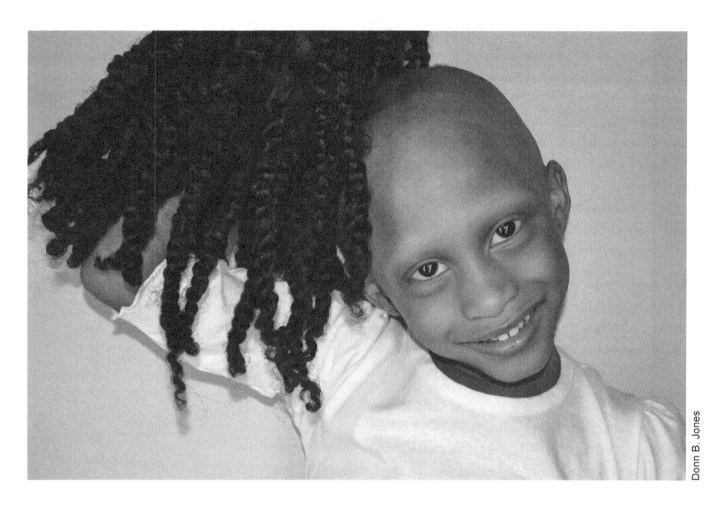

Donn B. Jones

Madison

I am four years old and was diagnosed when I was three. I get to wear lots of pretty hats and different wigs. I call them my crowns. Some of my friends tell me I'm bald, but everyone plays with me, likes to share stickers with me, and eats lunch with me.

I love having alopecia because it takes me to the doctor, and I love doctors. I want to be a doctor.

I don't know why my hair had to fall out. I wanted hair like my daddy's, all the way down to the floor.

I see a lot of people like me on my mommy's phone and on the iPad. We look all the time. They're bald like me.

I want to be a rockstar doctor with a medicine bag when I grow up. My name is Dr. Madison, and I have a pink waiting room.

"Madison likes to play dolls, color, and play with her sister Makaya and brother King King. She enjoys watching Lalaloopsy and Peppa Pig. Going outside and to the park is fun too. She especially enjoys going to birthday parties." - Mom

Madison's Mom

When my four year old daughter was diagnosed with alopecia, I was confused. I didn't know much about it, and didn't know anyone with it either. So, it was extremely alarming to have someone in my family with it and even more so, one of my children. We adorned her head with hats. Lots and lots of hats. Hats that were cute. Hats that were not so cute. Some that were small and others that were too big. All too often, these hats got in the way of Madison just being a "uniquely" normal four year old who wanted to run, jump, and have fun.

My husband and I decided to search for wigs. Unfortunately, there were many obstacles in the search. We tried to find something age appropriate and culturally fitting. We reached out to some of our social media friends for suggestions, and our request basically went viral. At least to us it did. People started offering to donate their hair, to cut their dreadlocks… They offered their time, advice, and solutions. It was amazing.

Our amazement soon turned into further disappointment as we hit more road blocks from some of the referrals to well-known organizations who accepts, processes, and uses donated human hair to create wigs for those suffering from hair loss. There we were with brave and selfless people ready and waiting to make the big chop for our little girl, and we had to basically turn them away. In our research, we found that most of these popular organizations for donated hair were not well-versed in dealing with dreadlocks, nor were they able to fulfill our request for a natural wig that was culturally fitting. We eventually collaborated with a great stylist who created a very special piece that fits Madison well.

As a family, we strive not to cover up Madison's alopecia but to be proactive advocates for her and this condition. So, we encourage Madison to constantly recognize that her inner beauty is what makes her outwardly beautiful and that with or without her crown, hat, or scarf, she is the epitome of beautiful. We instill in her the importance of peace and humility, cultural identification, and the strength to accept the individual uniqueness in all of us.

We also found the internet and social media to be very helpful. I show her pictures of other bald beauties so she understands she is not the only one. I always read comments others make regarding photos that are posted, and she is always excited to hear those. It truly takes a village, and we are growing a village.

A little over a year since her diagnosis, we have learned so much from Madison. This experience has positively affected us all and made us a stronger family unit. She radiates with such joy, confidence, and strength. Those around her can't help but be stronger, happier, and more confident. Alopecia is not who she is. It's just a small part of a bigger, successful, uniquely normal, and beautiful Madison.

Marina

I strongly believe that all obstacles or ordeals we are given is our compass, showing us the direction we should follow to become successful. If we treat it this way, we're always rewarded in the end…somehow.

For over twenty three years, I had been stuttering, but I managed to get a job as a radio presenter. When I was three, I woke up and found myself completely alone in the dark flat in the night. We lived in a small town in the National Park. That night, my dad was working a night shift. He worked as a veterinarian, and my mom was in Moscow for passing her exam at University. I couldn't understand why I was left in the dark alone and cried until I was exhausted and fell asleep. I don't remember when my dad came back but ever since then, I stuttered and couldn't talk properly when out in public. For years, I tried not to publicly talk at all but finally became fed up with it and decided to get my second degree in journalism. For over a year-and-a-half, while being a single mother to my young daughter, I took private classes with a well-known radio presenter in the '80s. She was amazing, and after I graduated from the institute, I immediately got a job as a correspondent in a radio station. I was then offered to host my own radio show. I couldn't have even dreamed about it before. Possibilities are endless when you really want something.

My alopecia developed when I was sixteen years old. It was a nightmare for me. I was losing hair so fast that I stopped going to school for six months until my parents bought me a wig. It was a real struggle. I hated my first wig. It was another challenge to get through, and now that I am thirty eight years old, I know passing through those tough times have made me stronger on the inside.

Alopecia helped launch my project for Alopecian women in Russia, where they can get any kind of support including a free photo shoot to feel beautiful and special. Over the years, I've taken up photography, decorating, drawing, yoga, and dancing. Dancing helped me reconnect with feeling feminine again after losing my hair.

The hope for my project is that other women may blossom in their beauty and to help them move through the pain. I am still wearing wigs in public because I love doing hair, but I am enjoying my natural look when I am on vacation, with friends, in the countryside, or practicing yoga in the city park.

I always wonder why one person is successful and another is not. I came up with the thought that the difference between losers and winners is quite simple – Losers are fixated on their problems, whatever they are, while winners just have no time to focus on these kinds of things. They eagerly discover new sides of life. I will continue trying to discover new sides of my life, step by step. I am really grateful for what I have in my life.

Marina is a TV producer, journalist, the founder of www.well-woman.ru project – a project for Alopecian women and is involved in art exhibitions organized by her father who is a sculptor.

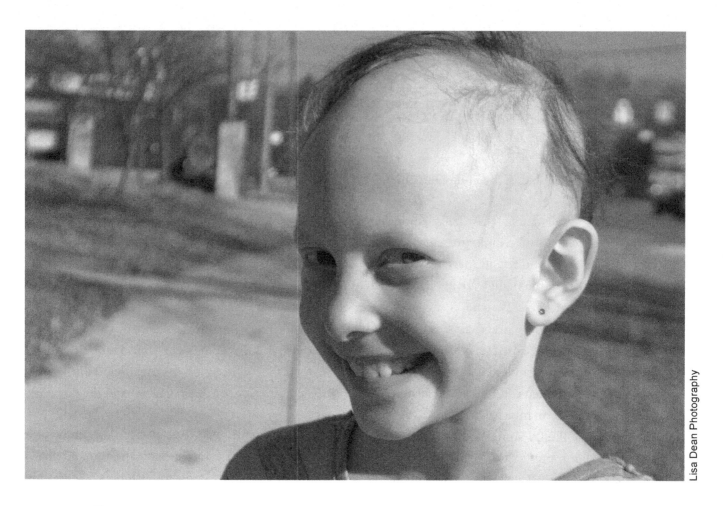

Lisa Dean Photography

Dakota

I am ten years old. I have alopecia universalis. I began to lose my hair when I was five. It started with patches, and I had those for about a year. During the summer of 2010, before first grade, I decided to shave my head. I decided to shave it because I felt that I didn't like my hair. It was always in my face. I felt good because I didn't have to comb or style it to cover the patches. My hair started to grow back in some areas. Then in January or February 2011, it all fell out. I did not like that it all fell out. It felt kind of scary at first to be bald, but then I kind of liked it. As soon as you find out about this disease, you can find friends with alopecia too. My friends think I am awesome, and they don't care about the way I look. Even though I don't like not being able to play with

my hair, I love having alopecia because I don't have to worry about doing my hair everyday

In 2011, I went to The Children's Alopecia Project, Alopeciapalooza, for the first time in Ohio. It changed my life because I got to hear other people's stories. I have been to camp with my family for the past four years. I've been to Ohio, North Carolina, Michigan, and New York. I met Miss Delaware, Kayla Martell, Georgia, and other amazing adults and kids with alopecia. Over the past four years of going to Alopeciapalooza, I feel that having alopecia is a loving gift from God.

Dakota enjoys dancing, sports, and babies. When she grows up, she wants to be a teacher. Dakota plans on attending her 5th Alopeciapalooza this year.

Help Along the Way

Sometimes, all it takes is the persuasion of a group of friends, a well-respected teacher, or a loving family member to help us take the next step toward our acceptance of alopecia. Timely remarks, personal realizations, and moments of celebration can cause ripple effects, almost instantaneously prompting movement in a forward direction.

"She stood in one photo with no hair and a glorious smile on her face." - **Sarah**

"A good friend pulled me aside and told me, 'Wake up to yourself. You're still the same person on the inside, and it's not life threatening.' " - **Judy**

"It was great fun, and it made me feel confident that my friends also had to go into school feeling different." - **Reuben**

"We started selling at events and shows, and I had to go out without my wig to these events. After all, that was the whole point, wasn't it?" - **Deirdre**

"It was like being rescued from a deserted island, for me." - **Joann**

"The director told me something that opened my eyes. 'I don't want perfect people on stage.' . . ." - **Sandra**

"My teacher, Mr. Steiner, shaved his head to support me . . ." - **Dino**

"The years went by, and one day while attending a birthday party at a restaurant, a lady approached me and gave me her business card for a modeling agency." - **Anna**

Sarah

Embracing My Baldness

I love being a bald woman. Honestly! I love embracing new ways of feeling beautiful, whether through big, dangly, brightly coloured earrings, some dark and alluring eye liner or even just the feeling of a cool breeze across my scalp. But my story doesn't begin with embracing my baldness. In fact, it doesn't even begin with being bald at all.

I was three years old when my mum first noticed patches of hair loss. I remember her putting my hair into three pigtails instead of two, to help cover a big patch at the back of my head. I stood up in class one day for "show and tell" and proudly presented my bald spots to the class. I can't imagine what the poor teacher must have been thinking. At that age, it was a game to me – I didn't know that it was going to stick around, and it didn't even register on my emotions.

As the years went on, I became more and more aware of my difference. I was determined no one would see my patches. My close friends all knew, and when playing sports or games, I would often ask if they could see my spots. They were so supportive. I was, and still am, blessed to be surrounded by generosity, kindness, and love in my friendships.

I went through a stage where I wore a headscarf to school every day. In hindsight, this was an odd decision to make, considering I was so worried about being different. But in my mind, a headscarf could be passed off as "normal" and hair loss most definitely could not. Hair loss meant there was something wrong with you, and it was probably your fault that it was falling out. I remember one day at lunchtime, being admonished by a teacher, as my headscarf "was not

48

appropriate school uniform," and I was to remove it immediately. I begged her to let me take it off in the bathroom, where I could check to make sure my hair was covering my patches, but she refused. I was mortified and embarrassed, not only about my patches but also because I was made to feel like I was somehow being bad or naughty.

I actually still had quite a lot of hair at this stage. Apart from my few patches, which were always falling out (then growing back and falling out somewhere else), I had thick long locks of hair. By high school, I was more comfortable with my patches, and by Uni, I even bravely cut my hair short, filled with the new courage of growing independence and a belief in myself that I didn't care about having alopecia.

Fast forward five years when I was teaching Drama and English in a small rural town. My colleagues and students knew about my alopecia, but I still tried to keep it under cover. I noticed that while more patches were developing, the others weren't growing back like they used to. As winter rolled in, I started wearing beanies every day. Before I knew it, winter was over. My hair was still not growing back, and I was completely and utterly dependant on my collection of beanies. I felt my only option was to shave off the hair I had left and start wearing wigs.

This brings me to my beautiful sister. She is a hairdresser (I know, the irony is wonderful), and so I visited her with my mum during school holidays, and she cut my hair short. We went wig shopping the next day, and I returned to school with not one, but three different wigs. If I was going to be a wig wearer, I was going to have some fun. I was always open about my alopecia with my students, and after they quenched their curiosity with a barrage of questions (Did I sleep in the wig? Do you have to wash it? Does it hurt?), they were completely accepting of me and my wigs. But I still could not brave going out bald.

I wrestled with the decision for a good six months. I wanted to go out without a wig on. I wanted to

feel strong enough and brave enough to show the world I was different and that it was ok and beautiful for a woman to be bald. Wasn't I always telling my students that they were gloriously unique, worthy, and beautiful? Yet somehow every morning, I would end up walking out the door with my good intentions bottled away and my wig firmly in place. The turning point for me was my auntie's funeral. She had won the battle against breast cancer, but it had returned in her liver, and she was gone within a few short months. Photos of her were displayed during the service, including ones taken during chemotherapy. She stood in one photo with no hair and a glorious smile on her face. I saw in that photo the beautiful woman I loved, and I understood in that moment that I would not wear my wig again.

That was two years ago now, and I have never regretted my decision. It hasn't always been easy, and I can still be hurt by the stare of a stranger, but I LOVE my body and truly, honestly, deeply believe that all women, with or without hair, can be strong, beautiful, and feminine.

As part of my PhD research, I wrote a verbatim play. Verbatim Theatre involves interviewing people on a set topic or event, recording these conversations, and then using the stories as stimulus for writing a play. I interviewed fifteen women across QLD who have alopecia and wrote a play called *bald heads & blue stars*, which premiered in August 2014. This has been an AMAZING experience for me. Meeting other women who have alopecia, sharing our stories, and working towards writing a play that enable us to share our stories with the public. People often ask me, "What does the blue stars part in the title mean?" and I often tell them, "You'll just have to come along and find out." I also think it's a beautiful way to end my story here.

I was facilitating a theatre in education project with second year university students. They were running

Sarah's Story Continues . . .

workshops at a local primary school that resulted in a short play, and I was visiting the schools to see each of these performances. After introducing myself, some of the students wanted to know why I had blue on my head. I thought, blue? What do they mean? Is there something stuck on my head? I then realised that because I shave off the small patches of hair I have left, this looked like blue to the children. So I explained that I have alopecia, and the white parts on my head are where the hair has fallen out, and the blue rough parts are where I still have hair. I let them touch my head, and they seemed to understand. I sat down next to one girl, ready to watch the performance. She looked at me in awe and said, "But who made it into blue stars?" And I thought, how beautiful. From her perspective, I have blue stars on my head. Now, I not only love my baldness, but I love my blue stars as well.

---

bald heads & blue stars premiered in August 2014, and through funding from the Australia Alopecia Areata Foundation (AAAF) the production was filmed and is now available on DVD through Artsworx. Sarah was honoured to interview fifteen remarkable women with alopecia and write their stories into performance. Over half of the storytellers were able to attend the performance on closing night, and the stories and connections (and hugs and tears) that followed were a wonderful experience. www.artsworx.com.au

Sarah is currently in the final year of her PhD, and re-working another verbatim play on youth mental health and wellbeing for a local schools tour. Since writing her story for Head On and performing in bald heads & blue stars, she has lost all of the hair on her scalp. So while there are no more "actual" blue stars for her, she thinks it's a lesson on perspective that she will always cherish.

Lina Hayes

Judy

Although I did not know it at the time, my alopecia journey began when I was twenty-four. I went to my hairdresser one Saturday and asked her to cut my hair very short and spiky on top, as was the fashion in those days. She told me she wouldn't be able to cut it too short because of my bald spot, to which I replied, "What bald spot?" She proceeded to give me a mirror, and to my surprise I saw a 15mm bald patch on the back of my scalp. Over the next couple months, the hair grew back, and I didn't think about it again.

At the same time, my mother was in hospital having a major operation and contracted a golden staff infection. She was transferred into isolation and remained in hospital for over six months on various types of medication. Upon her release, her hair started to fall out, and within a couple months it was all gone, including her eyebrows, eyelashes, and all body hair. We were told it was alopecia universalis and that it more than likely was caused from the stress and medications she had been taking. There was nothing that could be done to re-grow her hair.

Mum, being brought up through the depression, took this in stride, went shopping for a wig and got on with her life. She had never been one to put stock in her appearance and never wore makeup apart from lipstick if she was going out. She also did not discuss the situation with anyone. So, I really do not know how she felt, but I'm almost now sure she would have been crying at night at the loss of her beautiful tresses.

Over the next couple of decades, my "bald patch" would come and go, but I never even thought to link it to Mum's alopecia. I was forty-eight when I lost all my hair. Just prior to Christmas, I found another bald patch, and by the end of February all my hair was gone. It was falling out in clumps, on my pillow, in the shower. I was afraid to brush it because I ended up with more in the brush than on my head. I went to work with a scarf on to try and hide it, and a couple of young girls made some rude remarks. So, I went into the city and bought my first wig. I wasn't happy with the style, but the lady who sold it to me assured me it suited.

Mum was sympathetic, but we still did not discuss our feelings.

My husband and I went to the doctor, and I was referred to a specialist. I tried a number of different treatments, stopping short of injections. I had been doing a bit of research and had drawn my own conclusion that it was not curable and that I would probably never re-grow my hair either. It was at this point that I started to wonder if it was hereditary and worried if my own daughter would also be a sufferer.

I really missed my eyebrows and eyelashes much more than I missed my hair. It was easy to put a wig on, but it was much harder for me to do my eyebrows and lashes. I felt like one of those faceless dolls you see hiding in the corner of the room.

I was feeling very sorry for myself, and one day a good friend pulled me aside and told me, "Wake up to yourself. You're still the same person on the inside, and it's not life threatening." Sometimes, tough love is what you need, and from that moment on I decided to embrace my condition. I went online and found a support group. I went to workshops to learn how to draw on eyebrows and put on false eyelashes, and started to feel a little more human again.

Then one day, another friend told me about cosmetic tattooing. She had thinning eyebrows, was going to get hers done and asked if I would be interested in getting mine done too. After checking it out, I decided to go ahead. I felt so good once I had them done. They looked great, and I even got eyeliner on both the top and bottom lids of my eyes. The eyeliner hurt a lot. But as they say – "No pain, No gain."

Telling people about my condition was hard at first, as I really didn't want them to know I was bald. But when you wear a wig, it's hard to do some of the things you used to like swimming, running, and even going out on a windy day.

I then found a website for Freedom suction wigs and decided that no matter what the cost, I wanted one of those. I hated the feeling of scratchy, itchy hot wigs and the uncertainty of the weather blowing my wig off. A consultant came to my home, took a plaster cast of my head, and within a few months my wig arrived. It was great, and no matter what I did, it would not come off, as proved by being towed on an inflatable donut behind a speedboat. This was another positive step in my journey.

One of the highlights of my journey was being involved in a project to raise public awareness and acceptance of alopecia. *The Turning Heads Art Crown Project* began with an idea by Helen Beasley, a face and body artist from *Rainbow Face Painting and Body Art*, in collaboration with local photographer, Lina Hayes.

The project involved a number of people, ranging from age two to age sixty, who were all registered with AAAF (Australian Alopecia Areata Foundation). I was so excited to be asked to be a part of the project, that I flew 920 kilometres from Brisbane to Sydney to participate. I arrived on a Saturday morning, went to Helen's home, and met up with another woman who was there for the project. Helen painted a henna tattoo on both our heads, and we headed out to a local coffee shop to have photos taken. I had only ever been out in public once before without a wig on, and that had been a very short outing. I was scared at first, but with the support of the rest of the girls, I soon felt comfortable. After we left the coffee shop, we took more photos in a local park. People were approaching us and asking what we were doing, and it felt good to be able to explain to them about alopecia and the project. It was a wonderful experience and very empowering. I wish I had the courage to get a permanent tattoo.

We were able to achieve front page coverage in our local paper and an article on the project in a national magazine. The project images also inspired a song, "All of the Strands" written by Reuben Rose of Sydney Band, Redwoods, and were the subject of blogs all around the world. It's been amazing!

My husband has been very supportive throughout my journey, and he loves me just the way I am. At first, I found it hard to believe he could still love me looking the way I did, but his reassurances sank in, and I began to love myself again.

I now look at all the positives that alopecia has given me. No more waxing. No more shaving my legs. No more hairdressers, and I save heaps of money every year. Having the latest hair style can make you feel pretty, but you don't need hair to be beautiful.

Judy decided to get involved supporting others who have alopecia, and this past January took on the position of Branch Manager in Queensland for the Australia Alopecia Areata Foundation.

Dino De Luca

Reuben

I'm nine years old, and I first noticed I had alopecia when I was eight years old and my eyebrows and hair started coming out. I would look into the mirror every morning before school, and I just seemed to have less and less hair. I asked my mum to check my bed pillow because I was worried that it might need washed, and that was causing my hair to fall out. But as we started to look closely at my arms and legs, we noticed that all my hair was coming out, even my eyelashes!

One morning, my mum noticed I was crying while looking into the mirror. She asked me what was wrong, and I told her I was so worried that even my teeth would fall out. We then decided it was time to see a specialised doctor who told us that I had alopecia.

I was very upset, sad, and confused. I stopped wanting to go to school or my other activities like swimming, cubs, or football. I didn't like being with people I didn't know, especially older kids. I just wanted to hide and not go out.

My friends would ask why I was going bald, and it hurt me when they would say that. I still had some hair, but it was in patches and getting less every week. My friends were very good about it but just didn't understand why it was happening. My mum decided to properly tell my school about my alopecia so that they could tell the other pupils. I go to a small village primary school in our village of Aberuthven. It only has forty-two pupils. So, I know everyone. The head teacher, Mrs. Gordon, had a chat with me and made me feel good, and not to worry about my school work too much. She also explained to the whole school what was happening to me.

As the weeks went on, my hair got to a stage that it was looking a mess because it was so thin. So, my dad decided we should cut what was left off. He had an idea that we should have a bit of fun when we were doing it. We got one of my mum's friends, Kayleigh, who does amazing body and head art, to paint my head after we had shaved it off. Mum and dad also let me have a sleepover party the night before. The friends I asked to stay over also asked if they could have their hair shaved off to help me feel better about it, and not feel alone and isolated about my condition. So, in the morning, after the sleepover, all five of us sat in a row in our kitchen and had our hair shaved off. It was great fun, and it made me feel confident that my friends also had to go into school feeling different. Kayleigh then painted my head in this amazing mechanical design, and we had professional photographer, Dino De Luca, take some great pictures of me and my head design. I felt I looked really cool in my photos, and it gave me so much confidence, that I was doing more and more and feeling positive about my alopecia. The newspaper in Scotland heard about what we had done and decided it would make a great story for them. So, it was all over the papers as well.

On the day of the head paint, we started a Facebook page (called Reuben's World) showing pictures of my photoshoot with Dino and my daily life, hoping that other kids could see that they could have a positive experience from this condition. Through my page, I have been able to meet lots of people with alopecia and have also raised money for a charity that supports children in the UK with alopecia, called *BeBold*. I have had some great experiences since developing alopecia, which proves it shouldn't stop kids from having lots of fun – The best yet, was being selected to represent the Manchester City Football Club in front of over 50,000 people as official Mascot in their game against Chelsea FC. Amazing… When I grow up, I would love to be good enough to be a professional football player.

Reuben lives in Scotland, and states he "likes being cheeky. Not in a bad way. Just having fun and joking around." He is quite competitive - always trying to win at sports and games. He loves fast cars and animals and has two dogs, two guinea pigs, and a pony. One of his favourite things to do is ride on roller coasters, "Alton Towers has the best ones." Reuben and his sister, Poppy, can be heard and seen in the music video for the BeBold Alopecia Awareness Campaign and the theme song for BeBold's official hero, Captain BeBold, written and performed by Amy Hawthorn.

Maksimilian Dikarev

Deirdre
Bald, Bad Ass, and Facing the World Head On

I can distinctly remember screaming bloody murder as my sister, Aria, bent me over the tub and ruthlessly brushed the matted knots out of my hair. I was probably about ten years old and still remember crying from that pain like it was yesterday. Now, at thirty-seven, who would have known then I would cry so many tears over my hair. Not from the pain of the knots being brushed out, but from the pain of it not being there at all. I still feel that weird lump in my throat when I see old photos of myself with a full head of thick crazy curls, and more often when I look in the mirror and see my head now, completely bald. But I don't cry anymore. Now, I just wonder where did all that hair go? How is it possible that what was once so thick and unruly I could hardly fit it into a huge jaw clip, is now completely nonexistent? Why has my body chosen to attack itself in this cruel and bizarre way? There must be some larger reason fate has chosen me to walk this particular path.

I know there are millions of people out there with alopecia who can relate all too well to these thoughts and emotions. Meanwhile, those who go about their daily lives never knowing this strange affliction, can never seem to really relate. "It is only hair," they say. "At least you don't have cancer," they say. Oh, they are so clueless, even when they mean well. Most of the time, their words, even said with the best intentions, just hurt.

My name is Deirdre. I am a lawyer living in Miami, Florida. I have lived with alopecia areata for the past sixteen years. This disease has changed me. It has changed my life, my mind, and my heart. It has made me weak and vulnerable, battered my self-esteem, and heightened my insecurities… yet it has made me a stronger and better person at the same time. Ironic isn't it? Funny how a "little thing" like losing your hair can change the person you are, right down to your core. I always fancied myself a strong woman.

I knew what I wanted and who I was. I was kind of a bad ass, if I do say so myself. I was always the one who had their shit together. Confident, pretty, smart…my life was pretty charmed. Then, one day at age twenty-one, that would all turn on a dime. A dime…or really more of a quarter or fifty-cent piece. That was the size of the first bald spot I found while blow-drying my long curly hair. I was living in Spain at the time, studying abroad and having way more fun than should be allowed while "studying." I remember so clearly the instant I flipped my head over in the same way I had done a million times before, and saw it. A perfectly round and smooth bald spot. What the hell is that?! Panic immediately set in as I ran my fingers over it and felt how perfectly smooth it was. How can this be? What is this? I called my mother on a poorly connected transatlantic call and cried hysterical tears as I tried to tell her what I'd found. I remember her saying she couldn't understand a word I was saying. In hindsight, those words have come to be true in so many ways. No one in my life seems to truly understand what I am saying or feeling when it comes to my alopecia. They try. They have the best intentions. But they just don't get it.

The inevitable string of doctors, blood tests, and dermatologist appointments followed. "Your thyroid is fine. You are healthy." The eventual diagnosis: "You have alopecia areata." Huh? Alo-what? I mean who had even heard of this strange thing…certainly not me. Okay. So how do I cure it? Fix it doc. Make me better. What pill do I have to take? "Sorry, there is no cure. We don't even really know what causes it. But you must be stressed. You are so stressed." I swear, I have had people telling me for so many years that I am so stressed out, that it really stresses me out!

I remember sitting at my parents' prehistoric computer and doing an internet search for alopecia areata. What I found, horrified me far worse than their slow dial-up connection ever could. You mean, not only is there no cure for this thing, but that I could also lose all of my hair? I could even lose my eyebrows and eyelashes? This has got to be some kind of joke. I cried as I told my mom what I found. Her answer? "I

am sure that won't happen to you, honey." And for a long time it didn't. For years, I lived with patches, and I covered them well. I had so much hair that I did an amazing job of hiding the smooth patches that appeared seemingly out of nowhere and dotted my head like Swiss cheese. I went and got painful steroid injections directly into the patches. I tried creams and weird gels that made my skin red, itchy, and flaky. It was like playing whack-a-mole…Hit one patch, but another one would inevitably pop up nearby. Still, it was mostly an annoyance that only my close friends and family knew about.

On the surface, I still maintained the image of a pretty girl with a full head of hair. Under the surface, I was terrified, always thinking "what if?" and scrutinizing my patches in the mirror until I was blind. My husband still fell in love with me. He still thought I was beautiful. He was still able to lovingly caress my hair, or pull it when he was feeling kinky. I still felt like a woman. A woman with a secret but still a woman. Toward what turned out to be the end of my marriage (little did I know then), the patches started getting worse. Larger and larger. Growing into each other. More difficult to hide. I remember turning to my husband one day as I looked in the mirror and asking him, "Will you still love me if I go bald?" Now that I think of his answer, I should have sensed the end of our marriage on the horizon. He said, "Oh be quiet. You are not going to go bald, silly." You know, I always wished he had just said, "Yes, of course I will still love you." I did end up going bald completely, and no, he did not still love me. Although I don't really know if the two are even related in the reality of what happened with our marriage, I still think somewhere in the back of my mind that they are. My psyche has forever linked the events of going bald and losing love, even if the reasons he left me had nothing to do with me losing my hair. The mind will create crazy things for you to agonize over when you let it. But when he left, I still had hair. I only intelligently know this from the pictures I have that were taken around that time. When I think back to

Deirdre's Story Continues…

57

that horrible time in my life, I don't remember going bald. I think of myself as already bald. I now realize that I have mentally linked those losses, and I have to learn to unlink them if I want to find happiness. It has been a work in progress for some time.

Not so long after my ex-husband left me, the patches started to get really bad. I remember saying to my mom and sister, "I will NOT wear a wig. That is just ridiculous!" But alas, before long, there I was sitting in a wig store that was recommended to my mom by a friend who had a friend with cancer. "I guess I am doing this"…and I walked out a few hours and couple hundred dollars later with a wig. I remember saying to my mom, "What if people at work notice? I mean, how could my hair go from all thin and messed up, to perfect in one day's time?" She said to me, "People don't look at you as closely as you look at yourself." Ha! How true those words really are. The hair kept falling out at an alarming rate, and before long, there I was with one sad little patch at the top of my head and nothing else.

The next "life of an Alopecian" milestone was on the horizon; The Head Shave. My sister, bless her well-meaning heart, has never had a knack for subtlety. It must not run in the family because I lack that particular skill too. She turned to me one day and said, "God. Let's just shave that ridiculous thing off! It looks so stupid!" I looked in the mirror. She was right! I wasn't fooling anyone with the one little patch of hair directly in the middle of my head. I was bald, and holding on to this one sad little patch was not hiding that fact. I turned to her and said, "Ok. Let's do it." The next thing I remember, was sitting on the floor in the bathroom with her standing over me, razor in hand. "Don't cut me!" I squealed as she deftly shaved that sucker right off in a few quick strokes. That's it. I was bald. I was a bald woman. Of course, the wig went right back on when I left the house. It was like my armor; my shield from having to face the world head on as the bald woman that I was. I just wasn't ready for that yet.

All the hair on my head eventually stopped growing or just grew a little here and there, and I got into the habit of shaving it clean. I clearly remember thinking, "At least I still have my eyebrows and eyelashes! As long as they don't fall out, I can handle this." When I attended my first NAAF conference, I remember crying a lot through most of the sessions but also feeling empowered and strangely happy. I guess it just felt good to meet other people who really knew what I was going through. Really knew. That conference began my journey into coming to terms with my identity as an "Alopecian." Some people don't like that word I guess….maybe because it sounds like Martian? I do joke around sometimes that I look like an alien… trying to laugh at myself has helped some, but sometimes I think it is just another defense mechanism. Alopecia has certainly turned me into a self-psychoanalyst, if nothing else!

The year before my second NAAF conference, it happened. The thing that would prove to be the true turning point in my alopecia journey. The thing I had dreaded ever since that day when I did the first internet search on alopecia areata. My alopecia went from totalis to universalis. I lost my eyebrows, eyelashes, and most of my body hair. In a cruel twist of fate, my underarm hair and my pubic hair…precisely the hair I would have loved to get rid of and have paid tons of money and undergone many a painful waxing session to get rid of, is the only hair that has stuck with me through all of this! My brother lovingly stated, "That is like the cockroach hair that lives through the nuclear war." Ahhh, the eloquence of my brother. Now, I was not only a bald woman, but I was suddenly looking into the mirror and startling myself when I saw my reflection. A bald head is one thing to come to terms with, but the horror of seeing your face staring back at you with no eyebrows and eyelashes, is a feeling like no other. I still get the sense that it is not me. It is like some foreign invader that took over the image on the other side of the mirror. When I put my "eyebrows" on and look at myself, sometimes I think, "Oh, yeah.

There you are, Deirdre." I still don't let most people see me without eyebrows.

Losing my eyebrows and eyelashes threw me into a profound funk. I felt really uncomfortable in my own skin. Hiding behind wigs suddenly didn't seem as effective. I was going to be found out. It was just a matter of time. My sister, Aria, who seems to have her hand in many of the milestones along my alopecia journey, again stepped in to influence the way things would turn. She is a very talented jewelry designer and had stated several times that it would be cool to do an earring line using my bald head as the backdrop for displaying them. Every time she mentioned this, I agreed that yes that would be a cool idea in theory, but in practice, I just wasn't ready. That would mean really coming out of my "alopecia closet" and telling the world that I was bald. Something changed inside of me when the eyebrows and eyelashes made their exit. I started to feel like, "What the hell. People are going to find out now anyway. I might as well try to do something positive with this crappy turn of events." Maybe this project would help me come out on my own terms and help me deal with things. So one day while we were sitting in my mom's kitchen, Aria brought up the idea again. This time, fighting down the lump in my throat, I said yes, and B.A.L.D. was born. A new jewelry line with a name that stands for Bad Ass Lawyer and Designer. Me, the Bad Ass Lawyer and Aria, the Bad Ass Designer doing something together to try and bring awareness to alopecia, empower women with hair loss, and raise some money for alopecia charities like NAAF.

We jumped right in! Created a logo, built a website, and started building inventory. We did a photo shoot with a photographer that I happened to be dating at the time. People come into our lives for a reason, and this photographer happened to come into my life precisely when this project was being born. He was patient and kind and took amazing photos that made me feel sexy and beautiful, even without any hair. He was not the one for me, but I will always appreciate his place in my journey, and he will always

hold a place in my heart because of it. We started selling at events and shows, and I had to go out without my wig to these events. After all, that was the whole point, wasn't it? It wasn't easy, but people had great reactions, and it was even kind of fun to be the one everyone was looking at. We even did a segment for the local news. I decided to change my Facebook picture to one of the bald pictures. That was a big step. I remember thinking there would be no going back after that, and I was right. With one click of the mouse, I was telling a few hundred people, "Hey guess what? I am bald!" I think I actually wrote that very thing on my post. Creating the jewelry line hasn't turned into a huge financial success. We haven't made lots of money or gotten into tons of stores (yet!), but it has helped me to shed my mask and face the world as I truly am. It forced me to step out into my reality. I hope it has also helped me empower others in some way.

Through all of this, I have become very active with NAAF. I have become one of their Legislative liaisons and traveled twice to Washington D.C. to lobby for increased funding and improved patient care. I have walked the halls of Capitol Hill, bald, and sat in front of Legislative aides and showed them the face of this disease. I am a lawyer. I know how to talk and be persuasive, and I am using that skill the best way I can. I have gotten involved in my local NAAF support group and sat with other girls still hiding under wigs, even at an alopecia support group outside in the 90° Miami sun. I let them see me and my bald head, and encourage them to feel safe and secure enough in themselves to take off their wigs too. Some are not finding it so easy to do, which I can certainly understand. Everyone has to walk this crazy path in the alopecia road in their own way and at their own pace. Our support group recently had a huge Zumba event with several hundred people to raise money for NAAF. Guess who was the only bald woman in the entire room? My sister turned to me at that event and asked, "How are you the only bald one here?" and I said, "I'm not! I am just the only bald one not wearing

Deirdre's Story Continues ...

a wig!" Is it easy for me? No, it is not. Do I still feel strange walking out of the house with no wig on and getting the inevitable stares or questions about how my chemotherapy is going? Of course I do. But every time I do, I hold my head up, take a deep breath, and just do it. I just do it. Suck it up, Deirdre.

I still wear wigs. I am a lawyer, and I really feel like I need hair to maintain the professional image to be successful in my career. Maybe, that is a social construct I should be trying to fight, but for now, I am actually okay with it. What is important, is that I don't hide my alopecia anymore. I will readily tell people, even in a professional setting, that my hair is a wig. "Oh, you like my hairstyle? Thanks, you too can own it for $575.50! Yes, it is a wig. Yes, I am bald. I have alopecia. Oh you don't know what that is? Well let me tell you…" I have had this exact conversation so many times now, I have lost count. I am part of a professional networking group called BNI. We have about fifty professionals who meet weekly to refer each other business, and every month the group supports a charity. One month, I asked the group to support NAAF. I gave my pitch about having alopecia and how it has affected my life, talked about NAAF's great work… and I collected a few meager donations. The next week, I decided to make a real impact. I stood up in front of the group, most of whom had never seen me without hair, and took my hair off and put it right on the table in front of me. I made the same pitch I had made the week before, but bald. This time, I collected $1500.00. I am learning that showing people your vulnerability goes a long way. I am learning that being vulnerable is actually a show of strength.

Not everyone is Bad Ass enough to put the most secret thing about themselves out there for everyone to see and scrutinize. This process has helped me reconnect with that inner Bad Ass. She was in there all along but just got lost for a while. She still has her moments in hiding. Dating new men is always a hard time for her. She starts to hide behind the fear of rejection. She gets tested in the strangest ways.

The newest and current test is kind of an ironic one - some of my hair has started to grow back the past couple of months. But as this weird alopecia circus tends to go, the re-growth has been strange and patchy. Not the full head of hair I have had countless dreams about waking up to find magically returned overnight. But some strange design that makes me feel like an extra from a movie about post-apocalyptic survivors that have been living under the crust of the earth for twenty years. Weird patches of eyebrow hair, that is not enough to actually be a real eyebrow, but enough to make it more difficult to put my fake eyebrow temporary tattoos on. Leg hair just on my knees, just enough to actually have to shave again. And my family and friends getting excited and happy. "Your hair is growing back!" They can't understand why I am not excited. Why don't I love the fact that my once perfectly smooth head, now looks like some weird prickly map of the world and that I have to shave it again, and that now my $3000 vacuum prosthesis won't suction on properly? Why does this not overjoy me? Seriously? I would rather it just be smooth. Is it too much to ask for my damn hair to just make up its mind? Do you want to be here or don't you want to be? I want my body to make a decision! I realize this is just another chapter in the alopecia journey. Just another hurdle for the Bad Ass Bald Lawyer to conquer. Is she up to the task? She is. Does she have a choice? She does not. I do not. Yet another challenge to face, head on.

Lately, Deirdre is busy running her law firm, NERO Immigration Law, P.L. and teaching Spinning classes at local health clubs. She is very involved with the advocacy arm of the National Alopecia Areata Foundation and enjoys spending time sailing and traveling with her boyfriend, Eric, and giving lots of love to her dog, Marty. www.baldjewelry.com

Clare Xinghui Che

Joann
AA – My Journey to Acceptance

My journey with AA has encompassed almost my entire lifetime. I was first diagnosed at four years of age. I'm going to be sixty-three this month.

With the first bout of AA at four, I lost all my hair. I wore hats to kindergarten. I had remission and regrowth by six years of age but continued to have ongoing bouts, some severe, with AA throughout my childhood, teen, young and older adult years.

I can't remember how I felt at four about my hair loss, but by eight years of age I was very shy and self-conscious about it. I felt very, very alone. I knew no one else who had AA, and it wasn't something that was discussed in my family. I know my mom had a hard time with it because she would often mention what "beautiful" hair I used to have. I remember feeling ugly when she would say those words.

AA was my guilty secret. I was always thinking and worrying if someone "knew." It was quite a burden to carry, especially as a child and teen when you just want to be like everyone else.

Going to a hairdresser, having someone touch my hair, being asked why I was wearing a wig every day would fill me with dread. I carried on best as I could.

I met my husband-to-be in my late teens. At the time, I remember having a bald patch right at the front which I disguised with creative styling. One day, we were out and the wind was blowing. The wind. My enemy. I was frantically trying to hold my hair in place and he said to me, "Don't worry.

Joann's Story Continues . . .

I've seen that spot before." He loved me for me. Definitely a keeper.

He was my rock and the only one I could turn to when the AA became severe again in my early 40's. Still, he could not fully understand the devastation of losing my hair day by day, strand by strand. No way was I going to give up on my hair. I didn't know or want to know that I was fighting a losing battle. I tried treatment after treatment, with a horrendous allergic reaction on the last one available to me.

The hardest part of the hair loss for me, was accepting I had no control and never did. All the regrowths and remissions I had experienced throughout the years, were not because of anything I did. It was simply AA doing it's thing. I might have spared myself much grief had I only realized that sooner. I guess I just wanted the reassurance of knowing that I did everything I possibly could.

Cutting off the last lock of hair did bring me some peace. You can't stress when there's no more hair to lose. I was sad and depressed. It hurt to look at the stranger in the mirror. I did look and feel better with my wig on, but it could not compare to having my own hair. I didn't want my husband or children who were fourteen, eleven, and eight to see my bald head. I wore scarves and head coverings in the house.

AA can be very cruel. It took my eyebrows and lashes too. Losing all my hair was difficult, but losing those was even worse.

In March 2004, I started going on the internet. One day, I typed "alopecia areata" into a search engine. One of the sites that showed up was an alopecia areata support community. OMG!!!! I started to read the messages and look at the pictures.

I met a woman who lived about an hour's drive from me. It was like being rescued from a deserted island, for me.

I started to heal. To be able to express my grief and fears and have others who understood how I felt, helped me move toward acceptance in just a few months than all the prior years had.

I joined NAAF shortly thereafter. I can't express in words the peace that came over me when I saw so many other men, women, and children who looked like me. What an experience!!!

I sat in on the Women and AA support session and told my story there. It released a flood of emotions in me. I had never let go like that, and it felt so good to feel safe doing it there. They hugged me, and there wasn't a dry eye in the room. Everyone got it.

It was step by step to full acceptance from that point on. Each conference I attended, I came home stronger. At the first conference, I arrived in a wig. The following year, I was in a bandana and went out in public for the first time in my natural bald state. I felt as free as a bird. A wonderful lighthearted feeling.

I attended my eighth conference this year. I no longer feel challenged by my baldness. I know I look different from most people, but inside I'm who I've always been. My lack of hair doesn't change that.

I have reached full acceptance with my AA, late in life, but much sooner than if I had remained coping on my own. I no longer need support for myself, and at this time I'm helping those newly diagnosed and struggling. I want to give back what was given to me. True happiness and joy in living, confidence in myself, release from my fear and shame of others judging me. If I can make even the slightest difference to someone struggling toward their own acceptance and peace, there's no better feeling for me. There is so much strength to be found in facing something together instead of alone.

We often look at the negatives of having hair loss, but there is one important positive too. I have met some of the nicest people from all over the world. Good friends, whom I would never have known if not for AA. I feel that would be a greater loss than my hair.

I'm very glad that with the awareness and support available nowadays, no one newly diagnosed with AA has to cope on their own, as those of my generation did. The children and young people especially, are able to meet others their own age. How wonderful is that? They will grow up to be strong and confident adults.

As someone whose journey to acceptance and peace with AA is at an end, I'd like to pass on what I've learned, with hope that it may help others on their own journey at this time.

I've learned there are no quick answers or solutions to hair loss and that good health is more important than hair, hands down.

I've learned I'm not alone. There are millions of men, women, and children who are living their lives with hair loss, as I am. It's wonderful to have support in the hair loss journey, but even more rewarding to be able to give support to someone who needs your help.

I've learned it is best to take it day by day, where hair loss is concerned, and not cause myself unnecessary anguish for what may never happen and what I can't change, even if it does. The stronger emotions relating to hair loss do get better, and the sooner you can take control, the less hair loss will control you.

I've learned that people love and care about you for who you are, not for what you look like. Having hair loss can show you who your true friends are.

I've learned that at sixty-three, I don't look as I did in my 20's and 30's, and hair loss is just a small part of that. I may look different than other people, but it has nothing to do with what I accomplish if I set my mind to it.

I've learned that attitude can go a long way to how others will react or relate to me. You will never be exactly as you were before the hair loss but a much stronger and more compassionate person.

I've learned life doesn't wait for anyone, and that there is no going back, only forward. Having hair loss is life altering but not life ending. Life is precious, and we have no way of knowing how long we will be here. We have to take each day as the gift it is.

Joann has been a NAAF support person in the Toronto, Canada area for the past nine years. She also meets with those newly diagnosed with alopecia areata who need support and answers to their questions. Since retiring from the library system, Joann keeps busy reading, going to craft shows, and adding to her antique vintage collectibles as an ebay shopper.

Sandra

My name is Sandra, and I am thirty-four years old. I am Spanish, and live in a small town on the Mediterranean coast, near the city of Barcelona. Thirteen years ago, I developed alopecia. I was very stressed, and began to have several episodes of alopecia areata. Years later, I lost all my body hair. I remember how hard it was at first, not only for the loss of hair and feelings of depression, but because this was accompanied by chronic fatigue syndrome that made life very difficult for over ten years. Now, thanks to natural orthomolecular medicine, exercise, good nutrition, and relaxation, I have recovered part of the hair on my body, but not the head. Throughout this time, the support of my family, friends, and therapists has been fundamental.

To be bald in this society is not easy. I was a very shy and serious girl, and it took me a while to get used to seeing my new image and not hide. Now, when I look in the mirror, I like what I see and feel I am pretty, even more than when I had hair. There are moments when I would rather wear a headscarf and others when I prefer to go bald. I recognize the challenges I've been faced with, and they have made me very strong and have not got the better of me.

Everything has been a process, and little by little, my anger and my initial pain were transformed into love and strength. I am extremely keen to live in peace with who I am and to let the world see me with my imperfections.

I remember a particularly liberating time in the process. I had reached a point where I got tired of trying to do everything to ensure I grew hair. I was tired of waiting for the miracle that supposedly would bring back my happiness. One day, a friend suggested

I look in the mirror and tell my hair, "Dear hair: I do not know if you'll ever grow back. If you do, it will be a gift. If you don't, I am still who I am." I recognized the sorrow of having lost my hair and didn't let it invade everything. It was like staring into the mirror and seeing me for the first time.

While living with alopecia, dance and theater have been hugely powerful transformers. Art has taught me to look at myself in a more friendly way. I love dancing, and I wanted it to help express all my feelings and emotions.

I was involved in a performance, and I experienced a particularly difficult moment when I had to decide whether or not to go up to the stage and dance. I was so worried about being bald in front of the public, and the feeling completely invaded me. I remember having a conversation with the director of the performance, stating all my insecurities about getting up on the stage. He then told me something that opened my eyes: "I don't want perfect people on stage. I would like to show dancers, in one way or another, that they are human beings with their conflicts, their imperfections, and their virtues. That is the wealth and the value of work." These words made me realize the possibility that my appearance could provide something unique and special that other people did not have. I gave myself permission to go through the fear and show my dance and my hairless head. It was a wonderful experience and adds to all the acts of courage and love I have done to accept this image.

Today, I write with the same intention of love, and I am full of joy to share my story with you.

Sandra works as a movement teacher, doing classes and workshops, mainly in Barcelona, and occasionally around other parts of Spain. As a dancer, she is engaged in dance-theater projects in a performing arts center called ALAS-Artes en movimiento. Sandra is currently involved in a dance-theater performance called Fuego (Fire) to be released in Barcelona in October 2015.

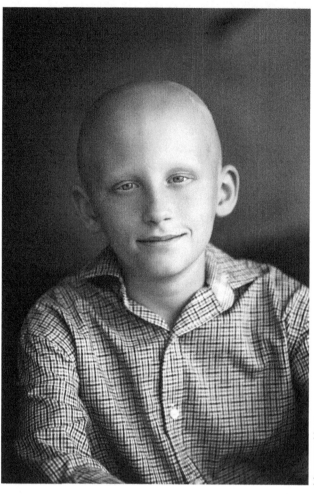

Vanessa Alves

Dino

My name is Dean. I go by the nickname, Dino. I am ten years old and in the fourth grade. I got alopecia when I was in the third grade. When I started losing my hair, I thought I was going to lose all of it because it was falling out so fast. I thought it would be weird because I always had a lot of hair, and my mom always spiked it up for me. I thought my friends would think I was weird. My friends all supported me though. If any kids ever laughed, they always stuck up for me. They still do. When I lost most of my hair, we decided I should shave off the rest. My teacher, Mr. Steiner, shaved his head to support me. My dad, some of his friends, and one of my soccer teammates shaved too.

There are many things I love about alopecia. I don't have to go get haircuts. Sometimes, I still have to go to the salon with my brothers though. I am really fast in the shower. I don't have any body hair, which I love! I also get a good laugh when they do head checks for lice at school.

The main thing I don't like about alopecia is when I see kids look at me and whisper. I think, "I know what you're saying. I can hear you." I don't like getting bit by mosquitos on my head. It seems to be an attraction for those little buggers. Scratches also seem to show up more on me.

Since I've lost all my hair, I have realized it doesn't really matter what other people think of you. What matters is how you feel about yourself, and I feel good about me. If there were a magic pill that could give me my hair back, I don't think I would want it. It probably wouldn't grow back the same anyway.

I'm not sure what I want to be when I grow up, but I know I want to be a leader.

"We had been trying a gluten free diet for some time. Even though we were seeing some stubble, it didn't turn out to be anything significant. One morning he said to me, 'I look in the mirror and I like what I see. I just want a peanut butter and jelly sandwich.'" - Mom

From a Mother's Eyes…

I remember the day we first saw something wrong. It was the last day of a beautiful summer filled with sports, sun, family, and fun. We took our three beautiful boys for their haircuts, a tradition since they were born. They were all born with beautiful full heads of hair. Dean a.k.a. Dino was an early surprise, born twelve weeks premature while we were on a business trip.

Dean was eight and entering third grade. Ever since he was a baby, we always spiked his hair. He is an adorable kid, and was always known for his "cool hair." The first thing his stylist noticed, was some patchiness on top, and then the big surprise – all the hair on his neckline was gone! How did I miss this? When did this happen? What is wrong with my son? It took all my strength not to pass out. I was speechless and scared.

We took him to his doctor the next day, and we were referred to a dermatologist. We were told it was alopecia. Nothing seemed to help. His hair just kept falling out. I cried so many nights and just didn't understand why this was happening to him. He is such a good kid. He is so smart and nice. He is a really nice kid. I saw a change in him too. He started acting silly. He's not usually overly silly, and it just wasn't him. I knew it was bothering him. The more I acknowledged it, the more he would get stressed. I stressed him out. Did I cause this? He couldn't be under stress. We just had the best summer ever!

The hair fell out quickly, and it bothered him to watch it fall. I suggested, on more than one occasion,

shaving it. He was worried his friends would make fun of him. It was heartbreaking. The last time I suggested shaving, we were on one of our early morning runs. I told him to ask his good friends' opinions to see what they said. I also emailed his teacher to let him know that he may ask them. Later that afternoon, Dino came home and said, "My teacher wants to shave his head too." The tears again…

We had a shave party that Sunday. A little friend, a couple of wonderful neighbors, and Dino's dad shaved with him. When we arrived at school, there was his teacher, bald! That started a whirlwind of media attention. He was a mini celebrity. People were shaving their heads for him. He'll tell you he doesn't like the attention, but I think these acts of genuine kindness helped him settle into who he is now. I miss my little boy. I feel like he has already grown up way too quickly.

I worry now about things I never worried about before. Will kids tease him? Will girls still want to date him? I know what a wonderful, beautiful boy he is. I just want everyone else to see it too.

It has been five months since we noticed those first spots and three months since he has been completely bald. He has starting losing his eyebrows and lashes now. I just try to step back and say to myself, "He is happy and he is healthy." What more can a parent ask for?

Dean is a very well rounded child who does well in school with little effort. He is a good athlete and loves to play soccer and tennis. He is well-liked and respected by his peers, teachers, and coaches. He is also a great big brother.

"I think that it's a big misconception that people with
alopecia who are wanting to wear a wig most of
the time are not secure with their look, bald."

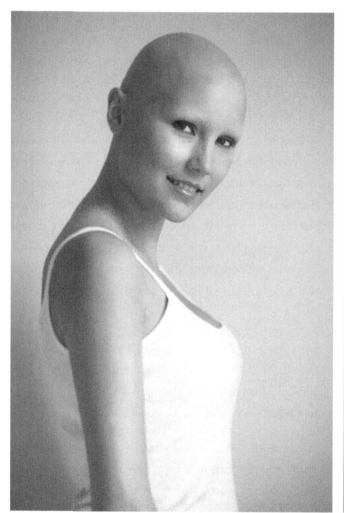

Anna

I was seven years old, and my hair fell out over two week's time. My family was devastated. I don't really remember much, but my dad had come home from a business trip and my hair had disappeared. When he left, I had a few patches but had most of my hair. When he returned, I had none. It was pretty horrible for him. We tried all sorts of medical cures. Since dad was a pilot, we could fly around the world trying all sorts of things. Nothing worked in the slightest. I put my foot down when steroid injections were suggested.

The years went by, and one day while attending a birthday party at a restaurant, a lady approached me and gave me her business card for a modeling agency. My mum called and set up a meeting. I was fourteen and wearing a wig when she first saw me. I was convinced that she wouldn't want me anymore when I told them I had no hair, but they were really surprised and excited once I explained my alopecia. They loved the way I looked, and it took off at full speed from there.

I was usually very shy, and had been bullied in school, but taking my wig off in front of strangers was much easier to me, even though I hadn't yet taken off my wig for my closest friends. I found separating my modeling life and personal life very easy. They were worlds apart. So, I never felt that they crossed over too much where I felt pressure to be one or the other.

Seeing how people in the industry reacted to my baldness, made me realize you didn't have to have stereotypical good looks to be beautiful. This realization helped me change my own perception of how I looked and felt about myself.

I'm completely comfortable as a bald woman but like to wear my wig for day to day life. I think that it's a big misconception that people with alopecia who are wanting to wear a wig most of the time are not secure with their look, bald. I'm a girly girl. I like having long hair to play with and change my look with. The sun is very harsh in New Zealand due to a massive hole in our ozone layer. So, it is also much safer for me to wear it.

I wouldn't be the person I am today, had the career, met the people I have, if I hadn't had alopecia. It completely turned my world upside down, but I love who I am today and realize alopecia is a part of what I am and who I am.

After several years of modeling and working in public relations, Anna is enjoying staying home with her twin boys. She looks forward to helping them understand that "beauty doesn't come from the outside, but within too. That it doesn't have to be what is traditionally defined as "beautiful." You need to look beyond that."

Capability

*"Each of us has been put on earth with the ability to do something well.
We cheat ourselves and the world if we don't use that ability as best we can."*

George Allen, Professional Football Coach

Music, athletics, arts…When we discover something that helps us heal, or find it already exists within us, it is easier to use these natural abilities and talents to convince and prove to us our full potential.

"My story brought out the passion of music in me." - **Sammy C**

"When I was in a writing class this past fall, it was the perfect opportunity to put something down on paper." - **Sydney**

"It was enough to make me realize I was good at something." - **Heather**

"I had a lot of internalized anger that I channeled in the water." - **Staciana**

"I needed to find something I loved, and keep doing it." - **Sophia**

"I will never give up because it's what I love to do and what I look forward to." - **Megan**

Justin Mein

Sammy C

I'm Sammy C, and I'm eighteen years old. When I was two, I was diagnosed with alopecia universalis. Throughout my life, I've been mocked, bullied, and even physically beaten. I've determined that a gem cannot be beautiful and shiny without a good polish.

I'm eighteen and still have alopecia. I know who I am. My personality is more vibrant than ever before, and it's all because of what I had to go through. I am not here to plead for people to come up with a cure. This is who I am, and I am positive that I will touch millions. My story brought out the passion of music in me. I started playing the piano when I was seven and guitar when I was fifteen. I've also been singing and rapping ever since the fifth grade.

I had an amazing opportunity of being on *The Voice*, season 5. There are multiple stages of auditions before the artist can hit the big screen, but luckily I was one of the sixty to qualify.

I didn't end up making a team, but just the fact that I made it to television was a huge success, not only for me, but for others who also have alopecia. It also encouraged others who have been bullied.

Bullying is a huge problem everywhere, and we need to speak up. I'm glad I can contribute to that campaign by telling my story. After the show, people contacted me to ask how I got through my struggles. It's a huge blessing to be an inspiration to people who have gone through the same thing.

Now, I'm working on my second album, recording music videos, and booking concerts. My hope is that I can continue to be an inspiration to people who are hurting. I believe I can change this planet with my story and my music. This is the mission exclusive to my existence. I won't stop until I achieve it.

Sammy C first appeared on NBC's "The Voice," season 5. Inspired by the judges feedback, Sammy dedicated himself to writing and composing, and produced his first album in late 2013. His work and natural talent as an MC and vocalist caught the attention of HipHop producer Jay Shanklin with MDI Records. In early 2014, Jay & Sammy C recorded Sammy's new hit single Eh Yo, which topped the charts on Hot Pop Radio. "The Chronicles of Insomnia" mixtape will soon be released.
Check him out at www.sammycmusic.com

Sydney

I am an early twenties college student, majoring in biochemistry and pre-med. I currently have lost all my hair to alopecia and have dealt with the psychological and social effects it has had. I know how hard it is to be a girl and slowly lose your hair. I hope to be a general family practitioner one day and be able to share and show empathy with my patients. I've written a children's book about my story and I hope when others read it, they can share in my feelings and the happiness

when truly finding yourself through alopecia.

My book became a part of my reality due to everything I experienced. I was ten years old when I was diagnosed with alopecia areata, but it was only ever just small velvety smooth patches of scalp that eventually grew back. I didn't have any obvious signs of alopecia again until three years ago, right after I graduated high school. I was shocked to discover the smooth feeling of my scalp while getting ready one day.

It's a devastating and frightening experience at any age. Hair loss in women is hard to deal with because society has made us all think our hair defines us and makes us beautiful. Society is wrong. Hair doesn't define a person. What you do with your life and who you are is what defines you.

I watched as my hair fell out over the next year and a half. After having twenty to seventy steroid injections in my scalp every six weeks, I figured out hair wasn't what defined me. Even though I have a high pain threshold, those injections caused me to be lightheaded and in pain. They weren't doing anything for me when I was at school and having to keep up with my aggressive course work in biology and chemistry. By October of 2013, I had no hair anywhere on my body. Talk about being a psychological and emotional mess, and still pushing through school and life.

I had a point to prove to an elderly woman who told me I couldn't be a lady without hair. Wigs were a terrible feeling against my scalp, and they were too much maintenance for me being a biology and chemistry major and being in a lab everyday.

Hiding behind scarves and being insecure, was also wearing on me. My boyfriend left me, after we'd been dating for almost a year, when I needed his support the most. I didn't know how I felt about having to shave my head or being asked to model hats for *Wishes Together*. It was all so much to adapt to and take in at one time.

Through all the tears, and the support my family and friends were giving me, I needed a release. I needed to write down some of what I was feeling so I could understand it all. When I was in a writing class this past fall, it was the perfect opportunity to put something down on paper. That's when the story for the book began.

The book is called *The Curse of the Fates* and is my story, in fiction. It is about a twelve-year-old girl named Lottie who is experiencing losing her hair to alopecia. She doesn't understand why the fates have cursed her with something so traumatic. Lottie experiences the psychological and social effects of losing her hair, and finds out which friends are true to her and how they are there to be with her, not for her hair. She rides the roller coaster alopecia puts you through emotionally, and eventually goes to see a "witch" to try and make her hair come back. In the end, it just comes down to being healthy, happy, and hopeful. I never anticipated being encouraged to send my story into a publishing company, around Christmas break.

With the support of my professors, the librarians at Concordia University, and my family, I got my story refined and sent in to multiple children's publishing companies. By January 2014, a publisher picked up my words, and I was in the process of getting a book published. I worked with them on getting the book layout and manuscript set up and refined. They let me bring in Katy Jackson, from London, as my illustrator, who did a fantastic job. Katy helped give my words life and images that portrayed what I was trying to get across.

The book process was long and tedious, but in the end I believe it was worth it. It's made me a better person and helped me accept having no hair. It's been my coping mechanism. I'm hoping it can provide hope and comfort for those also affected by alopecia, either directly or indirectly. I want to spread awareness and educate society and communities about alopecia to make it okay for others with their own insecurities. I have already received videos and thank you notes from women and children affected by alopecia who have read my story. They give me hope and strength to keep pushing myself on. They are the difference I am trying to make. They make me face the public and accept alopecia as I am. Everything I have gone through with alopecia has given me the motivation to try and make a difference in my life and the lives of others.

Sydney is currently finishing up her junior year of college and degrees, and has a few book and speaking events in the upcoming months to promote alopecia awareness and to educate others.

Heather

Ever since I could remember, I always looked in the mirror and thought, "I like the way I look, but I would look 100 times better if I had hair." I always concentrated on the one thing I didn't have and everyone else around me did. That kind of negative thinking consumed my thought process every day since I was five years old.

"What would my life be like with that girl's hair?" "How much better at sports would I be if I had hair?" "How many boys would pay attention to me if I looked like that girl with her hair?" It was exhausting to live with this relentless negativity and insecurity, and I was unable to focus on anything else.

People will always compare themselves to others, but I had the ultimate comparison: an identical twin. My sister, Jen, has never been diagnosed with alopecia. Although I love and admire her so much because she has been by my side through it all, I did envy her when I was younger. Who doesn't envy a beautiful, athletic girl with the most gorgeous long, shiny blonde hair?

Luckily, I was fortunate enough to have a family that could afford for me to wear wigs. Going to the wig store felt like Christmas morning. I finally didn't have to stand out in the crowd as the little bald girl, or so I thought. Initially, they would make me feel so happy, but eventually I would still feel different because nobody else I knew wore wigs. Once again, my feelings of insecurity would emerge.

My parents worked hard to involve me in activities from the time I was diagnosed. I played competitive soccer and basketball until high school, and then discovered volleyball and fell in love with the sport. My most self-conscious moments were when I played sports. I never wanted my teammates, or anyone really, to see me without a wig. So I would tape it down, tie the long itchy hair back, and wear the thing in 90° weather if I had to. As much as I hated it, there was no other option for me. The negative thoughts would be overflowing in my head while I tried to convince myself that when I got hair, I wouldn't have to care about this and would be such a better player.

Even though I was never completely confident when playing sports, I never used my hair loss as an excuse to give up. My sister and I grew up with natural athletic ability and talent, which definitely helped boost my self-esteem. It was enough to make me realize that I was good at something.

"When is this insecurity ever going to go away?" I finally discovered what it would take. Thanks to my sister, best friend Rosie, and a pair of nail clippers, I was finally able to rid my negative thinking. I always thought I would never be happy unless all my hair grew back.

I was diagnosed with AA when I was five, and I used to set goals for the anticipated year I would grow all my hair back. After elementary school…then middle school… and then finally high school. I did grow 60% of it back, which led me to set the next goal for after college. Then there was the dreaded day I brushed my hair, and the brush started filling up with hair. Each day, I became more worried. Discouraged and defeated, I finally came to the realization the goal I wanted to accomplish so badly was not going to end in my favor. Making an anticipated "end date" didn't give me any control over it, but finally getting rid of the hair myself, did.

The nail clippers weren't ideal, but it's all we had. I was finally in control of my hair loss. As the hair fell down to the ground, so did my negative thoughts. It was the most liberating experience that surprisingly gave me a sense of relief. I didn't realize this would be the outcome and honestly didn't think I would ever experience this peace of mind.

I decided that this was a once in a lifetime experience I wanted to share with anyone and everyone who was interested in my story. I knew it was going to be painful, but wanted to show off my bald head with my "peace of mind" right where everyone could see it. I decided to get a tattoo with a sunflower (my favorite flower), with a peace sign in the middle and the stem forming the word *Of* in cursive. The pain was worth it. When people ask about my tattoo, I am able to explain, with a smile on my face, about my hair loss to those who have never heard of alopecia. I could finally use all that energy to start making realistic goals for myself. Goals that had nothing to do with hair.

During college, I realized that I wanted to help people figure out how to overcome obstacles. One of the biggest goals I had for myself was to pursue a career where I could feel fulfilled by helping others. After completing my degree in Recreation Therapy, I landed my first full-time job as a therapist. I worked with adults who had severe and profound intellectual and physical disabilities. We did everything from going on nature walks around campus, to a four day vacation. It was challenging at times, especially with the level of care and support they required, but what I ended up discovering about myself was that I have mastered the ability to adapt.

Overcoming adversity wouldn't have been as possible without my amazing group of friends and loving and supportive family who always made every effort to make sure I felt comfortable with myself. I am also lucky to have met my bald family. Just to know you are not alone is the best feeling a girl with alopecia can have. So the last thing I have to say to alopecia is THANK YOU!

Ignacio Di Biaggio

Heather works as a recreation therapist, is a competitive volleyball player, and spends a great deal of her free time traveling around the world. She recently returned from a trip to Dubai and Cape Town where her tattoo drew the positive attention of locals and tourists alike.

Staciana

"This isn't me…Who is this?" I thought as I stared at the 12-year-old bald girl looking back at me. My dad had just shaved off the remnants of my hair, and as I looked in the mirror, all I could repeat was, "Why?…Why me?" That afternoon, I lay on the floor and cried until I had no more tears to shed. I cried and sang along to Patsy Cline's greatest hits over and over, trying to sing the sadness out of me while "falling to pieces."

Three months earlier, I stood in front of that same mirror and brushed my long brown hair. I was getting ready for school and thinking to myself, "I look so cute today." I was an optimistic child and wanted to fit in with the cool kids at school. So, I tried to style my hair the same way they did, thinking it would earn friendships. As I combed my hair, I had to continuously clean out the brush. The trashcan was filling up quickly. I ran to my mom, as a normal

dramatic pre-teen would and said, "Mom! I'm dying!" She laughed at me with nervous concern and said, "I don't think you're dying, but let's go to the doctor and see what's wrong." We went to multiple doctors and all had the same answer. "You're fine. You're not dying. You have alopecia areata, which is causing your hair to fall out. We don't know the cause. We don't know how much will fall out. It could come back at any time, and it could fall out again at any time. But you're fine." I thought to myself, "How is this FINE?! I am a 12-year-old girl going bald. This is NOT fine!" They discussed my options to try and grow my hair back. They suggested topical steroid creams and cortisone injections into my scalp. Neither had a high success rate of stopping hair loss or promoting hair growth, and I would be dependent on these treatments for the rest of my life. I decided the medicines and pain weren't for me.

Three months later, after waking up to hair all over my pillow each night and clumps falling out in the shower, most of my hair was gone. My dad insisted he shave my head. I knew the few strands that were left looked terrible, but I could not prepare myself for the image of the bald girl standing before me. I wore hats and scarves in public and at school for all of 7th grade. I became introverted and nervous, wanting to hide under my hat and disappear. Normally silly and bubbly, I grew more depressed and scared to go out in public. But swimming saved me.

My older sister and I swam before we walked. We spent hours at the pool, pretending to be mermaids. My love for the water exceeded everything else. There was a calmness in the water that made me feel whole and free. We joined the local YMCA swim team when I was six and swam competitively for all of our childhood. When I began to lose my hair, I knew I didn't want to stop swimming. I thought it would be foolish to wear a wig. I laughed and thought, "Here I am swimming in the pool, and there goes my wig floating away…" So, I decided to rock my bald head at practice. I explained to my swim team friends what was going on, and their reaction was priceless. "Cool! You are going to swim faster!"

My hair almost completely came back the summer after 7th grade. I had the best summer: swimming and not wearing hats. I felt free. Free from hiding, free from worry, happy that my prayers were answered. But at the beginning of 8th grade, it all started to fall out again. I wasn't sad anymore. I was angry. I was angry at the uncertainty. I was angry that I didn't have any control over it. I was angry that I wasn't normal like every other 8th grader. I was angry that I would have to lose the happiness and freedom that I enjoyed all summer, and even more angry that I would have to deal with this my whole life. My anger motivated me to stop wearing hats and hiding in public. I didn't want to hope and pray and then be disappointed. So, I would have to embrace it.

The first day of school without a hat was the hardest day of my life. I was fearful, but determined. I walked to school looking at the ground, putting one foot in front of the other, telling myself, "I can do this." I ignored the kids laughing and teasing. I ignored the stares. I ignored it all. At the same time, my swimming started to improve. I had a lot of internalized anger that I channeled in the water. I put my head down, and worked as hard as I could to push my body to its limits every day. I loved that I didn't need hair to swim fast. It didn't matter that I was bald in the water. In fact, it felt amazing to have the cold-water rush over my head as I swam. I slowly progressed, dropping time every year until I made my first national team and competed in the Goodwill Games in 1998, at age sixteen. I had started swimming with the Irvine Novaquatics in 1997, where Amanda Beard trained. She had swam in the 1996 Olympics, and I watched her race in awe. We were the same age, swam the same event, and now I had the opportunity to race her every day. She gave me the confidence to believe I could make an Olympic team, and that's all I thought about for three years as I trained thirty hours a week. I made the 2000 USA Olympic Team in the 100 Breaststroke by .001 of a second, the smallest margin possible, and swam in the 400 x 100 medley relay that won gold in Sydney. I believe I would not have made that team had I not had alopecia universalis. The condition motivated me to prove I didn't need hair. It made me angry, which I used to train harder each day. And ultimately, as my teammates said that fateful first day at practice, my hair loss "made me faster." Fast enough, even if it was only one-one hundredth of a second fast enough, to achieve my dream of becoming an Olympian.

Staciana still enjoys swimming, and recently discovered a love for yoga that continues to inspire her to fully embrace life. Spending the last several years traveling the world, Staciana and her family have recently returned home to California, looking to discover their next adventure together.

Sophia

Throughout life, everyone is faced with their own set of battles to overcome. I just consider mine a bit different than my friends. At the age of two, my hair started rapidly falling out in patches until I was completely bald. It progressively grew back by the time I turned five. Fall out, grow back, repeat. That was a process I became all too familiar with by the time I was a teenager. Throughout most of my school years, I felt too ashamed and embarrassed to draw any type of attention to myself. It always felt as if someone was judging me, especially when I walked into the first day of middle school without any eyelashes.

Even though I have never known life without alopecia, I've spent a lot of time feeling like my identity was completely taken away from me. My junior year of high school was a major turning point for me. I was in the position where I had enough hair to cover most of my bald spots; however, going to school and trying to act like nothing was wrong got old pretty quickly. I would come home, lock myself in my room, and analyze every single bald spot until I couldn't force myself to look in a mirror anymore. I even missed my junior prom because of this. If I heard one more person talk about how they were planning to do their hair that special night, I might have exploded. At that point, I was willing to do anything to experience how it felt to have a full head of hair for one day. Just twenty-four hours was all I wanted. I knew I needed to find a way to get myself out of this funk.

I needed to find something I loved, and keep doing it. The answer was simple…music and softball. Music gave me a sense of comfort. I knew I could come home from school, no matter what kind of day I had, pick up my guitar and play for hours. It instantly became my biggest escape. Softball gave me a source of acceptance. To my teammates, it didn't matter how scarce my eyebrows were or if I could get my hair into the perfect ponytail. They became my best friends and were there for me when I needed them the most. Together, guitar and softball became the perfect distractions.

Although having hair on my head during this time is a blessing, the anxiety of waking up without any is still there. I wake up two hours before school starts to make sure there are no new spots and that all the ones I do have, are covered. I still find that I'm extra paranoid about whether one of the spots is showing, even though I know most of them can't be seen. The thought of going to college and telling my roommate about my alopecia is something I think about often. I'm turning eighteen now, and still facing these same challenges. I've learned to accept myself for who I am, and the many other lessons along the way.

I now realize that hair doesn't define you. I once read a quote that said, "I am not this hair. I am not this skin. I am the soul that lies within." This may have taken me long to learn, but once I did, it completely changed my perspective in a positive way. Whether I am going through a fall out or regrowth stage, I am still the same Sophia. There were times when my alopecia would lead people to flip up my hair and laugh at my bald spots, but at a certain point, it stops mattering. I knew that whether I had no hair on my head or a full head of hair, my personality would ultimately stay the same. I'd still have the same morals, likes, and dislikes.

I have lived through an abundance of ups and downs and have come out of every single one alive. This entire process has made me a stronger person than I could ever imagine. The more positive I have been with all of this, the easier it has become to handle. Once I saw that I wasn't going through this alone, a huge weight lifted off my shoulders. I realized that if I was looking up to someone experiencing this, whose strength seemed like something I could never reach, maybe somebody was doing the same with me. I always try to remember that my story of survival could serve as an inspiration to someone else.

Sophia enjoys playing softball and the guitar, and plans on attending college in the fall. She continues to focus on the present because "We have no idea what the future has planned for us."

Jennifer Starcher

Megan

I would like to send a message in hope of inspiring others. I was diagnosed with alopecia when I was eight years old. I am twenty years old now and have been living with it for twelve years.

We first noticed my hair loss one day when I put my hair in a ponytail for school and saw the bottom half of my hair was gone. We went to the doctor, and I was diagnosed with alopecia areata. It's really tough for a young girl to live with hair loss. Hair is one of those things that makes us feel girly and pretty. Being eight years old, living with alopecia wasn't too bad. It didn't exactly bother me because I had only lost the bottom half of my hair, which wasn't very noticeable. It was easier to keep it to myself. After about a year, it all grew back, until middle school when I started

80

losing a lot more hair. I was losing it at the top of my head, which everyone could notice! I didn't know how to hide it or cover it. I tried using powders to blend it, and even tried hair pieces later on. But that didn't keep people from noticing. There was a group of about five boys who bullied me all the time. It was extremely traumatizing. I hated and dreaded school because of the bullying. Every day, they would say horrible things and make fun of me in front of everyone. It's shocking that others can actually have the heart, or lack there-of, to do so much to one person. Who would think that simply losing your hair would be such a hard thing to overcome? Because of my choice of career path in skating and being bullied in school, I switched to homeschooling. I am so glad I made this decision. It made things a lot easier to deal with, and helped me focus more on what was most important to me.

After all the bullying I went through, I had a difficult time accepting it. I was very depressed and didn't feel like a normal girl. I never understood why it was happening to me, but eventually I finally accepted it. I stopped caring about the hatred, and I got over it. The stronger I became, the better it was for me. I learned to own it, and now I absolutely love it! I love wearing wigs and playing around with them, or not even wearing one at all. I want to spread the message to always be yourself and own what happens to you. You are the way you are for a reason, and that's amazing! Everything happens for a reason. I've found that now I can turn it into a way to help others. I want to raise awareness for alopecia and bullying. I want to make a name for myself, so later down the road I can use it to help others. My biggest goal in life is to become as successful as I can in order to give back as much as I can.

My biggest passion in life is figure skating, which has pretty much kept me sane through having alopecia. I've been skating for fifteen years and competing for eight. I'm very devoted to my skating. Although I've had multiple set-backs from serious back injuries, I will never give up because it's what I love to do and what I look forward to. Without skating, I don't know where I would be today. Skating is what pushed me through everything.

My accomplishments as a figure skater include being a US gold medalist, North Atlantic Regional Champion, a three time national showcase qualifier, and one time national showcase competitor, finishing in 7th place in the nation. My biggest goal for this year is to get into the show business side of skating by becoming part of a professional live ice show. I'm also a huge fitness fanatic! I love yoga, lifting weights, aerial arts, and hoop dancing. Another artistic interest of mine is modeling. I was signed with a modeling agency at the age of fifteen, but just in the past few years have become more involved with it. I've been able to work with different photographers, and recently had a four page spread and article written in a magazine.

In the future, when I'm done with ice shows and everything else, I plan on joining my family's business. I can also see myself branching off and doing something more independent. Just recently, I became certified in teaching yoga. My main goal is to help people with health conditions through my yoga. After becoming a certified instructor, it made me want to learn more. I've now found that I'm very interested in personal training to help disabled and/or mentally challenged people.

I have beaten a few odds with my back and skating, and I couldn't be more thankful. I want others to experience what I was so lucky to have. Being able to give options to others, especially to the ones who can prove to be so much more, is important.

Giving others the ability to heal is one of Megan's ultimate goals. She would like to put a studio together that would help those who are disabled, with personal training and figure skating as methods of therapy.

Unconditional Love

"There are only two lasting bequests we can hope to give our children.
One of these is roots, the other, wings."
Johann Wolfgang von Goethe, German Poet

As parents, we always want the best for our children, whether they have alopecia or not. We are given many opportunities to help them grow into mature adults who can handle a multitude of responsibilities. With alopecia, the lessons we would typically teach them as they grow older present themselves much earlier than expected. We search high and low for a cure, for some type of resolution, and finally realize that choices are what ultimately help our children embrace their difference. Choices to be whoever they want to be, wear whatever they want or don't want on their head, and the freedom to discover all of this in their own time.

"My perspective these days is pretty simple…Confidence…Attitude…Education." - **Abby's Mom**

"She needed to suffer in silence so I would not really understand what was going on . . ." - **Diogo**

"It was time for me to stop living in fear, to stop hiding and face my truth." - **Rachel**

"I feel good, happy, and grateful that I have alopecia." - **Isabel**

". . . and so my journey began…I did it for my Isabel." - **Allison (Isabel's Mom)**

"What I'm waiting for now is that he can accept it, and throw the
bandana away so he will feel free and strong." - **Alexis** *(Vangelis' Dad)*

"I am happy that me and my dad are the same." - **Vangelis**

"I know my family will always take care of me and my sister." - **Jasmine**

". . . you will be okay because you have your family to take care of you." - **Joanna**

"We love them so much, and help them build their confidence . . ." - **Jasmine & Joanna's Dad**

"I feel good about my alopecia because it doesn't bother me." - **Maya**

". . . we believe that knowledge is power." - **Maya's Mom**

Angela Lang Photography

Abby

I am four years old, and I have had alopecia since I was three. I feel good about my alopecia. My friends feel good about my alopecia too. I like looking like Curious George, wearing hats and headbands. A girl named Angelina also has alopecia. She works at the frozen yogurt shop. I want to be a princess when I grow up. I like to play princesses and jump all day.

Abby's Mom - "My perspective these days is pretty simple…"

1. **Confidence** – Build Abby's confidence, and praise/kiss/love her bald head. Every chance I get, I kiss it. Make sure she knows she can do anything she wants – no matter what.

2. **Attitude** – Abby will model our attitude about everything. The first six weeks, we were fairly distraught and sad, but we have come a long way. We try to be involved in as many alopecia related events we can, and let Abby see others without hair and make it all positive. We have made many new friends!

3. **Education** – People are curious and concerned. I try to take any annoying questions (Does she have cancer?) in a positive light. Abby will see how I react to these questions, so we have to just be kind. I have sent out a letter at Abby's preschool, and also made a little business card with Abby's picture on it so she (or I) can hand it out to people who inquire. This Christmas, I plan to send the NAAF quarterly newsletter out to close family and friends.

Abby loves princesses and My Little Pony. Apples and noodles are her favorite foods. She is learning how to swim and enjoys gymnastics and ballet class. She can spell her name and never misses having a treat after dinner, especially if it's chocolate.

Diogo

I am twenty one years old. I was diagnosed with alopecia universalis at the age of four, and today this disease is a part of my life. I have already accepted alopecia as a part of me and so I am already "mentally resolved." Not having any hair on my body is completely normal for me.

Before I start digging in my story, I want to write down something that I consider important to those who are suffering from alopecia at the moment: No one is absolutely less than anyone else just because he/she does not have hair! I mean, what is really valuable in a person is his/her "essence," not the exterior appearance! When you accept this and achieve this state of conformation, life gets shiny again.

Now, my story. I was only four years old when my hair first started to fall. The first indicator of having something unusual was the random and small lacks of hair. Who is really worried with this when you can easily hide them by just combing the hair? At that time, all I needed to do was comb my hair to the side of the spots and I was ready to go. Simple, right? No, not that simple. Those spots multiplied, and I really did not understand why this was happening to me. Moreover, my family did not know what it was

84

because as you may know, alopecia is not totally a hereditary disease, and we never had a registered case of alopecia before. I remember waking up and seeing my pillow covered with hair. Lots of hair! Although I barely remember that time, I do remember seeing my nearest family suffering with this unknown situation. I can understand that it is not easy to see a relative losing his hair. Once he had always been healthy, day after day. Then not knowing why this was happening, was confusing. What I cannot imagine is how my mother felt during those years because she needed to suffer in silence so I would not really understand what was going on, and so I could have a "normal" life like the other kids. And I always did. I had a normal life back then, and I also have a normal life now.

I cannot deny that I heard some unhappy and uncomfortable comments when I was younger. As everyone knows, kids can be very mean to each other. I learned it by myself because sometimes I heard comments related to not having hair. I think, nowadays, those who suffer from this disease need to raise his/her head and think that even though people are mean, we cannot give importance to those comments. People usually talk about what they do not know, not giving any importance to other people's feelings. In fact, we need to have the discernment to understand this and take it as a realized truth. Once we get that, our life is so much easier!

My family has always been there for me, in the good and bad situations of my life. They are my shelter. For that reason, my childhood was so "natural," and I can say, nowadays, that I am psychologically healthy because of them. I have a twin brother, who I don't consider very like to me (even though everyone says the opposite). It could be because he does not have alopecia. My twin brother and I are the type of brothers who are still very emotionally dependent on each other. It is really good having someone to talk with at any time of my day. Although we are studying at different places now, we are still very close.

A characteristic of mine I think was mostly influenced by not having hair, is that I do not like finding hair on my stuff! It makes me "uncomfortable," but I do not really know why! It is kind of funny!

Bruno Nabiça

Diogo lives in Portugal and studies Human Resources Management at Polytechnic Institute of Setubal. He is very interested in all the areas of study that can relate to people development, whether in an individual or in a team perspective, such as Psychology, Sociology, Happiness, and so on. Diogo loves to visit Lisbon, the capital city of Portugal – which is his favorite city – to spend his spare time laughing and joking with his friends and doing other stuff a person in his 20's likes to do.

Rachel

My alopecia story started four-and-a-half years ago. I remember it vividly. I was lying on my side, on my daughter's bed, while reading her a story. I lifted my head, placing my hand through my hair to hold my head up. That is when I felt it. I knew instantly what it was. The perfection of the circular shape; alopecia. I had studied it in beauty school. I had a moment of panic and just seemed to know my life was about to change. I went to my doctor soon after and was referred to a dermatologist. They told me it could be due to stress or hormone imbalances, and could be temporary. I had just had my second daughter. I began testing to find out the cause for my hair loss. Nothing was found except a new spot on the side of my head, which began to rapidly grow. I began steroid injections in my scalp as my hair continued to fall out. I went through a gamut of treatments and supplements. I searched conventional, natural, homeopathic, and naturopathic avenues. I went cosmic and tried reiki. I consulted famous medical psychics and other various energy work and healing. I sought out Chinese doctors and acupuncture. I regularly used the acupuncture tool that was hammered on my head until my scalp bled. I put creams on my head that

severely burned the skin. I took every herb and vitamin that might possibly bring back my hair, and spent literally thousands of dollars trying to find a reason and cure for my hair loss. It was all to no avail. I was living in hats and watching handfuls of hair come out of my head. I received the diagnosis that it was autoimmune alopecia, not a result of hormone imbalances. By this time, I had virtually no hair left. I decided it was time for a wig. I could no longer keep my hair loss a secret. I was so embarrassed and ashamed. I felt ugly and unfeminine. The irony was that I was a hairstylist and had been for over fifteen years. I knew the option to be bald was there, but at the time, this was inconceivable to me. How could a female hairstylist be successful and bald in an industry based on looks?

At this same time, my husband of almost twenty years and I divorced. The two major life events were significant that they happened together. They both forced me to really look at myself, to find my true self because I had nothing left to identify ME with. I had temporarily left my hairstyling career to raise children, and moved to a new state for my then husband's job. I had lost everything I identified myself with; hair, career, and being a wife all at once. I felt lost and unsure of who I was. Having two young girls to think about though, I couldn't wallow or be held down by these negative events. I had them with great intention, and from day one was dedicated to being the model of the type of woman I was trying to raise them to be. So I found my boot straps and started pulling like I never had before. I thought how I would want them to respond in this situation. Both events showed me how I needed to relook at how I define myself, and how much judgment I had toward myself and others. It caused me to look at my entire value system and beliefs of beauty and femininity. I sought out a support system of friends, therapists, and family which proved to be the beginning of finding me. They offered support; let me cry; let me get angry; let me go through the grieving process of losing my hair. I gave myself space to move through the process.

At that point, my wig was necessary in my process because it allowed me not to have to address my hair loss when out in public or for moments of my life when I just couldn't. On my journey with alopecia, I searched high and low to find a wig that was somewhat affordable, but was also something I could work with to make look like real hair and be as comfortable as possible. Along with a good friend of mine who was a hairstylist, we learned by trial and error how to cut them to work for me. I sought out others in the guarded wig industry to learn how to work with wigs in different ways. Receiving as much advanced training as I could, I knew there was quite a bit that could be done to create more comfort with the cap, and create a cut and style to make the wig not look so "wiggy," and feel like me. I painstakingly altered a wig for myself that looked so good people stopped to compliment me on how much they liked my hair. Wearing a wig gave me time to accept my alopecia, grieve over losing my hair, and come to terms that I was also losing a part of me.

I never wore my wig at home with my children. I hated wearing it. It was hot, itchy, and I was beginning to resent the notion that I felt like I needed to hide and be ashamed of my lack of hair. At the same time, I was living in terror that someone would see me without it. I struggled with why I felt so ashamed that I would be

that uncomfortable to make others comfortable, for people who didn't even know me. It bothered my girls that I was so afraid to go out in public without it or let anyone know about my alopecia. I was hoping it would go away, or I'd find something that would cure it and I wouldn't have to deal with it. Not the case for me. One of the pivotal moments in my journey with hair loss was a conversation with my daughters. They asked me why I lived like this, and both said, "If I had alopecia, I would just be brave and be bald." In that moment, I realized I was teaching them to stay small and not own who they were. What I wanted to teach them was to be bold, take chances, live their lives to the fullest, and embrace and love themselves. The only way to teach them to be strong, self-loving, happy, confident, successful, and independent women was to show them by example. It was time for me to stop living in fear, to stop hiding and face my truth.

I decided in that moment, I wasn't going to do it anymore. I began to work on educating myself further, revamping my career and my place in it as a bald hairstylist. I had to be brave. A poem by David Whtye called *Step Close In* is my mantra, "Take the first step, the step you don't want to take…" I began taking those steps, keeping awareness of what I was feeling; fear, anxiety, or whatever it was at the moment. I just kept going. Every time I found I embraced my alopecia more or was more open about it, amazing things would open either within myself or in my life. My alopecia was turning into more of a gift than I could ever have imagined. I began to talk about it and share my experience with people. I found there were many others out there who just wanted to find someone who understood and could help them in their process, their journey. I could offer understanding, compassion, options, choices, and suggestions on how to be creative and live with hair loss. I could also give back some control to at least allow a person to look the way they need to, so they can continue on their journey with whatever it was they were dealing with. I have found I can be a facilitator, helping ease the process of hair loss for someone else, something I wish I would have found early in my experience.

Rachel's Story Continues…

I personally don't think women should feel like they have to wear wigs. I understand, however, that dealing with hair loss is a process, and for me I needed time to figure it all out. My wig gave that to me. So, my work in offering wig services is to help with that part of the process, to give women the power to choose and hopefully inspire them to see what their options are.

I have become fueled by my alopecia. I now live without my wig. Being uncovered, I notice people noticing me. But it is not as difficult as I had thought it would be. I truly feel it is no different than if I had a purple mohawk. It's different, eye-catching, and raises curiosity. I look at it as an opportunity to educate, bring awareness, and inspire people to be more open and compassionate in their lives.

When I discovered I had lost the ability to hide who I really was in losing my hair, I found humility, openness, enormous amounts of consideration and compassion, and most importantly, awareness of myself and others around me. Not having hair exposes the real you. My alopecia not only showed me myself, but helped me look at others in a whole new light. We all have our battles and difficulties in life. For some of us, they are visible. For others, they are not. For those like me, we have the option to camouflage it until we are ready to share it. I have been beyond humbled by my alopecia. I feel like with the loss of my hair, I lost my armor. In the journey that led me to living uncovered, I shed the heavy facade I was carrying around and freed myself. It has taught me how and where to find inner strength. I found how to stand in my truth, be authentic, and be completely at ease with it all. I am far from perfect, but even in all my imperfections, I see beauty. I see beauty in everyone. Alopecia has taught me how to redefine beauty for myself and how I find it in the world.

Some of my many goals are to make some strides for change, and influence my industry to bring more awareness and openness around hair loss. The hair industry is not stepping up to the needs of women facing hair loss. For various reasons, hair loss is on the rise in our country. There should be more education available to stylists to serve hair loss clients better, and to have more support from companies to offer better options for women. Better quality, less expensive wigs should be available, along with scalp treatments and head massages in a private setting available in salons. A woman should not have to lose the salon experience just because she loses her hair. Cutting and styling wigs is still working with hair. For a woman, going to get her hair cut is more than just about the hair. It is a way to take care of herself, be pampered, and empowered to make a choice in how she looks. While I bring options and support to women facing hair loss, I also want the reality of seeing a bald woman to not be so foreign. Being a bald female hairstylist has brought challenges for me personally, but it has more often than not brought incredible fulfillment and joy at seeing how offering the services I do, coupled with my experience and understanding, can give people options and help on their journeys. If a woman can get to a point where she feels good, she can make strides in gaining confidence and work toward healing and moving past whatever she is dealing with on any level. I am still discovering the gifts my alopecia has brought me. Each day, I find more reasons to be grateful for who and what alopecia brings me in my life. I have met the most amazing people, my fiancé included, and have had the most unbelievable experiences because of it. I have more happiness and satisfaction in my life than ever before. Thank you alopecia! Thank you for changing my life, opening my eyes and my heart. Thank you for the gift of learning to let go; for being the cataclysm that led me to my purpose and to finding my authentic self. I am so grateful for my alopecia and the chance to share my journey, and maybe help ease the process of hair loss for others.

Rachel is currently running, "Fringe Benefits," a specialty program for hair loss clients in the salon she works in. She and her fiancé are the current Sonoma/Napa County NAAF support group leaders, and are actively involved with NAAF. She is also on the Lead Council for the American Cancer Society, working with the "Look Good, Feel Better" program. She has begun public speaking, using her own alopecia story as a platform to bring awareness for alopecia to encourage more compassion and tolerance in the community.

Isabel

I am five years old. I was two and four months old when I got alopecia. I feel good, happy, and grateful that I have alopecia. I love not having hair and that I don't have to brush it. I love hair, but I love not having it because hair gets lots of knots in it. My friends make me feel happy. They are kind to me. I like when they do that. Sometimes, kids who don't know me laugh at me because I have alopecia. When that happens, I don't feel happy and it hurts my feelings. I don't know anyone else who has alopecia other than my mom. When I grow up, I want to be a mom. Something fun I like to do is get ice cream with daddy and mommy, Evin, and Anna. I like to go to the park, sledding, skiing, and drawing. I really like swimming. I like to do everything. I like that me and my mom both have alopecia. I think it's good.

"Isabel is a very kind and sweet little girl. She is happy, cheerful, and full of adventure and curiosity. She is very confident in everything she does, and it shows in the way she is not afraid to take on a new challenge. She is very active and loves to learn new skills like archery, skiing, swimming, gymnastics, and karate. She is a natural athlete and excels at whatever sport she is trying. She also loves to draw, write, and read and is very confident in her work and expressing herself. She is helpful and always willing to jump in and lend a hand. She loves cooking, Play-Doh, and doing fun gooey science experiments. She has a silly side. She loves to make us laugh by making silly faces and doing silly things. She is not afraid to be herself and follow her own path. She is confident in her choices and the way she expresses herself, from her clothes to her demeanor." - Mom

Allison

On June 7, 2012, I stepped out of the car and walked into the grocery store with my head free of my cranial prosthesis. For the first time in twenty years, I left my crutch, my wig, at home and showed the world my true self. I was liberated, anxious, and proud. I looked in the mirror, and what I saw back was beauty, strength, and love. I knew I had to share it with the world for one reason only, to make this world a more compassionate, kinder, gentler place for my daughter, and so my journey began... I did it for my Isabel.

The courage one finds for their child is an amazing thing. I had to have it now more than ever for my daughter. At two, Isabel was diagnosed with alopecia areata. As a mother, I was in a unique situation because I grew up with alopecia from the age of five. Thirty five years later, and it is a part of me. It was something I continually had to make peace with as my condition changed from areata to totalis, from my natural hair with bald spots, to complete baldness to wearing wigs. At times, it was difficult. I had my up days and down days, but I tried to keep it in perspective and not let it take over my life. Instead, I used my condition to motivate and push me to be stronger. It actually made

me strive for more. I never let alopecia stand in my way from attaining my dreams. I was determined to be seen as Allison, not a girl with alopecia. It would not define me or stop me. I did all that I set out to do: bachelor's degree, sorority, marriage to love of my life, travel, master's degree, art educator, three beautiful children. I was outgoing, took risks, and lived life. I was happy and content with life. Things were going along as planned. Until I had an accident one month after our move to Washington.

It was Cyber Monday. I raced down the stairs, after putting the kids to bed, to do some on-line Christmas shopping when I slipped on the last two steps and broke a vertebra and two ribs. Nice clean breaks. No other damage. I came home from the hospital, unable to walk up the stairs, hold my children or care for them. It was very difficult for all three of them. New home, new place and now after only knowing my care, I sent my two youngest off to daycare. It was very hard for my then two and three year old. Two months later is when I saw the two round patches on the top of Isabel's perfect little head. I just cried.

My peace with alopecia was over. It is one thing to have it yourself, but to see my beautiful baby with it broke my heart. The guilt came gushing in like a flood that would not stop. Not only was it my genes that caused this in my perfect beautiful baby girl, but it was my accident, my inability to take care of her adequately for two months as I recovered, that caused this. I knew she had it. I believe that the stress of this event was the onset of her condition. I made the appointment for the dermatologist more as a formality. I knew the words she would say, "Your daughter has alopecia areata." At that time, I had no idea what course Isabel's alopecia would take, but by the summer we knew she was going to lose it all. Very quickly, she progressed to alopecia totalis; eyebrows, eyelashes, scalp hair was gone.

This opened up old wounds and made me re-evaluate my relationship with alopecia. I had to get honest, get real, and figure out how I wanted to handle this with Isabel. I had to take a hard look at my life. How did this condition affect me? Yes, I had a great life and was strong and took risks, but there were more times than I'd like to admit that I did not. I didn't jump into the pool. I didn't try that new sport. I didn't stand into the wind or take that risk for fear of someone discovering my secret, that I was wearing a wig and that I had alopecia. Of course my family and friends knew, and I was open and would talk about it, but I wasn't fully free to be myself.

Now, as a mother raising a child with alopecia, I had lots of questions I needed to ask myself. How would I raise her with this condition? What insight could I pass along to Isabel? What things would I change for her about how I was raised? What could I make better for her? I knew without a moment's hesitation, I would not put her through any medical treatment like I was. She was way too young. I would show her that she needn't hide her condition, but let it shine. Be your true authentic self. This is when I realized I would need to lead her by example. It was

time for me to shed my wig and be her role model. The world is different now - more accepting, more open to diversity, change, individualism. It's more compassionate now. It's time for change.

Isabel's alopecia has been a gift to me. It has allowed me to shed my wig. It has brought new friendship and unexpected love from so many strangers into our lives. It has allowed me to be an example to so many women and children whom have lost their hair. Yes, we can live life bald, and it can be wonderful. It was difficult at first. The stares and questions, but I was new to this way. As time went by and I got more comfortable, it became natural. Now, it doesn't even dawn on me that I am out bald until someone brings it to my attention. Then, I smile. Two-and-half years later, I couldn't imagine going back to wearing a wig. It's freeing. It's unrestricting. It's given me strength and a newfound confidence. There are so many benefits from it. I have so much time now that I don't have to "do" my hair. I don't have to worry about lice. Sorry haired people, but yuck! I can jump in the water and play so freely with my kids. I love it. I do. It's great!

I am proud of the role model I have become for my daughter, for all my children. Every day, I teach them and everyone I come into contact with, tolerance, compassion, and to embrace one another's differences. Isabel's journey so far has been great. We put it right out there so others know what is going on. We try to educate people of our condition and are open to talk about it and answer any questions they might have. She is only five, but she is so strong. She has not had any negative situations thus far. We know as time goes on, she will have questions and may want to experiment with wigs, treatments, and so on. We will be there to support and help her as she grows up. As her mother and someone who has lived with alopecia, I know she will be fine and will have a wonderful life full of love, laughter, friendship, and adventures. She will know she is beauty, strength, and love just the way she is.

After working alongside her husband for several years, Allison changed directions, went back to school, and obtained a Master's degree in Education. She worked as an art teacher until the birth of her first child, and her job title grew to include the role of a stay-at-home mother. She now enjoys traveling and is looking forward to a month-long trip through Europe with her three children.

Alexis and Vangelis

Alexis

The problem started when I was ten years old, and now I am nearly fifty years old. I had a lot of therapies and the hair came back, but started to fall out again at other places. Psychologically, I was in a bad state. All the time, I was afraid the other children would see it, even though they knew and never said anything about it. When I grew older, the patches became bigger, and my confidence was at zero. When my hair was all nearly gone, I decided to have my wife shave the rest too. The first contact with outsiders was very hard. We came out of winter, where I could no longer hide under a hat. Summer started, where we have to gain our money in tourism. Nobody said anything and just accepted my situation. Now, I have adjusted and got used to my bald head, and I don't think about it anymore at all.

When my son started losing his hair, everything came back again. I know what he will go through, and the situation seems like a big mountain. The biggest question is, "Why?" I feel sad, angry, and responsible. I am happy that my son and I don't have another health issue. I always used to look at Vangelis when he got up in the morning and fixed his hair with gel, and I was so proud and happy to see him that way. The lack of this now and seeing him so different, kills me. What I'm waiting for now is that he can accept it and throw the bandana away so he will feel free and strong.

Vangelis

I'm Vangelis. I'm almost eleven years old, and I have had alopecia totalis for one year now. I feel a little bit sad that I am bald, but my friends are behind me. I have a beautiful head, but I dislike that I have to wear a bandana. I do know somebody else with alopecia. He is my dad. I am happy that my dad and me are the same. He makes me laugh when he says that we have to be careful with our long hair. When I grow up, I want to be a pilot. I like to draw boats, like the Titanic. I also like to play football, and I'm learning basketball.

Alexis and Vangelis share a special bond because of their alopecia. Alexis' wish for Vangelis is to have a sense of freedom, comfort, and strength regardless of his alopecia. Through this experience of writing and having photos taken, the entire family has begun to understand the tremendous impact alopecia has had on Alexis, and the need for Vangelis' experience to be different.

Lydia Rawie

Jasmine

I feel that having hair is really great because I get to do fun stuff with it like putting it in braids or ponytails, and also putting it into buns and other cool designs I want. It is fine by me however I want it to be.

I feel really happy for my sister because I know that she is a helpful sister, and also that she is confident and brave even if people look at her and laugh. I know that we are going to help each other get through this together.

When I was a little baby, I got alopecia areata too. I was fine with my hair loss because I knew that my family would always protect me and make me brave about the hair loss. Then, when I was six or seven, my hair grew back.

I do not dislike my hair being lost because I know that the people who don't have hair are always brave, are risk takers and express themselves. It doesn't matter if you have hair. It does matter that you know you like your own self.

What I like to do for fun is to play soccer and go to dance class. I like to do both of these things because they are a really good exercise for your body, and they can be fun. It is also fun when you have the spirit.

Having hair loss means so much for me, my sister, and my parents. I know that if other people have lost their hair too, they are brave. I know that me, and mostly my sister, can be brave in the world.

I know my family will always take care of us. When we were little kids, they were so proud of us because we were being brave and confident in ourselves.

Joanna

My name is Joanna, and I have alopecia areata. I am nine years old. I have a sister, a mom, a dad, and a pet lizard, and they love me for who I am.

People ask me what do my friends think of me, and I say they love me for who I am and not what I look like. They see what's on the inside and not what's on the outside. I have two good friends who love me because I am kind to them.

I got alopecia when I was four years old. When you get it when you're a child, you will be okay because you have your family to take care of you. My sister had it before me, and it started to grow back. I am happy for her, but it took me five years to not be jealous of what she has. It took me years to understand that other people have hair loss and just wanted to be loved too.

People ask me how does it feel to have alopecia areata, and I feel like it's okay for people to have hair loss because I do. We are like a pack full of bravery. People think I have cancer, but I do not have it. Because if I had cancer, I would have been sick! I understand because people don't know what alopecia is, and it is okay.

Something that I dislike about alopecia areata is if people have it, like me, they get bullied and called names. I bet that happens all the time.

I like to play soccer because I can teach people that if you don't have hair, you don't have to stop doing what you love to do. You just be yourself through it.

Mom and Dad

Being a mother of twins who both have alopecia areata was so hard in the beginning. My heart was broken. I even blamed God for it, asking "Why me?" In the beginning, I felt like I wanted to fight when people looked at my girls. At the time, no one was helping me. I told my doctor I was stressed out with the girls' hair loss. He left the room and came back with some paperwork about NAAF. NAAF changed my life. I went to a support group, and if I felt sad or upset, I'd call Annette from NAAF, and she would make me feel better.

Even though I cry once in a while and have feelings about wanting both my daughters to have hair, even for just a day, I am a very proud mom. They are both good daughters who are good dancers and singers.

I decided to sign my girls up for activities like mommy & me dancing, soccer, and mommy & me tiny tots because I wanted my girls to know they are beautiful and not alone. I'm not going to hide them in the closet because they don't have hair. When they have activities or before the start of the new school year, I write a letter about what the girls have, just to educate about what alopecia areata and universalis are all about.

I am Juan, the proud father of Jasmine and Joanna. In the beginning, like Joy, I was very confused and angry of what was happening to my twins. I also asked God why this happened to us, and I blamed myself for not being a good father at the time. I remember brushing their hair in the morning was the hardest moment. It will carry with me forever, seeing how the hair was falling from the scalp, and every day holding each piece was really breaking my heart. I was very lucky to have a flexible schedule at work, year after year, from tiny tots until now. They are now in the fourth grade. I was always able to drop them off at school in the morning, and have not yet missed a field trip or a soccer game. We have also always been at their big dancing stage performances. They both give us so much joyful, happy, and proud moments. I am mostly the follower at home, and Joy is the leader. I am very lucky to have her as the mother of my twins. After she found NAAF, we got educated! Our lives changed for the better. I thank God for guiding us through our journey. The emotional hurt will never go away, but we know how to control it now. We educate the girls at home, as well as our friends and family, teachers, coaches, and dance instructors.

Our kids are well known in our commuinity. We love them so much and help them build their confidence by letting them know they are beautiful inside and out and that they can carry on a normal life like everyone else.

Joanna and Jasmine are smart in academics and enjoy playing soccer. They both love to dance, and they are the love of their parents' lives.

Maya

I am seven years old. I feel good about alopecia because it doesn't bother me. I think my friends feel good about alopecia too because they don't really care that I have no hair, but they do care a lot about me. My friends, Marie-Eve and Emma, tell me they like me without hair and that I am pretty without it. A few things I like about alopecia - I love that my dad paints my head and that I don't have to wash my hair. I don't really like not being able to brush my real hair or being different from other people. I met some new friends at CANAAF who have alopecia. I also know a lady named Carolle, and I like her very much.

Like many other children Maya's age, she is very active. She loves to dance, sing, skate, swim, do arts and crafts, and most of all — she loves gymnastics.

Maya's Mom and Dad's Perspective

Maya started to lose her hair when she was two-and-a-half years old, and by three her alopecia had progressed to totalis. At that time, we didn't know what alopecia was and had no idea what was happening. By the time we figured out what alopecia was all about and pulled ourselves together, Maya was four years old and had started school. We made the decision to concentrate on Maya and give her ALL of our undivided attention. We felt that she not only deserved this, but would need this growing up (especially in her teenage years).

For us, it has been an emotional roller coaster. Back when Maya lost her hair, there were more downs than ups, but now we rarely have down moments. Don't get me wrong, it is still very difficult for us to see how strong Maya has to be at such a young age, not to mention how mature she has become compared to other children her age. Maya's uplifting personality and tremendous inner strength have helped all of us cope with the frustrations.

The way we have coped and dealt with Maya's alopecia is somewhat of a loaded question. Back when Maya lost her hair, her dad and I made a celebration out of it. There came a point when we decided to shave Maya's head, as she had only a few strands left. Maya shaved dad's head, followed by him shaving hers. We then took her out to celebrate and show off their new hairdos. My husband and I noticed many adults looking at Maya and making comments like, "poor little girl," "that's so sad," etc. We even had an older gentleman walk up to us and give us money to buy Maya a little something. It got to the point where going out was uncomfortable because none of us liked the attention. Parents would also pull their children away when they asked us why Maya had no hair. This was hurtful to us because the children were just asking out of curiosity. We began coaching Maya and role playing on how to answer the children's questions because there was nothing to be ashamed about. We would also tell the parents that it was okay that their children had questions and encouraged them to ask Maya why she didn't have hair. Maya has been able to answer this question from the very beginning. We've taken a proactive approach by creating awareness because we believe that knowledge is power. If people are aware of alopecia and Maya's story, they will be less inclined to tease her and/or say hurtful remarks. This approach has been beneficial to all of us. Not only have we created awareness, we have also developed a large support system in the process. A letter is sent out to every parent in Maya's school every September, educating them on alopecia. A letter is also given to her coaches and teammates of any sport she joins. I have developed a presentation and delivered the presentation to her school at the principal's request. Her dad and I have organized a Dragon Boat team called *Team Alo*. Our dragon boat team consists of twenty-five people who participate in an annual Dragon Boat festival every July. Our greatest supporters are Maya and her friends. They can be found at the beach swimming and playing in the sand during the race; however, when the boat passes by, they stop everything and cheer us on by screaming and singing the *Team Alo* song. During the festival, my hair stylist donates his time by attending the festival and cutting ponytails to donate to a *Wigs for Kids* program that Maya belongs to. The men on our team, as well as other men on other teams have their heads shaved in solidarity on race day. Last year, I had my head shaved for Maya and sported my do for approximately four months when she asked me to grow my hair back. We have been interviewed by our local news, radio stations, and newspapers to share Maya's story. It has been a fun-filled four years for Maya and us. The outcome has exceeded our expectations. The best part of all of this is seeing how much confidence Maya has gained.

To make a long story short, the way we cope and deal with this is by giving Maya tons of love and attention and educating and creating alopecia awareness.

What Our Children Teach Us

"It's not only children who grow. Parents do too. As much as we watch to see what our children do with their lives, they are watching us to see what we do with ours. I can't tell my children to reach for the sun. All I can do is reach for it, myself."

Joyce Maynard, American Writer

The lessons we learn from our children are just as important as the ones they learn from us. As parents, we often get caught up in feeling powerless in a situation beyond our control. Then, one day we open our eyes to discover our beautiful, wonderful child is teaching us a lesson in determination. They are wise beyond their years, and in those moments, they help restore our faith in our own abilities to once again lead.

"Well I don't care. I don't let hair define who I am." - **Destiny**

"She has an inner strength that I don't see in most people." - **Destiny's Mom**

"As Elsa said in Frozen, 'Let it go and be free.' That's what I'm doing." - **Kaiya**

". . . but the beauty within my daughter has come out, and boy does it shine." - **Kaiya's Dad**

"I feel okay about alopecia. It's who I am. Everyone is different." - **Jackson**

". . . alopecia has given him and our entire family a reason to step forward." - **Jackson's Mom**

"When I grow up, I want to be an alopecia model." - **Sophie**

"She is the strongest person I know." - **Sophie's Mom**

". . .but I will certainly try to help kids with alopecia . . ." - **André**

"The wisdom of an eight year old is a remarkable thing." - **André's Mom**

"So, I decided to try and raise money to help find a cure for those who don't want it." - **Bailey**

Renee Nicole Photography

Destiny's Words of Wisdom

"Here's how I think of it - Most babies are born without hair. So, why does hair matter now?
Well it doesn't. Today, our society is focusing on hair. Well I don't care.
I don't let hair define who I am. I am my own individual who is not trying to be like
everyone else because I am myself, and no one can change who I am but me."

Destiny

I am Destiny. I am thirteen years old. I was twelve at the time I developed alopecia, but it all started a year ago when I got a bald patch. I told my mom about it, and she set up a doctor's appointment for me. As time passed, my doctor appointment finally came. I was eager but nervous. Eager because I wanted to know what was going on with me and nervous because I thought I had cancer. More time passed, and weeks later we got a call from the doctors saying I don't have cancer, but I have alopecia. This was really hard for me to cope with because as you know, many girls depend on their hair. I started to wear hats/berets, and people started wondering why. Then I started wearing sew in hair and wigs. I was afraid someone would try to pull my wig off, but I haven't had that problem. Many of my friends would spend the night, and that would be my time to tell them. I try to tell my friends little by little. People used to tease me about wearing wigs. I would cry to my mom, and it would make me feel horribly sad. Some days, I wouldn't even want to go to school. We tried many things to help my hair grow back, such as Rogaine, Clobetasol, squaric acid, and we even tried Cortisone injections in my head. The injections helped the spots that were bald but made more hair fall out in other areas that weren't bald. These shots were very painful, but I had to be a brave soul at the time.

It was very frustrating playing sports because I was afraid that my wig would fall off. I stress all the time because I'm afraid my hair will not grow back. But I try not to stress because it makes my hair fall out even more. I have been to a support group, and it was one of the greatest experiences ever. I was able to see and learn about the different types of alopecia and meet new friends who know the sadness I feel. We still keep in touch and meet up and go out to eat, which makes me feel free because I don't have to worry about being judged by anyone. It is now October, and I have learned to cope with this because I am getting older and many of my friends support me and talk to me. They tell me I'm beautiful no matter what, and they understand more about alopecia. My sisters and brother have helped me by talking to me. They are the best siblings ever, especially because they cope as well as I do. One of my sisters, Sabrina, cut off her hair and donated it to me. My other sister, Andreece, said she would too. One of them wrote about me in her college essay, which makes me feel lucky and proud to have a family as caring as mine. My mother is one of the best. She does anything to cheer me up to make sure I feel comfortable with my hair. One of my favorite quotes to help me remember what's important is, "I am not my hair. I am not my skin. I am the soul that is within." Now, I am better at dealing with this. I try to not stress, and I stay as positive as I can. My hair has shown a MAJOR improvement on growing, and I am proud of myself for staying strong and not caring about opinions as much as I used to.

It's been two months since I originally wrote my story. I stopped using squaric acid or any other prescriptions for alopecia. One day, I was reading on Google about things to make my hair grow, and I found this vinegar shampoo. My mom ordered it, and ever since I started using this shampoo, I noticed how thick my hair has gotten. As my hair got thicker, I got more confident. On January 29th, it was about 7:20 p.m., and I had just gotten out of the shower. I was looking in the mirror, thinking about how pretty wigs were, but how unhappy I was to hide who I truly was and how uncomfortable I was. Although wigs are cute, they are not so comfortable. The next morning, I woke up and realized I was sick of hiding who I really was. So, I put on a headband to cover up the bald patches I still had and wore my hair natural and curly. When I arrived at school, I was really nervous about what others would say. I walked down the long, crowded hallway and watched as everyone stared at me. I heard everyone whisper and point as I walked to class. Everyone complimented me that day, and I started to gain confidence and not really care what others thought of my hair.

Destiny's Mother

Destiny was diagnosed with alopecia areata a little over a year ago. I remember it like it was yesterday. I noticed a bald spot on the back of her head. I often kept a bottle of hair removal cream in the shower. So, I asked her if she accidentally used it instead of the conditioner that usually sat right next to it. She assured me that she hadn't. Over the next three months, I continued to watch as the spot got bigger and bigger. I wondered what could be causing this. "Lord, please don't let my baby be sick!" I thought. It was then that I scheduled her doctor appointment. They did blood work and examined her scalp. Two weeks later, I got a call that she had alopecia areata and was instructed to schedule another appointment to discuss this disease and treatment options. My feelings during the appointment jumped from sadness, hopelessness, and devastation, to relief that my daughter wasn't ill. As she sat there crying, I tried everything to hold back my tears, which didn't work by the way. I wanted to hold my baby and tell her everything would be back to normal soon, but my heart knew this was not the truth. This diagnosis would change life as we knew it.

We first started out using Clobetasol and Rogaine for the spot. As many more spots started to appear, the medication became less effective. We continued treatment for three months. In the meantime, we tried sew-n-weaves and wigs to cover the spots. The doctor then recommended cortisone shots in Destiny's scalp. I left this decision completely up to her. She decided she wanted to go through with the injections.

She was so brave with her first set of shots. I, on the other hand, not so much. I sobbed the whole way through. I felt really guilty. After all, who was I to break down when it was happening to her and she was handling it so well? As her Mom, my heart broke for her. She continued shots for four months. The results were just okay. We would see new hair growth, but it would fall right back out. The amount of physical pain she was experiencing from the injections compared to the amount of hair she grew, didn't seem worth it anymore. We were then referred to a specialist in dermatology.

Destiny has been through so much this past year. Being teased for something that is out of her control has been the hardest part to deal with. Kids can truly be cruel at this age. Despite all of this, Destiny remains very humble. She is gaining more confidence daily. Her inner light shines brighter than anyone I know. She has an inner strength that I don't see in most people.

A year later, I am able to see the blessings that have come from this. It has made us a stronger family. I no longer focus on the negative. Each day, as a family, we put one foot in front of the other. We know that there are many children who suffer medically and have health concerns beyond belief. Destiny is a healthy, happy young lady who counts her blessings instead of counting the hairs on her head. She is beginning to embrace who she is as a whole. Every part of it. I am so proud and blessed to be her Mommy!

My advice to parents who are new to this, is to encourage your children to love themselves for all that they are. Appearance is only skin deep. Our insides are what make us beautiful!

"Destiny is an athlete, a great student, a little sister, daughter, poet, and last but not least, an Alopecian. She is exactly who she was created to be." - Mom

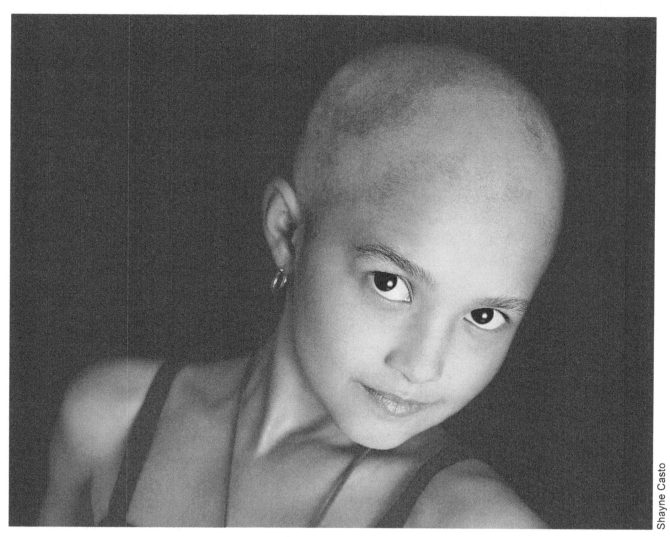

Shayne Casto

Kaiya

Hakuna Matata - it means no worries. That's my motto. Hi, my name is Kaiya. I am eight years old. I have had alopecia areata for three months now. I am moving on to third grade. My mom found my first spot April 2nd. That was when I was still seven. Right now, I am bald on the front top of my head, sides, and the back of my head. I still have hair though, but not much. When it first started, I wanted to wear head wraps. But now when my mom says I have to, sometimes I don't want to. Once in a while, I feel embarrassed but when I do, I talk to my mom and that makes me feel better. Whenever I am sad or want to talk about something, I always ask my mom if we could talk, and when I'm done talking to her I always feel better. Mostly, I think having alopecia areata is cool because I get to wear really pretty head wraps, and I'm beautiful even without a head wrap. It does not matter how you look on the outside that counts. It is how you look on the inside that counts, and you don't have to have hair to be pretty. My mom showed me a lady who was on *So You Think You Can Dance*. She did not have hair anywhere on her body, and she danced bald! My mom said that she was so beautiful that she made my mom want to be bald. My mom says that if I lose all of my hair, she will cut off all her hair too. That's my story. As Elsa said in Frozen, "Let it go and be free." That's what I'm doing.

Kaiya is actively involved in community service. She plays soccer and attends dance class with her friends. In her upcoming recital, she has a solo singing a Shrek song. She does it all without covering up her head, and when people ask, she proudly tells them it's alopecia.

Kaiya's Mom

My name is Charisse, and my daughter has alopecia areata. I stumbled upon your website from a post on Alopecia World. I was looking for other parents going through a similar situation. After showing my daughter your site and what you are doing, she wrote a message about herself and shared it with her teachers at summer camp today and finally exposed her head to her friend. Through writing her story and then sharing it with others, she said she felt free and felt relief.

We've all been dealing with this. Sometimes, my emotions make it feel like it is me and not her. She has the best attitude and has helped us be brave like her.

Kaiya's Dad

The bible says that a woman's hair is a crown of beauty for her. The Bible also says that beauty comes from within. As a father that loves his family very much, I never want any harm to come to them. This "alopecia" was a silent pest that took my daughter's crown away and harmed my family. I never thought I would see the day that I would have to shave my daughter's head. The day I shaved her head, I cried because it's not normal. It is a constant battle within me, and I try to not let it affect me so I can be strong for my wife and daughter…but it's hard to do sometimes. Months have passed, and we are still dealing with this pest that won't go away. It has changed our family, but the beauty within my daughter has come out, and boy does it shine. I still get sad from time to time, but my daughter does not let it bother her, and she doesn't even skip a beat.

When life throws you lemons, you make lemonade. This is true in our case. We have learned to deal with it as a family by open communication and not trying to hide it. This is my daughter now. Her hair does not define her, but it's who she is on the inside that does. We are grateful that it is not a terminal illness but it did affect me in the same way when we first found out. To all the fathers out there dealing with this, be strong for your family, and treat your child as a loving father would. Cry with them. Laugh with them. Talk with them, and remember, you and your family are not alone.

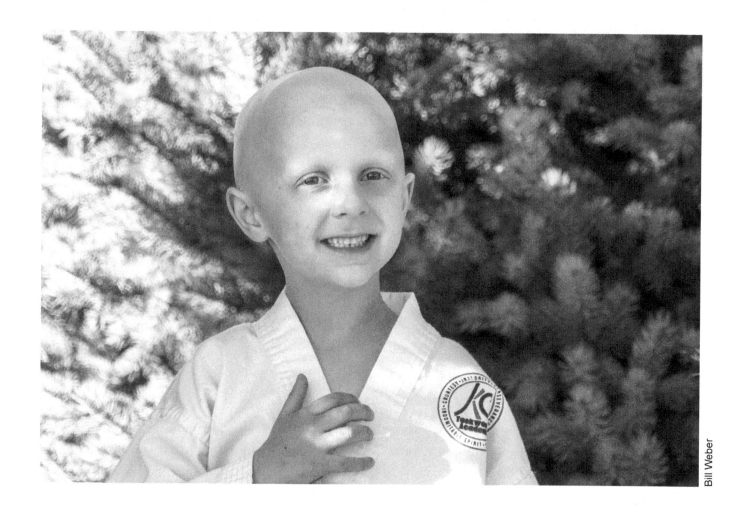

Bill Weber

Jackson

I'm five, and my mom told me I first got alopecia when I was three. I was four when I became completely bald. I feel okay about alopecia (he says with a shrug and a grin). It's who I am. Everyone is different. I have lots of friends. They like my alopecia because they like me. I don't really like that I have to wear a hat a lot so I don't get sunburned or cut when I'm playing, but it's okay. I have lots of hats.

I have other friends with alopecia who I've met at alopecia meetings. I'd like to be a fireman when I grow up or Spiderman's helper. I could work with my daddy or mommy. My mom said I still have lots of time to decide. I like to play superheroes, swim, take tae kwan do, play on the Wii, and go hiking. I also like to go on mommy-son dates and to play with my family and friends.

Jackson is a vibrant, happy kiddo who enjoys everything... truly! He's one of those kids who aims to both experience and see the best in every situation, and particularly loves taking Tae Kwan Do, playing with his sister and friends, going swimming, and spending time with family. He has a wonderful spirit that includes an old soul personality. As his mother often says - people may first notice him because he has no hair, but they remember him for a thousand other reasons.

Jackson's Mom
Appreciating Alopecia

There's a saying in life that first impressions count, and the reality is that includes how you look. While I don't consider myself a vain person - after all, I skip workouts and almost always eat dessert - I do believe that looks matter. Judge me if you will, but I've been raised to see the truth in society... not always the ideals. So, when a small bald spot on my son's head was diagnosed as alopecia and rapidly advanced to over 90% of his body's hair falling out, I couldn't help but fast forward to what life would be like for my little boy. Suddenly, I envisioned my happy toddler as a struggling teen who was being judged for - you guessed it - his bald head. I imagined how he'd have a crush on a girl in college and despite his captivating eyes and charm, he'd be ignored by not only this girl but many others. The list went on and on, and there were many nights I cried myself to sleep as I watched my son become bald at only four years old.

I'm proud to say the sadness that came with my son's alopecia diagnosis quickly receded after some long, internal talks with myself and more importantly, time spent with my son. My sweet, now five year old boy is still the same happy guy who wakes up full of life and curiosity every day. He's as silly as he's always been and smarter than ever. He's possibly the sweetest five year old I know, yet has a wise and serious way about him. He is - quite frankly - one of the coolest, most fascinating persons I know... and I swear I'm not just saying that because I'm his mom (wink, wink).

The reality is, my son and I - along with my entire family and our entire alopecia family - are lucky. The diagnosis of alopecia wasn't an easy one and certainly one that no one wishes for. But it could be worse.

When we walk into a room together, I know what people are thinking. After all, bald children are always used as poster models for well-known charities. Without even saying what these charities represent,

I know YOU know what I'm referring to... and this is the same thing most people think when they first meet or see my son. Fortunately, that potentially deadly diagnosis was not what we received that crisp October day in 2013. Instead, we were told my son has alopecia. Thankfully, that's something we can live with. And living is, very simply, exactly what we do. Nothing has happened to make my son step back in life, but rather alopecia has given him and our entire family a reason to step forward. We're grateful for health, happiness, and each other... as well as opportunities my son and my daughter both will have as life stands in front of us. Not all children have this luxury, and that reality never escapes too far from my thoughts.

There are still nights I lay wondering about my son's future but not in the same sad fashion I used to. Instead, I wonder how my son will be able to gain even more confidence, strength, and character as a result of alopecia versus becoming an outcast, depressed, or the kid that gets made fun of. I also imagine there will be moments he will wonder "Why me?" - as any preteen, teen or even adult may - and then I imagine the best way to handle those conversations. My imagination even runs wild and allows me to believe his alopecia is meant to be... truly making him stand out in a crowd. I pray for the strength to teach him how to be remembered for something other than his bald head, even if his bald head is what he is first recognized for. You see, I don't believe alopecia defines my son - although I'm no fool to think it won't impact who he is. It is part of my little man, the same way his big brown eyes and his cute little strut are. And for all those reasons, I'm so proud he's mine.

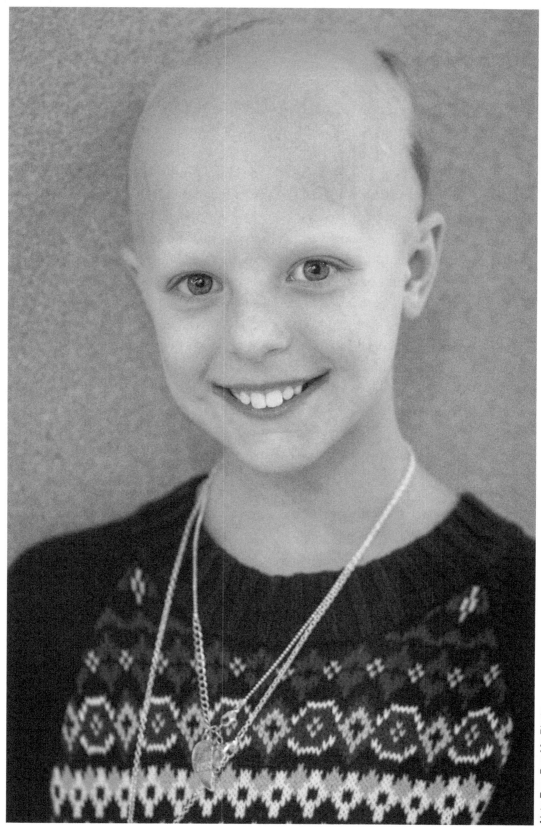

Sophie

I am nine years old. I got alopecia one month before my fifth birthday. Alopecia doesn't really bother me, but sometimes I want my hair back. Most of the time, I am okay not having my hair. My friends don't even notice I have alopecia. If they do, they don't treat me any different. Since I don't have hair to brush, there are no knots to hurt when I brush. It allows me to swim faster. Having alopecia, allows me to go to alopecia conferences like the ones in Texas and California. If I choose not to wear my hat or a wig, people who don't know me will stare at me and ask questions. Sometimes, I do just want to have my hair. There is a boy at my school named Michael, and also all the kids and adults at the alopecia support groups and conferences who also have alopecia.

When I grow up, I want to be an alopecia model.

Sophie enjoys playing with her friends, playing games with her family, and going to the mall and to the movies. She enjoys Facetiming with her friends and loves her iPad. She loves arts and crafts. There are also moments where she likes to just be with herself.

Sophie's Mom

Sophia was born in good health and for the most part was always in good spirits. She had a personality that captivated anyone she encountered. After her eighteen month immunizations, she was hospitalized with a febrile seizure. Soon after, she developed allergies to dairy, egg, and numerous environmental allergens. October 15th, I noticed her first spot of hair missing when she was five. She lost 75% of her hair the first time around, but then it grew back to below her shoulders. She kept it until three years, to the day, that her hair had originally fallen out. This time, it started as the size of a pencil eraser, and within two to three months she lost her entire head of hair, followed by her eyebrows and partial loss of her eyelashes.

She is the strongest person I know, but not only that, she is smart, kind, spunky, and beautiful inside and out. She's the life of the party wherever we go. We became very active with NAAF soon after she was diagnosed. I became a support group leader for the D.C. metro area. I believe this has been the foundation to why we both have embraced alopecia like we have. Sophia and I have now been able to attend two NAAF conferences and our third later this year. What an impact these conferences have made for us. After last summer's conference, Sophia came home with the confidence and courage to go out in public without a hat for the first time. The second day of school, this year, she took her wig off and shared her condition with her classmates. Now, depending on her outfit, she might wear her wig, a hat or just go as her beautiful bald self. She's quite the fashionista. Alopecia does not stop her love of life or dampen her bright spirits. We just had our 2nd annual Bowling for Baldness fundraiser for NAAF, selling out the alley with over 300 bowlers, an amazing online silent auction, and a grand raffle bringing in $33,880. Alopecia isn't beating us. We are beating it.

Will it grow back again? Only time will tell, but more than likely it will not. As her mother, I have made it my goal to assist her on her journey from girl to teen, into a young woman bestowing the confidence that she illuminates every day now. May her journey be painless and steadfast - with her beautiful head high and her dazzling smile always shining. That is a mother's wish!

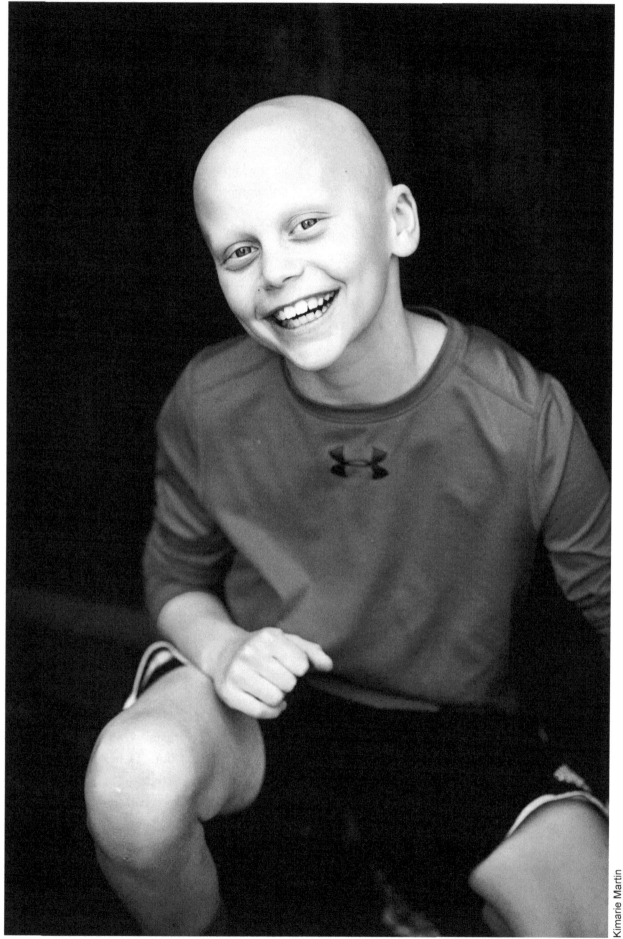

André

I'm ten years old and have had alopecia for about three years. It was confusing at first. We didn't know what it was, but I felt better knowing it wasn't actually hurting me. When I had four to five patches, I decided one day to just shave it. My sister cut her hair into a faux hawk to be supportive. I don't like to be the center of attention because of alopecia, but I can now say I'm comfortable with myself. A few things awesome about alopecia is that sometimes I can wear really crazy hats, and I don't have to waste fifteen minutes brushing my hair in the morning. I also get fifteen dollars deposited in my savings account when my sister and brother get their hair cut because I'm not spending it.

Ryan Shazier, now a professional football player who was then going to college at Ohio State, came to my school to talk to the kids about bullying. He told them to not tease me because he would have a problem with that, especially because he also has alopecia. When I grow up, I don't know whether I will be a professional athlete or not (although I would like that!), but I will certainly try to help kids with alopecia if I can.

"André loves sports, and his favorites are soccer, wrestling, and baseball. André loves to play the trombone and read. He has a cultivated sense of humor, a quick wit, and a kind heart. He is a sensitive soul with compassion for others and a fierce passion for social justice. André's memory serves him well. He often reminds us of the things we have forgotten. If he is right or thinks he is right — be prepared for an argument." - Mom

André's Mom

André started losing his hair three years ago in June. He had been sick with fevers and fatigue for the first part of the month. He underwent a workup for anemia, but everything was negative. I was worried that it was something more serious, so it was a huge sense of relief to find out he was OK. In July, I noticed a round patch of hair loss on the top of his head as I was sunblocking him for the pool. Then, he told me kids were asking why he didn't have eyebrows. Did he have eyebrows? That was a moment. I hadn't noticed they were gone. Within a week, he was off to sleep away camp with his sister. By the time he came home and I did my post camp lice check, I saw that he had lost about a third of his hair. We quickly went back to the pediatrician and had an appointment with the dermatologist within a week. August: alopecia. No Lupus. Thank God. Many treatment options were discussed – topical steroids, chemical irritants, injections. We started with the steroids. We ended with the steroids. "This isn't working and it's a waste of my time." André stated. The wisdom of an eight year old is a remarkable thing. André was completely hairless by October. A fantastic barber, a wonderful dermatologist, and many friends supported us along the way. No, we aren't going to put a wig on a little boy. No, we aren't going to pursue injections or clinical trials. It's hair. It's not easy. It's not deadly either. As a parent, my emotions have run the gamut from despair to pride. I have watched my child hang his head. I have also watched him strut. Last year, he and his friend did a fundraiser for the *Children's Alopecia Project* at school. I love my son so much. I am so proud of him. Alopecia doesn't get you good grades, sports success, or popularity. It's not an excuse to skip the study time, slack off, or shy away. It has allowed for tremendous maturity, empathy, and emotional strength not typically accessed in childhood. We take it a day at a time.

Bailey

It took a while to find out I had alopecia. My mom took me to many different doctors. I went to a place where they would rub my head, a place where they would poke my head, and we went to every place possible to try and find an answer. I was about three and didn't know much about them at the time. One of the doctors didn't know what it was but said I should start having twenty shots a month, and well...we didn't really like that. It was getting hard for me, and I was starting to think something was wrong. My mom took me to one more doctor – still no answer. My parents then took me to a specialist who said, "That's alopecia," and that's how I learned about alopecia. My mom had a hard time with it because she had to have her head shaved, for medical reasons, when she was a kid, and she remembers it being very hard. I think the thought of having a daughter without hair kind of upset her. I don't really remember much after that, but I do remember going to school and making friends.

I've had many amazing opportunities because of alopecia. I've been able to meet people like Charlie Villanueva and communicate with other amazing people who have alopecia. I've been to so many professional sport games where I've met mascots and athletes. So, that was pretty amazing. I've also been to alopecia support group pool parties that have been fun and life-changing. My dad, brother, and I met Rachel and her daughters (the M&Ms) at one of these pool parties. They are a huge part of our lives, and we're all a family now. I think alopecia has helped me be the strong person I am now. My dad helped me learn to care a little less about how people look at me. I used to be scared and ashamed, but since people have been pointing and staring at me for a while, I've learned to talk to people and educate them about alopecia. I've talked to everyone at my school, and

I'll talk to random people in the grocery store when they ask how my treatment is going. But sometimes, when people ask questions and assume I have cancer, it makes me feel bad because there is nothing really wrong with me medically. All that's different is I don't have any hair. People just assume I'm sick, and that doesn't make me feel very good.

I went to a basketball game with other people who had alopecia and saw how some people don't want alopecia. So, I decided to try and raise money to help find a cure for those who don't want it. I decided to do a big fundraiser at school. Me, my mom, and my dad all helped. I wrote out a speech, went around to every classroom and explained how alopecia was an autoimmune disease, and for the younger kids I explained how my brain had been programmed to say my hair was bad, just like a cold was bad but that I was not actually sick. They were all very supportive. I put a jar in each classroom, collecting spare change. I started each class out with a quarter, and each day kids started throwing pennies in. I even found a ten dollar bill in one. It was amazing to see how supportive all my classmates were and how everybody else was so amazing too. They asked good questions, like "Is it contagious?" I explained it is something that is inside me, and I'm pretty much going to have it for a looooonng time. Even if there was a cure, I explained I wouldn't want to take it because having alopecia is just one of the things that make me - me. There are many others, but it is quite an extraordinary one. I ended up raising over $650.00, and I was ecstatic. It meant that some of my friends who have alopecia and don't like it, are getting closer to finding a cure, and that makes me so happy. Our family has had many fundraisers over the last seven years, and we have raised over $10,000.00 for NAAF.

"Alopecia doesn't slow Bailey down at all. She spends a lot of time doing the things she loves the most: reading, drawing, playing sports and musical instruments, learning about science, and having incredible adventures. Alopecia has actually encouraged her to be more outgoing." - Dad

Realizations

*"Vulnerability is about showing up and being seen. It's tough to do that
when we're terrified about what people might see or think."*
Brené Brown, Research Professor

Pushing ourselves to take that first step toward sharing our alopecia experience with others is just the first of many. We challenge ourselves to do as many before us have done. Put one foot in front of the other, admit we are vulnerable, trust others to accept us, and ultimately allow ourselves to realize who we are and what we are capable of.

". . . I decided that for me personally, there was no choice." - **Sue**

"It began to dawn on me that it wasn't my hair . . ." - **Kevin**

"I finally got the chance to look up at the world around me." - **Allison**

"I chose to take myself on, no matter how immensely painful and vulnerable it was." - **Rebecca**

"That was two years ago. I didn't expect to feel very different since that day, but I do." - **Tanya**

"I finally reached the top of the hill, and my friends greeted me as usual. Just as usual!" - **Steph**

"My truth and my reality was that I wasn't just losing hair . . ." - **Dante**

*"By opening up and sharing, I soon discovered I was giving others
in my life an invitation to be close to me."* - **Erin**

"Over the years, I learned that I never gave them enough credit." - **Caitlin**

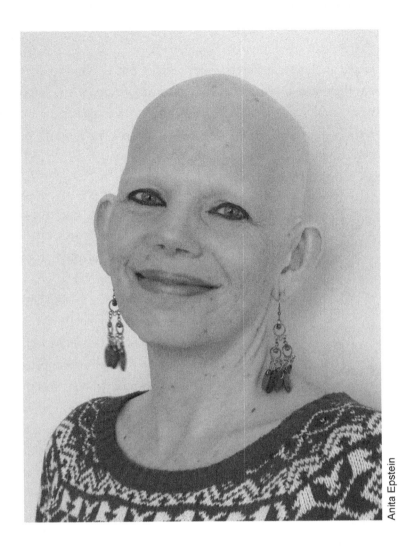

Anita Epstein

Sue
Alopecia: Two Stories

The *Waterhouse Girl* was the first story I wrote with a view to publication about thirteen years ago. I sent it to Michael Morpurgo, who rang me to tell me that it had moved him and that it was "beautifully written." He placed it into the hands of his editor at Harper Collins, strongly recommending it, but although she agreed with his verdict, she turned it down. A big, bright bubble burst! And that's when I gave up, for a while, on being an author.

But the story didn't end there and if publication in 2009 is an end to the story, it's a very different one from anything I could have imagined then - because if *The Waterhouse Girl* had been accepted at that time in my life, it would have been published under a pseudonym. I would have been desperate to preserve

my secret! Daisy Waterhouse is a girl with alopecia – total hair loss – and she's brave, generous, and funny even though her life becomes very difficult, especially at school. I based it on my own experience of losing all my hair thirty-three years ago, and when I wrote it I was hiding fearfully under a wig. I lacked Daisy's courage. And once I realised it was never going to grow back, I expected to continue hiding fearfully for the rest of my life.

I was twenty-four when I noticed a bald patch I couldn't see, covered by my thick, curly hair at the back of my scalp. Even when I was told it was "quite big," it never occurred to me that I would lose every hair on my body – which I did, over four months.

Sue's Story Continues . . .

Because alopecia is not considered an illness, sufferers are often acutely aware that they are not cancer patients enduring chemotherapy. We don't really NEED hair, except when it's chilly out there. But it's a hard thing to live without because ours is an image-conscious society which judges people by appearance. Hair is big business, but for most women it's also a big deal, emotionally and psychologically. I used to look in the mirror and see myself as alien, a freak, a baby, unattractive and unfeminine. And the other me, the one in the good wig, felt like an impostor and almost equally vulnerable – because any day, any time, my fraud could be exposed. On one memorable occasion, before I began using double-sided tape, my wig was blown off by a sudden gust of wind on a school playground. It was a free lesson for me, but inside that building were about fifteen hundred teenage boys, some of whom must surely have been gazing out of the window. I chased it, grabbed it, shoved it back in place, and leaned against a wall. With my heart thumping and tears beginning to overwhelm me, I thought, I'll have to resign. I thought, I'll go home, and I won't come back. Instead, I talked and cried with the nurses in the school sanatorium, put my smile on, and walked back to my classroom as if nothing had happened. There's no choice. After that, I was acutely aware of the eyes on me around the school, but I just kept mine ahead and held my head high, telling myself the giggling and whispering were nothing to do with me.

By the time I wrote my story, I was wearing the most fabulous, state-of-the-art wigs and receiving compliments on my beautiful hair! But I was only fooling the world rather more successfully. However classy the wig, it has to have an edge and my fringe was liable to be blown upwards on a windy day on a sports field. I was teaching young children, one of whom would occasionally ask, "Do you wear a wig?" I was the kind of teacher who aimed to be authentic, as truthful and open as possible – but I lied or evaded. "You cheeky thing!" I'd say, playfully but dismissively, with a smile. When I got home from work, the first thing I'd do was remove the wig with a deep sense of

relief – but if I had to cross my own front room, I'd duck down under the window and crawl just in case someone was passing – even my neighbours. That's how afraid I was, and it's no way to live.

It was my novel – or my character – that made the difference for me. In a way, of course, writing it was therapy. But she isn't me, and nothing that happens to her has been part of my experience except the hair loss. So, I've adapted from life and fictionalised real feeling. The novel is broader and deeper now, with more humour, eco-activism, an older boy for Daisy to adore, and a whale! But it carries the words, "Beautifully Written" by Michael Morpurgo on the front cover and has two photos on the back of me with and without a wig. Because when it was published, I decided that for me personally, there was no choice. I was an author now. I was in love with a man who loved me plus or minus hair, and I was older and tougher too! I had to talk openly in schools, libraries, and bookshops, to the press, and on the radio about alopecia. I hoped it would encourage others, but it also helped me. Walking through my home town bareheaded (during the summer!) felt liberating after all the tears, anxiety, and the years of damaged self-esteem. I won't pretend the first time was easy, or the second or third either, but it's a step I was ready and determined to take, and I'm glad I did. After all, I should be old enough now not to care what people might think and to find the strength, with the support of those who love me, to be myself. Since all my stories are about courage and our right as individuals to be different (often a hard thing for young people to be), I knew it was about time I walked the walk.

Sadly, because my book is published by a publisher with no budget for promotion and because I hadn't been on TV, it didn't reach as many readers, with or without alopecia, as I'd hoped. I wasn't on Facebook. Twitter didn't exist, and it was mainly children and teenagers in the schools I visited (to run writing workshops) who knew that I, or Daisy existed. But her story, and mine, made an impact on these young people. A teenage boy wrote to me afterwards, "You made me a better person." I had many emails from girls who saw the shallowness of our society and were inspired by my message: that our identity, as unique individuals, is a question of heart and soul, our attitudes and beliefs, the way we interact with other human beings in the world – NOT appearance! And that it's not just O.K. to be different – it's good! In fact, being true to ourselves is bigger and braver and cooler than pretending, just so we can follow the crowd. It's a message for everyone, and it's about respect.

Just occasionally, I found when I visited a school to inspire children to write, that there was a pupil there with alopecia. One seven year old I hadn't even spotted in the audience, came to find me afterwards to give me a tearful hug without words. But of course, it's better if I know in advance and can make sure that the help I give is the kind the young person chooses. A couple of years ago, I was asked by an alopecia support group in Wales to visit a school where a fourteen-year-old girl called Chloe was losing her hair. She still had a pony tail, but a hair band covered the bare skin at the front – and a boy had pulled it off. After arranging with Chloe how it would all go, I began my story, stopping to say, "So, I have alopecia and so does Chloe Jones." Chloe, who'd been sitting at the front, rose and stood beside me. I put my arm round her, and the whole hall applauded her, spontaneously. The teachers cried, and I was struggling. But having owned alopecia, she sat down – and her life changed. She's told me so. People apologised for being mean; others said they understood and told her how brave she was. She went to Sea Cadets a few days later and gave a talk on alopecia. We're still in touch, and she's still grateful. But what did I do? I was there, as an author, to help her to tackle alopecia head-on – or come out, if you like – and that means the end of being a victim and the start of taking control. OF COURSE, her life hasn't been all plain sailing (in spite of Sea Cadets!), but she found her courage that day and she's not letting go of it. It's a mark of her new strength that she's happy to be named by me when I tell this story. She loved my book too and still remembers how it helped. Chloe wears hats and scarves; that's her choice and that's important. Mine, now, is to go bareheaded whenever the British weather allows. But I have a dear friend, a strong, capable woman, who wears a wig in the world, looks fabulous and is fabulous. As individuals, we all have the right to live with our alopecia in our own way. What matters, is finding the strength not to be defeated because we're so much bigger than alopecia can ever be.

There have been other opportunities to support young alopecia sufferers, but I've always hoped that out there, without my knowledge, there might be other young people who'd been helped by *The Waterhouse Girl*. Just a few weeks ago, I arrived at a school to be greeted by a teacher who was thrilled to meet me because when her daughter lost her hair, she Googled alopecia and my book came up. She bought it. They read it together, and "it made such a difference." I was delighted and moved. On returning home, I did the same kind of search, but I wasn't there. I realised that at the time she looked, I'd just been featured in a U.K. magazine and an Australian online mag for women – so she'd been lucky. I also realised that other children couldn't find the same support through my book if they didn't know it existed. That's why I contacted Alopecia UK, the biggest alopecia charity in Britain, which has now invited me to be an ambassador. This will mean supporting a lot more young people like Chloe in the future, by visiting schools, and with my novel too. I've begun tweeting and reached many people with alopecia, all of them with their own stories. My story – the one I wrote when I was frightened, in spite of my wig and my smiles and my teacher act – was a new beginning for me, and I'm thankful because thanks to Daisy, the eleven-year-old girl I created, I can now be me.

Sue Hampton is author of over twenty titles for all ages. This year, she has taken on the important role of Ambassador for Alopecia UK, a public figure providing encouragement to those with alopecia in and around the United Kingdom. Look for the sequel to "The Waterhouse Girl," called "Crazy Daise" coming out this year. www.suehamptonauthor.uk

Kevin

My experience with alopecia has been a positive one, although it didn't seem like it would be at first. There are some lessons in life that are easy and some that are difficult, but a good lesson well learned is worth a bit of trouble. In the end, I believe having alopecia stimulated personal growth and made me a better person than I was before.

Alopecia is a mysterious condition, and anyone who has it can tell you doctors don't have many answers. In fact, the answers they do have are usually given as a list of possibilities such as, "It could be caused by your genes," or "It could be stress related. It may go into remission, or it may not. Steroids might cause remission, or acupuncture might cause remission." Perhaps there are simply different causes for different people.

In my story, I believe alopecia was brought on by stress. It began for me at a time when I placed myself in a situation I had not prepared for. At twenty-one years old, I decided to leave home for college in Arizona. It was a new place, a new school, and I was totally on my own in the sense that there was no one there I knew. My goals were to compete on the track team, keep the record of straight A's I had kept in junior college, and of course meet new people. But from the moment I got there, I found myself fighting an uphill battle.

Everything that could go wrong, did. Moving into my new place didn't go smoothly. I had trouble registering for the classes I wanted. The workload from classes was much higher than expected. I found myself burning through the money I had saved and barely keeping up with my coursework. Relationships with some of my friends and loved ones seemed strained, and then I got hit with the big news. The track coach had found someone with better stats to replace me and decided he would not take me on the team.

With all of these concerns weighing me down, I began to lose track of the big picture and became more and more fixated on small matters. This, of course, increased my stress level because even the small setbacks grew to take up the whole of my concentration. I remember developing the feeling that I was constantly running out of time. After a month or two of this, my hair began to fall out.

I remember waking up with more hair on my pillow than usual and getting in the habit of brushing it off my keyboard while doing homework. The fan in my bedroom had blown extra hairs onto the wall and stuck them there in a little line, like a border around the top of the walls. Not sure what was happening, I went to get a haircut thinking I had let my hair grow out too long, and that's why I was shedding more than usual. The haircut was an interesting experience because I could feel the brittleness of my hair during the cut, and it hurt and itched when the barber pulled at it. The shedding did not stop after the haircut, and a couple days later a friend from school pointed out that I had a completely bald patch on the side of my head.

Over the next eight months, the bald patch continued to spread to include every hair on my body. I reached out to doctors and friends for help and support. Both groups were equally unsuccessful in their efforts. The doctors simply lacked the ability to treat the root cause. The human immune system is very complex and is still not well understood by the medical world. My first diagnosis was something called *valley fever*, which is a fungus that lives in the Arizona dust and can infect you through your lungs. Hair loss is not usually a symptom though, and the second diagnosis was alopecia. I was then sent to a dermatologist, which seemed like a strange choice for a person with an immune system disorder.

Kevin's Story Continues . . .

They could prescribe Prednisone though, and that succeeded in temporarily restoring my hair, but it was unhealthy to continue treatment for any length of time. The friends and family I turned to during this time gave me words of support, compassion, and pity, but it did not restore my confidence. Good friends are always willing to help, but seeking support can put a burden on relationships. In this case, it was not necessary, as the solution to my perceived problem was elsewhere.

Losing my hair at twenty-one years old, one of my biggest concerns, as you might imagine, was girls and whether I would still be attractive to them. I did notice a negative impact at first, although not a universally negative one. Being very determined to solve this problem, I wondered why I was sometimes having negative interactions and sometimes positive ones when my lack of hair was obviously staying constant. At times when I was thinking about my appearance, I noticed that everything went less smooth than at the times I forgot I was hairless. It began to dawn on me that it wasn't my hair, but my attitude and behavior that was having the biggest effect.

I resolved to be more outgoing than I had before and to make the extra effort when meeting new people so I could be more in control of my self-image. The benefits of this new approach began immediately. I changed schools to run track at CSU Stanislaus and after one semester became the team captain. I won a seat on the student senate around the same time. I also formed many valuable friendships, and some of those friends came down to try out for *American Ninja Warrior* with me. These skills are invaluable now for my work on the show. They have given me the confidence to be on screen and some of the knowledge about what I should do when I am there.

American Ninja Warrior has been an amazing and life changing experience. I am amazed by the outpouring of support I have received from the alopecia community. One of the common themes I hear is that it's nice to have someone you can root for with alopecia on T.V. because it's usually the villains who are totally hairless. I have always loved to push myself to master different stunts, obstacles, and challenges. Training and competing in the *American Ninja Warrior* competition feels natural and right to me. I am also fascinated by the incredibly talented and completely crazy people I have met through the show, and I hope to keep doing it for a while.

On the show, I had the opportunity to talk about my alopecia, and I did my best to show the positive feeling I have come to have about it. The lessons that alopecia have pushed me to learn have helped me immeasurably, and I do believe I am happier today because of them. It has caused me to become more confident and to seek big challenges, and of course it also makes me more aerodynamic.

Kevin is currently training hard for the next season of "American Ninja Warrior." In addition, he organizes competitions so more people can experience the fun of obstacle courses. Due to his involvement with the show, he's had many messages from young people with alopecia, and he tries to help build their confidence by encouraging them to embrace their individuality.

Allison

My mother made me (yes, made me) take piano lessons when I was little. I was awful, which meant the practice time was always extended. One night in second grade, I was at my nightly scale routine when she came over to the bench and asked to see the back of my head. I always wore my hair in a ponytail, and she lifted the pony and asked, "Did you cut your hair?"

To be fair, I had cut my bangs several times because my dad usually took it upon himself to cut our hair (with an upside down green Tupperware bowl on our heads), and it always looked a little crooked. My brother would tell me to cut my hair on a dare, and I would. So the question wasn't that far-fetched.

Allison's Story Continues . . .

"No," I responded. She asked my dad and sister to come over, and they started looking over every inch of my head. I could not understand why everyone seemed panicked. My mom asked my dad to call our neighbor who was a doctor, but an orthopedic one. She took me in the bathroom and had me hold the mirror up to see the back of my head. It only took one look at my head and one look at my mother to know something was very wrong.

Looking back, the night my alopecia was discovered changed so many things for me. I became the girl with "cooties." No one talked or played with me and parents did not come near me. I went to a Catholic school, and my teacher told me that if I prayed enough, my hair would come back. That was the beginning of my awkward stage that, in a way, still continues today.

My mother was amazing. She went in like a bull. We went to many doctors in our hometown, and one by one they determined they had no idea what could be happening. My mother, who had three children and a full-time job, was relentless. She would spend hours on the phone each night trying to get answers. Then, one day my mom told me were going to take the day off school to go to the big hospital in another city. I swear I heard angels sing because by this point my hair was in bad shape, and I was also not fond of school. My hair looked as if it had been through a fight with a lawn mower. Almost 60% was gone, and I had completely shut the world off.

I was diagnosed with alopecia areata in a big city by a highly qualified physician who ran a multitude of tests. To this day, I can remember what great shoes the doctor would wear. I could never look her in the eye but always looked forward to seeing her every four weeks. Strange as it may be, I would look forward to the appointments with her. She was smart, pretty, and had the best shoes. She asked me about my hair loss without ever giving me a strange look. Even though

those appointments would bring hundreds of shots to my head and usually some blood tests, I still loved her and those shoes

Those were my adolescent years. I spent my time playing with my brother after school and on weekends. I did well in school but never really liked it or trusted my classmates. My hair came and went, but I always looked like a hot mess. At the end of high school, all my hair came back. Not to miss a moment, I got a perm and a can of Aqua Net hairspray. My motto was, "As big as it could get." Making sure every strand stood on end was the daily routine.

College came and went. I got married, and boom, there was hair everywhere. I was working my way up the corporate ladder and found myself feeling like I was back in the classroom again. Scared, worried, and just when everything looked so perfect – my hair had a different idea. It tends to fall out around the back of my head. Sometimes more than others. Sometimes easy to disguise and sometimes not. My coworkers never asked. We never talked about it, and life went on. The funny thing is, I knew they could see it, but they never said a word.

I made it all the way to Vice President of the company, and the long awaited call finally came. Home Shopping Network wanted to hire me as a host. I thought this was great. Not because I wanted to go on television, but because I would not be traveling five days a week. I could spend time with my daughter, move to the Florida sunshine and relax a little.

When you enter the world of television, the gleam of a camera lens or lighted set is both unfamiliar and exhilarating. You're suddenly center stage and away from your daily morning walk with the dog. You're in front of a waiting audience. I never intended to set foot in the entertainment industry, and now I find myself reflecting back on a career that has allowed me to record more hours of live television than Jay Leno,

Conan O'Brien, and Rachel Ray combined. I never thought I would reach those numbers, especially while living with alopecia in a world where bad hair days cannot be hidden, and trusted teleprompters are nowhere to be seen.

When beginning my time as a show host and television personality, I was forced to confront my alopecia before millions of viewers and conquer my own apprehensions about sharing my experiences with my audience. It only took about fifteen years behind the camera. Yes, I just forwarded fifteen years. Television was a game of chess with alopecia. Dodging hairstylists and guests, and spending hours in my home figuring which way to make my bangs go to cover a spot up. It was a daily struggle, and it was exhausting.

Then it all changed.

One morning when I got off air at 2 am, I looked in the mirror to see one of the hair pieces falling down. Fifteen years of hiding, hairpieces, hairspray, spray on hair, and standing "stage left" so the customers would never see the right thin side of my hair, left me feeling exhausted. I needed help. The little girl I had been would never have known what to say or who to say it to. I sat at my desk and began my search. I realized I could reach out for help and also be able to help anyone with this terrible, terrifying, life altering, and lonely disease. For the first time in my life, I could admit how this one gene had changed my life.

During the summer of 2011, I spoke to a group of fellow alopecia areata families. Getting there was not easy. I had to admit to myself that I could tell my boss at the network and finally own this disease. Once I gave that speech, my life changed. I finally got the chance to look up at the world around me. I wasn't looking at people, wondering what they thought about me. I was telling them, and it felt good. I am not broken, and I certainly don't have "cooties." Yep, at the age of forty-five, I realized that I did not have cooties. Sounds silly in a way, but the truth was that I had never moved forward from the moment I first lost my hair.

Over the years, some have told me that they were surprised about my having alopecia. "You don't have the bad kind," they would say. I think some think that if you have not lost it all, it is not as bad. Well, I did lose it all. Some came back, and it continues to be a struggle to hold onto every strand. They also forget that all the symptoms on the inside are the same. It has always felt strange to be judged on what kind of alopecia is worse than another. They are all just as serious and challenging, and they all bring us together.

Living with alopecia for the last forty years has been a journey. I am lucky. Not the, "I won the lotto" kind of lucky, but the kind of luck to have alopecia areata. I believe it has been a path filled with friends and family that have led me to make difficult and rewarding decisions about how I see the world. Alopecia has left me with a gift, one to see beyond what others prize; how they appear physically to the world. Is it easy? No. Important? Yes. We want to say that we are the same as everyone else, but in fact, we are not. We have the chance to truly look at others for who they are, not what they look like. When I see my friends who have alopecia, they look me in the eye when they are talking and listening.

Allison is a best-selling cookbook author, chef, and television host. Growing up in the chocolate industry was the beginning of a love affair that started Allison on a journey for a life filled with delicious and innovative cuisine. Allison has been featured on The Food Network, and can be seen in more than 80 million homes as a host on EVINE Live, a leader in retail broadcasting. As a classically trained chef, she brings together her love of food and the memories they create.

Rebecca
Do or Die

I was in Granada, Nicaragua for a yoga teaching training course in March 2014. After twenty-five years of living with alopecia areata, I finally decided it was do or die. No more wig, no more scarf. After spending all those years covering up and hiding, I figured it was time to try something new. It proved to be the ultimate painful and challenging experience of my life, but I was ready for it.

All my life, it was very difficult to accept myself as I truly was, as opposed to who I wanted to be. I had so much inspiration from other bald people and had seen so many others who were "owning it." So, why couldn't I? I had a tremendous amount of emotional support from my family, friends, and community. So, what was wrong? I finally realized the only thing in my way was me. I was tired of living my life as a prisoner to my beautiful collection of scarves and stunning European 100% human hair wig. No more space. No more time for what was prohibiting me from living a life worth living.

The first two weeks of walking the streets of Granada and exploring the restaurants and sights were awful. I felt people staring at me, and I thought for sure they were thinking how I looked like a boy or how strange and ugly I was. Here's the kicker…those were my thoughts, not theirs. I didn't go up and ask them, "Hey, what do you think about my look?" What if, just what if they were thinking, "Wow, what a striking woman that is" or "That girl is bald, but she sure does look happy and confident." What did I do? I can tell you what I didn't do, which was go grab my scarf or wig and cover up. I persisted.

Three weeks in, without expecting it, something shifted. I was less preoccupied with my appearance than the previous few weeks. I felt more comfortable and safe. I still didn't like looking in the mirror at this point, but I wasn't caring as much what other people were thinking. Then, I noticed I didn't feel people staring at me like before. This was so perplexing because I didn't change my look. I really believe in the power of our thoughts, but it was hard to believe that a change in my perspective could change my entire reality as I knew it.

Now, six months later as I write my story, the layers of insecurities and judgments have been shed along with my wig and scarves. I chose to take myself on, no matter how immensely painful and vulnerable it was. By doing so, I created space for transformation. Ultimately, living with alopecia areata has guided me to freedom. Freedom to discover who I really am. I accept who I am. Now, I am free.

Rebecca's inspiration was to open herself up to the flow of life. Nicaraguan-American, she wanted to connect with her culture and heritage. The flow of life brought her to Little Corn Island in the Caribbean Sea. She is now the Wellness Director for a 5-star resort, teaches yoga and meditation, and is pursuing an online master's degree in clinical nutrition.

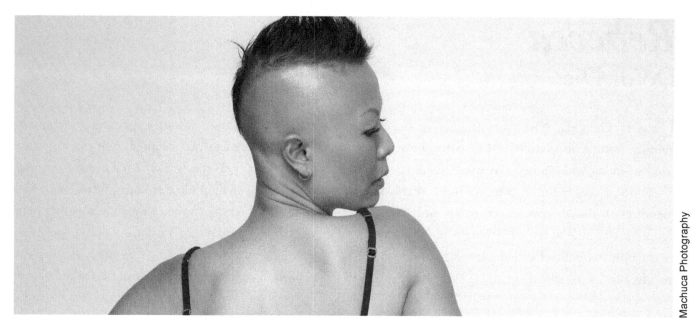

Tanya

When I was ten, I had a full head of shiny, healthy black hair. Then in three weeks, I lost all of it. Alopecia hit me hard in so many ways.

Before alopecia, my mom used to doll me up and tell me how pretty I looked. I was a happy and confident kid at school. I was friends with everyone in class, even though my sense of humor was a bit mean, and I sometimes hurt other kids' feelings without knowing it.

As my hair fell out, I felt ugly and vulnerable. Praises from my mom were replaced with concerns. She'd exclude me from photos being taken because she didn't want me to feel bad when I saw them, which made me feel bad. At school, I became extremely cautious about what I said. I stopped joking around because I worried if I accidentally hurt someone's feelings, they'd have a comeback ready for me: "Well, you're bald!"

My mom did something great for me though. She had a chat with the teacher about my hair, and the teacher then shared with the class. I was never made fun of. However, at the same time, there was no voice in my life saying, "You're awesome the way you are!" Instead, my parents and I tried everything under the sun to cure me. My hair would come and go but never grew back 100%.

As a teen, my self-esteem plummeted, and I decided becoming model-skinny would make my life better. I dropped to 90 lbs. and absolutely damaged my health. The worst part about it was my thinking, "If this means I've weakened my immune system, then maybe my hair will grow back!" Here I had just damaged my digestive and nervous systems, yet I was still concerned about my hair! But I was right... my hair completely grew back for the first time. But I was also wrong... my hair fell out a year later and didn't grow at all for seventeen years. I've since learned that no amount of hair growth justifies compromising my health.

Over the years, I became an expert at finding convincing and comfortable wigs. I was reminded less and less of my alopecia and was feeling confident again. I decided to start a support group in Vancouver to help others feel good about themselves too. I was so lucky to have the most amazing people join the group! We quickly bonded, the way life-long friends would. We shared hilarious and emotional stories. We inspired each other too.

I was super inspired by Dana in our group. She had been AU for just a couple of years. One afternoon, she was downtown by herself, and being away from people who might know her, she thought it was a good opportunity to take her wig off and go into Starbucks for a cup of coffee. And she did! I was so blown away. Knowing Dana, this wasn't easy for her, but she did it. I told my mom the story, and she was impressed too. She said, "Wow. For most people, just having coffee by yourself in a coffee shop is hard!"

It's ironic that I started the group to help others, but I ended up getting the most from it. After telling so many members they looked good without hair (and they did!) and hearing cool stories like Dana's, I finally realized I could maybe look good without hair too. We are so irrational and critical of ourselves sometimes, aren't we?

I've always loved yoga, but never tried hot yoga because of my wig. So, a hot yoga class was perfect as my first wigless experience. It was hard. For the first two classes, I convinced myself I needed to wrap a towel around my head to absorb the sweat. In reality, I was just chickening out. By the third class though, I did it! I was self-conscious at first but felt amazing and free by the end. After class, I had a shower and put on my splendid wig. I was out the door while others were still blow-drying their hair. It was a winning moment.

On my birthday, three months later, I was ready to tell everyone I had alopecia. I posted a video on Facebook, showing my friends what I looked like without a wig, and told them, "From now on, I'm going to have fun with alopecia!" I got so many encouraging words from friends, and over 300 people shared the video. I cried a lot of happy tears that day.

That was two years ago. I didn't expect to feel very different since that day, but I do. Hiding my alopecia turned out to be a big burden on me. Only after this burden was lifted, did I see how much I had limited myself and what it feels like to be free.

Since then, I have done so many things. When I vagabonded to Shanghai, I had a roommate for the first time in my life. When I backpacked in Thailand, I stayed at cheap and fun hostels instead of alone in a boring hotel room, and I met so many people. I learned to scuba dive and saw the most incredible sea life. I jumped my heart out at a trampoline park. I rode a mechanical bull like a pro. I surfed in a wave machine (not like a pro). I played on every single inflatable at the inflatable water park. Now, I don't let worrying about my hair keep me from enjoying anything I want to experience.

I tried online dating without a wig. In my dating profile, I posted photos of me with and without a wig and talked about my alopecia journey. I received two hundred messages in two days, and I appreciated every single sincere message.

I went on first dates without a wig. On one date, a guy came over to tell me I looked beautiful and kissed my hand in front of my date. Three girls bought me a drink and asked to have a photo taken with me. (Not in a lusty way, but in a "Girl, you rock!" kind of way.)

I know from my group that I'm not the only one. Women often come over to tell us we look amazing bald. As for men - for a long time, I thought it was impossible to find a guy who can accept the hairless me. Notice, I say "accept" because I couldn't imagine any more than that. It turns out, there are more than enough people who not only accept you but appreciate you. Sometimes, they are attracted to the bald look, and sometimes they respect the way you handle your alopecia, and most often, it's both.

Now, I too can appreciate my alopecia. I go bald (In the photos, I have a mohawk, but it comes and goes) or wear one of my nineteen wigs. I have so much fun and versatility with it, the haired people are jealous.

It took me twenty-three years to see my alopecia in a positive light. I think it took so long because I closed myself off to the world. Once I started listening to stories from others with alopecia, my mind grew and opened up. I think we all have it in us to give alopecia a positive spin and to love ourselves the way we are!

Tanya is the president at Knot Theory www.knotheory.com. She spends her time designing, playing on her laptop, and travelling. She just started The Alopecia Channel on YouTube. Come see where it's at, or even better, be a guest on her channel!

Jessica DeLorenzo

Steph

Six years ago, I walked up the street to my bus stop, extremely nervous. I was a 10-year-old girl about to start my first day of fifth grade. I wore a new outfit and carried a new backpack, but there was something else different about me that was making me so anxious. I walked up that street with my twin sister by my side, sporting a completely uncovered bald head.

It had been almost two years since we'd seen the first signs of my alopecia. My bald spot had appeared a month after I turned nine, but since our pediatrician shrugged it off, saying I'd been playing with my hair – my diagnosis didn't come until several months later, after I'd seen various doctors who had ruled everything else out with a bunch of tests. By then, I had lost all the hair on my head and had begun

126

wearing hats. I felt that as long as I wore a hat, no one would know I was bald.

A year after my alopecia first appeared, I entered fourth grade just like the previous year. I brought a note to my nice teacher, explaining my condition and asking permission to wear hats. No one was allowed to wear hats in school, and I'm sure my classmates noticed I did. Some kids in school bullied my friends and me, inventing a game called "germs"- sort of like cooties for specific people. They would pass around Stephanie "germs," picked up from anything I touched, as though it were some undesirable thing. This went on for several months until my teacher stepped in, and that was easily resolved.

By the end of fourth grade, I'd met an older girl who had alopecia, and I'd had my hat fall off enough times that I made the decision to stop wearing it. By the time I started fifth grade, I'd done enough "test runs" of going bald in public but still felt terrified at what my friends would think.

So on this day, I finally reached the top of the hill, and my friends greeted me as usual. Just as usual! They didn't care and treated me the same even though I was bald. I was so relieved and happy. I expected them to act awkward or surprised to see me without anything on my head, but they weren't. That's when I realized that even though I'd been using it to hide, the hat hadn't hidden my baldness. They'd probably known about it for a long time. That first day, mom worried about me walking into school bald and thought it best to walk in surrounded by friends. That didn't seem right at the time, and now that I knew my friends accepted me, I wasn't nervous at all. I didn't need to be protected by a crowd just to enter the classroom. I walked into the school without a problem. I don't even remember the rest of the day. I even went on to explain my condition on the school news later that year. People said it took courage, but for me, it hadn't been difficult.

Reaching that bus stop had been the hard part. It had been a relief for me, and my sister too, because people had always come to her to ask questions about why I was bald.

Almost seven years have passed since then, and so much has happened. I've always felt a great need to explain my condition to everyone I can. I'd rather they not assume and wonder. Don't mistake me for some extremely confident person, though. I've always been pretty shy and self-conscious in social situations until I get to know people. But that has begun to change since reaching high school. I started being more social and joined many activities including swim team. At the end of meets, when we all high five or shake hands with the other team, I make sure to stand straight with a bare head. It's as if I'm announcing, "Here I am. Bald, beautiful, and not sick!"

I've also participated twice in the "I'm OK" panel at *Alopeciapalooza*, a camp for kids with alopecia organized by *The Children's Alopecia Project*. It involved answering questions from kids and their families. Sometime in the near future, I'd like to do something special, although I don't know what, for alopecia awareness.

This past September, I walked into my school, almost seventeen, ready to start junior year – Not nervous at all.

Stephanie swims for the school team and plays flute in the marching band. She also enjoys science, art, and writing. Since writing her story, she followed through on raising awareness for alopecia by making a video, "Find out why I'm bald" and posting it on YouTube and Facebook.

128

Dante

Life has its share of challenges. That is a truth that's shared by everyone. For me, one of my biggest challenges growing up was external but caused many internal issues; alopecia areata. I was first diagnosed with alopecia when I was about eight years old, when bald spots started forming on my scalp. One small bald spot quickly progressed to an entire scalp full of quarter sized bald spots. After visiting my doctor and being given several prescriptions, my hair grew back. When I was fifteen, I was combing my hair and preparing for school. It was the week of midterm testing during my eighth grade year. I woke up that morning nervous and anxious to get to school to complete the state required exams. After showering and brushing my teeth, I stood in the mirror and began to pluck out my mini afro like I ordinarily did. That particular morning, with each pluck of the pick came a patch of hair uprooted from my scalp. In a rush to make it to school on time, I grabbed a head covering and rushed out of door. Adversity introduced itself to me without even being invited.

I felt so misunderstood. My physical adversity made me a target for bullies. "Spots, Crater Head, and Baldy" were just a few of the horrible names I was called. For several years, my physical issue caused me to grow insecure. I never left home without a head covering because I didn't want to deal with people's ignorance. I was willing to wear coverings in uncomfortable temperatures because I was so insecure with who I was, and more so who I felt I wasn't. For years, I was imprisoned in my mind by other people's perceptions of me.

Friends and family often tried their best to encourage me. "It's just hair..." was something I heard often.

For me, it wasn't just hair. It was a part of my identity that was missing which created a new identity, that at the time I did not want. My truth and my reality was that I wasn't just losing hair, but I was losing myself due to the social effects of this physical issue. Finally, I got sick and tired of being a slave to my issue and decided to do something about it. It wasn't until I shaved my head bald that I realized I was beautiful with or without hair. I still felt the social weight of my condition for a few months. After about three months, the need to shave grew less necessary, as the hair stopped growing back. I had progressed from alopecia areata to alopecia universalis, which meant I was losing all of my body hair. Instead of allowing this unfavorable situation to break me, I looked deep within myself and found the strength to keep moving forward in spite of it all. I encouraged myself daily and told myself I was beautiful until I believed it. I took off the head coverings after the hair stopped growing back and embraced the beautiful being I saw in the mirror each day. I gave up fear and envy and exchanged it for freedom to be myself and love who I was.

Everyone has a struggle they must work to overcome. Find the strength to validate yourself and see yourself as beautiful. It's easy to list everything you're not and everything you don't look like, but it takes strength to embrace who you are and love yourself for being you. You may be someone who is living with alopecia and feel you're too different to be accepted. The truth is, as long as you accept that you have alopecia and alopecia doesn't have you, you can live in peace.

In Dante's self-published inspirational testimonial entitled, "Free to Be Me: I Am Not My Issues," he details his experiences of living with and overcoming the effects of alopecia, along with other issues he faced during childhood, including abuse, rejection, and uncertainty — all things that helped build him into the man he is today. Today, he is free to be himself, with no disclaimers. www.danteworth.com

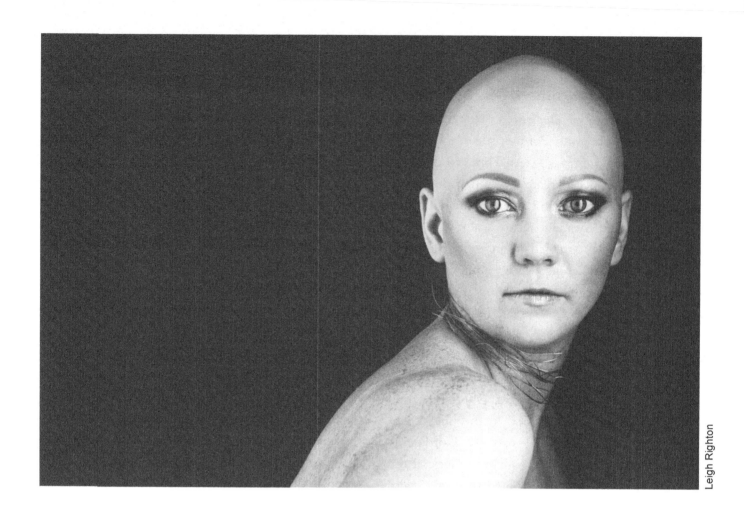

Erin

It felt like my fairy godmother had granted me a wish. I was thirteen years old, and I literally woke up with hair that could only be described as "a miracle." The night before, I had gone to bed with normal long, red, and straight hair and awoke the next day with perfect auburn ringlets. I soon became known as "the girl with the amazing hair."

As an adult, my life was going along at a pretty standard pace. I went to University, travelled, got the perfect teaching job, and subsequently got married. I was soon absorbed in my married life, to the point where I felt I had lost a sense of myself. Six years later, shortly after my marriage ended, my hair fell out. Not just little bits of hair – all of it.

In February 2010, I was a participant in the Vancouver Winter Olympic opening and closing ceremonies, just four months after the end of my marriage. Within two weeks, from opening ceremony to closing ceremony, I had completely lost my hair. Just like that, the gift of my beautiful red curls had been taken away, almost as quickly as they had appeared.

I had started taking personal development courses during the first year of my alopecia and found that after a year of devastation, confusion, and discomfort in my own skin – I needed to dedicate more time and energy into figuring out who I really was. I didn't know how to move through life without a wig and up to this point had always worn one, even at home.

My undergraduate work had been in psychology, and I found a counseling program that gave me the opportunity to do some soul searching. I made acceptance my goal; both me accepting myself, and accepting how others might react. I had been outwardly concerned with what people might think because something bad had happened in my life, and I thought it looked like I couldn't cope; hence all my hair falling out.

I soon discovered a different confidence and beauty I didn't realize I possessed. After three years of gradually revealing my alopecia to the world around me, I finally fully embraced my new identity. As a teacher, my last step was to share the story with my students at an all boy's school. It was important for me to show up authentically in all areas of my life and not to hide my true self anymore. I decided to place trust in the fullness of my experience. The result was overwhelming support and encouragement from staff, parents, and my 9-year-old students. While wearing my wig, I shared my story and told them I'd be showing up to school without my wig, and they responded with encouragement, "We want to see the real you." When I took it off, I heard, "You look so much brighter." The response was unwaveringly warm and embracing, and they met me where I was.

That is where I learned the power of what I bring. What I present and go out into the world with, is what I will be met with. By opening up and sharing, I soon discovered I was giving others in my life an invitation to be close to me. The response from people, when you show yourself as vulnerable, is that they also want to connect and share their own experiences with you. Trusting in a friendly world opens doors to a friendly world.

Erin currently continues teaching elementary school boys, and pursuing a private counselling practice to help women with their body and self-image, called Renew YOU Counselling - Empowering Women's Body and Self-Image. She is active in her figure skating community as an ice dancer, and makes fitness, personal development, and travel a priority in her free time.

Jordan Jennings

Caitlin

I find two things hard to believe - One, that I am twenty-seven and technically an "adult" and two - I've had alopecia for more than half my life. When I first realized this, I sat back and thought, "Wow. It's hard to picture my life without it." My attitude toward alopecia has undergone a huge change over the years. When I was diagnosed at twelve, I was scared of the uncertainty, angry that I had alopecia, and sad. Very sad because I did not know anyone else who looked like me, and I missed having hair.

It was partly my fault that I felt so alone because I isolated myself. My parents suggested the annual alopecia conference, but I refused. If I went, that meant I really had alopecia. And at thirteen, I was not willing to accept that. For the first year, I did not tell my two best friends. At the time, I still had a partial head of hair and only wanted to hide it. My biggest fear was rejection. And really, in hindsight, I was projecting my fear onto them because my internal battle of acceptance was raging.

My friends and family have always been very supportive. I'm blessed to have the parents I do. They let me work through things in my own time. It was my choice to stop treatment after the first year. It was my choice to attend my first alopecia conference, and it was my choice to go bald in public. I always sensed their protective, and at times, defensive demeanor. I know it's caused them pain. They've mentioned several times when I have struggled, that they wish they could "go through it for me." I don't think I'll fully understand their perspective until I have children of my own.

My friends have always been supportive too. When I first told them, I was very brief and they said, "Okay." I think they were confused and unsure what to make of it. I kept the painful part of those initial years to myself because I didn't want to "burden them." Over the years, as I've accepted it more, I've become much more open. Now, they feel free to ask questions if there's something they don't understand. They also feel comfortable educating others. Over the years, I learned that I never gave them enough credit. I didn't appreciate their capacity for acceptance.

One of my defining "alopecia" moments was when I met a woman, during my junior year of high school, who had breast cancer. She was a mom of a soccer teammate, and she amazed me. I had never seen a bald woman before. For a few years, I had been contemplating not wearing my wig anymore. I knew deep down that was how I would feel most comfortable, but I wasn't ready. Seeing her in the stands during games and at other school events inspired me to attend my first alopecia conference. It was the summer before my senior year, and after that I was unstoppable. Meeting other kids like me was mind-blowing. I realized I was not alone. These people were happy and doing things in their lives. For years, I had let alopecia dictate what I did, but I was tired of that. After the conference, I went home and met with my high school principal and vice principal who were extremely supportive and accommodating. He sent a letter I wrote to the entire school, telling them about alopecia and that I would be going bald in public. I started receiving letters and calls saying how brave I was. Even to write about it now is surreal. At the same time, I didn't feel brave – I just wanted to be me.

On the first day of school, I gave a speech about courage in front of 500 students and faculty. I got a standing ovation, and everyone cried. A few months later, I was elected homecoming queen. The moment they called my name and I received the crown that was bought especially for my bald head is something I will never forget. It was the ultimate gesture of acceptance.

The local newspaper found out about me and wrote an article which donned the front page. Through that, other people with alopecia in the area contacted me. At the end of the day, attending that first alopecia conference started a chain of events that changed me.

The next big moment in my alopecia journey happened senior year of college. I wrote my senior thesis on women, alopecia, identity, and gender norms. While interviewing twenty-three women, I realized, "Caitlin, you still have some stuff to work on." Deep down, I still struggled with feeling attractive. I think that comes from developing alopecia at the start of adolescence.

I found a therapist I clicked really well with, and after some emotional digging, I was "released." Although alopecia is a part of who I am, it's not all I am. I learned that in therapy too.

After receiving her Masters in Social Work, with a concentration in interpersonal practice and mental health, Caitlin began her journey as a therapist. Having alopecia makes her a better therapist who feels she can empathize, to a greater degree, due to living with alopecia. She knows what it's like to be different – even if that difference is something invisible like depression – "I can feel your pain."

"We gain strength, and courage, and confidence by each experience in which we really stop to look fear in the face...we must do that which we think we cannot."

Eleanor Roosevelt

Pushing the Limits

We are all influenced by the world around us. Limitations, whether they are ones we put on ourselves, or ones imposed on us by others, are everywhere. As a result, our struggle becomes a very private battle. When our intolerance for the barriers that have been set before us spur an act of rebellion, one bold step is all it takes.

"So, after being told to keep my hair loss a secret for a year . . ." - **Georgia**

"So, I began to think about what life would be like without covering up." - **Anthony**

"I decided that one of us ought to get a head tattoo…and I decided it was up to me." - **Joyce**

*"I began pursuing modeling again, despite being told
I could never model without hair of my own."* - **Mikaya**

*"After I stopped worrying about what others thought and concentrated
on my job, my results and confidence improved."* - **Dean**

"I've now made the decision to tattoo my eyebrows and not wear wigs anymore." - **Sarah**

"After a lot of debate, I finally jumped in." - **Angelica**

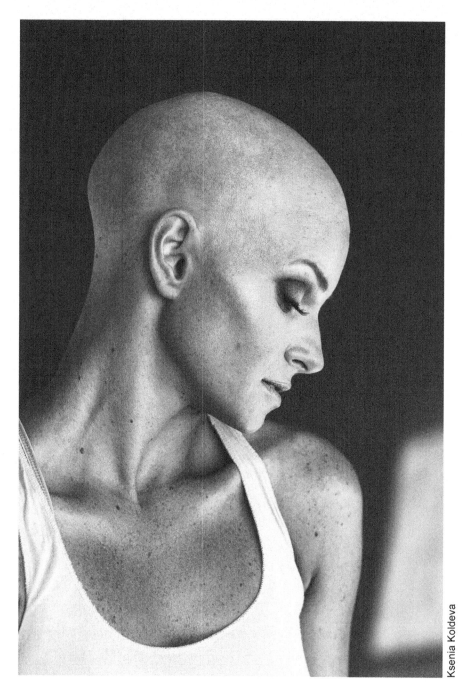

Ksenia Koldeva

Georgia

I must confess, I am a little sick of my story at this point. When my hair fell out, I was a hair model and actress. I'm a little embarrassed to say my appearance was how I made a living. So, after being told to keep my hair loss a secret for a year and detesting every second of it, I decided to do the complete opposite and tell my story to the world. All I wanted was for no one else to have to keep their alopecia a secret. As a result, I've now had the honor of telling my hair loss

story thousands of times to reporters, interviewers, all ages of kids in school, and the many Alopecians I have had the joy and privilege of meeting over the last seven years since that first spot appeared just above my right ear.

So, instead of sharing my hair loss story, I'll share with you some of the things that never would have happened if I hadn't lost my hair.

I would never have had a wig-wearing party with the girls in the Mar Vista Projects and seen them laugh as they traded wigs while taking on new personalities, and I never would have felt their little hands all over my head as they searched for spikey and smooth spots.

I wouldn't have met Cameron, my "little sister," who was nine when I met her. She didn't even know what alopecia was. When people asked her if she had cancer, she would say, "Yes." She figured maybe she did. She hated wigs and didn't want eyebrows drawn on. She just wanted to be herself. Cameron helped me look at why I wore wigs and showed me what really being ok with yourself looked like.

I would never have discovered what it feels like to receive thousands of incredible hugs from the cutest bald and patchy headed kids you could ever imagine.

I may never have learned that when people love you, they don't want you to wear something that isn't you. They think you, without all the fake hair, is the best version of you. My brother once said, "When there is no hair in the way, we can really see your eyes and who you really are."

I never would have got away with shaving my legs only once a month.

I may never have had the honor of opening up my email thousands of times to read one that started with, "I have never told anyone else this before, but…"

I may never have learned the Calvin Klein model I dated was completely self-consumed and cared more about whether he could catch my alopecia than kissing me.

I may never have learned that 98% of women in Hollywood don't use all their own hair, and they spend thousands of dollars on having hair "put in" every year. When I go out with a wig on, at least two women will tell me they want my hair. My response, "You can have it – it isn't mine!"

I would have never received a YouTube message from an 18-year-old girl who believed she would never ever get a boyfriend because of her alopecia, become friends with her and a year later see her status on Facebook change to "In a relationship."

I would never have learned that you can tell a lot about a man by the kind of hair he likes his girlfriend to have. FYI – Guys who say, "I'd prefer you keep the wig on around me," aren't worth a second date.

I may never have had the chance to sit opposite a 10-year-old girl who was threatening to kill herself because she felt fat, tell her I know what it is like to look in the mirror and not see what you want to, and that it will get better. Then, look into her eyes and see that she really did feel understood. That girl is now fifteen years old.

I may never have been forced to notice all the other parts of me that are beautiful. Before I lost my hair, I used to tell everyone the only part of me that I liked was my hair, and now I really like all the parts of me – and the parts I like the most are on the inside of me.

I may never have learned that everyone out there is just dying for a chance to be honest and share who they really are. Losing my hair was the greatest key to opening up any friendship, breaking down any wall, and connecting to anyone who was just looking for a chance to be themselves.

And I may never have been asked to share my story.

Georgia continues to play and work in the entertainment industry, but spends all her heart, thoughts, and most of her time on improving the lives and futures of all children. She loves continuing her work with her young Alopecian friends while developing Arts Bridging the Gap - her non-profit organization that creates arts education programs for underserved youth to improve their academic, social, and emotional success. Everything she does now is in pursuit of happiness for all children. Even all of her race-running, swimming, and fitness work is to encourage her kids to be healthy, fit, and go beyond what they think they can accomplish.

Leslie Hassler

Anthony

Alopecia areata. Even as I type the "areata" part, I see the red underline thing telling me that it's not a word. It is, autocorrect. IT IS! It's more than a clinical term though. For me, its associations encompass fear, rejection, hiding, but also bravery, compassion, and acceptance. I never knew why I had bald spots on my head, and no one else did either. So, they were just a big mystery that no one could explain. My immune system was confused, something like that.

It was never something I focused on, but there were certain times growing up where I would be swimming and could feel people staring at me. The wind would blow, and the soccer ball would roll out of bounds as people would stand still and gawk. Then came the teasing. Let me tell you, kids can have this uncanny ability to tease mercilessly. I used to feel like the only way to not get teased was to cover up or wear a hat. So, that's what I started to do. Cover up. All the while I was hiding, I so desperately wanted to be seen.

In the midst of this secret, all I wanted was to communicate my feelings. So, I became an actor. I developed my passion for theater and felt very much at home on the stage, where makeup and costumes were part of the charm. I continued my studies of acting into college, and once I graduated I began my career as a professional actor. My alopecia was something I had compartmentalized so well that very few of my close friends even knew that I had it. If I didn't acknowledge it, it wasn't there. Right? Well, things have a way of finding their way to the surface.

It was during a big television gig, that the condition I had always kept under wraps began to get bad enough so that I couldn't ignore it. It was during this time that I lost half the hair on my head, along with both eyebrows and most all of my eyelashes. This was happening while being on a show with millions of viewers a week. I don't know how I kept it together. I tried the steroid injections, the ointments that burned my scalp underneath hair pieces, penciling in eyebrows before red carpet parties - hoping that they wouldn't notice my makeup.

I'm a strong person, but the pressure was getting to be too great. I managed to still book work with partial regrowth and makeup, but I knew I couldn't do this forever. So, I began to think about what life would be like without covering up. This was terrifying to me. I felt like I was risking annihilation by showing people what I actually looked like. But the need for authenticity began to outweigh my fear of not being accepted. Over the course of a few years, I began to develop the courage to stop wearing makeup and then to let my spots be seen.

At first, I was waiting for something painful to happen, but there was nothing. There was no impact to the imaginary crash I was bracing myself for. It felt like the people who truly loved me came forward in my need to be accepted, but I see now that they were with me all along. There was the other bunch too, who had problems with my not caring anymore and who wanted me to cover up. I recognized in them that they were still scared of exposing themselves and whatever it was that they were hiding, and needed compassion most of all.

I fully feel for those who are still scared to be seen. Their judgment is an indicator of their fear. Knowing this helps dismantle when someone isn't being kind. I was and am very fortunate to have such loving friends and family, and even business relationships who helped guide me through this murky water. Not everyone with alopecia has such a support system, and some don't want to be exposed. I encourage you to do your best and lead by example with self-love. Change doesn't happen overnight. It didn't with me anyway. To me, it happens in each moment of compassion you can bring to yourself and to others who also have their fears and insecurities.

My journey has been one of allowing myself to be seen. I have shaved my head, don't bother with makeup, and my career as an actor has been benefiting ever since. Most people think my look is really cool, but what's more important is that I feel that I like the way I look. Everyone has the right to feel free to be who they are, and I wish them luck on their path to self-acceptance and self-love.

Anthony Carrigan resides in both Los Angeles and New York. He is dedicated to bringing forth a positive message in the entertainment industry, and playing fun and dynamic characters. In his spare time, he volunteers at Comfort Zone camp (a bereavement camp for kids who have lost a parent or loved one) practices tai chi, and gets outdoors whenever possible.

Celia Strickler

Joyce
Alopecia - It's Not for Everyone…

Being a bald woman is not the kind of thing most women would aspire to. I did not seek this out as a lifestyle – or a style – or a way of life. Baldness found me. I am fortunate that I have become enamored with this development in my life and style. Being hair-free has led me on a journey that has taken me to places and introduced me to people I never would have found as a "haired" person. As I sit here, I can honestly say I am thankful for these adventures – and yes, I am thankful that I am a bald woman.

I have had alopecia for more than fifty years. Nothing about this was easy, but to get into the details does not add value to my story. From the age of twelve until twenty-four, I experienced bouts of alopecia areata, after which my hair fully returned and remained for almost thirty years. I believed I was cured. Wrong. When my son told me his hair was falling out, I was devastated. This is when I tried to make a deal with God, "Leave my son out of this!" That didn't really work out. Within a couple of weeks, my own hair was falling out again. Before long, we were both bald. Here I was – fifty-something – and losing my hair. At some point, I realized it was all going this time, and to some extent, I was relieved. I was no longer waiting for this to happen. It was done. Whew! It wasn't long before I was googling to learn more about alopecia and chatting online with people who became and remain my friends to this day. My first visit to a NAAF conference was life changing and forged even more life-long friendships. I attend as often as is financially and logistically possible

140

My son inspired my first major adventure as a bald woman – getting a tattoo on my head. My son displays many beautiful works of art on his person. I love tattoo art (and have a few of my own). I decided that one of us ought to get a head tattoo. When he told me that he wasn't interested in doing this, I decided it was up to me. As fate would have it, Miami Ink was a fairly new offering on The Learning Channel (TLC) at that time. It was a reality show about tattoo artists and stories of their clients. Online, I found a link to "apply to get a tattoo on Miami Ink." I sent my application, including my plea to help me make a statement to the bald population (whether from alopecia or other causes). You do not have to hide your head or be ashamed because you have no hair. I did it! In July 2006, I got my tattoo in Miami. All of the folks involved with the show were FABULOUS. The show aired in October 2006.

Choosing to get a butterfly as a tattoo was a no-brainer – this was truly my metamorphosis. One day, I was just another woman with bad hair – through alopecia, I was reborn with a sweet little bald head – a blank canvas. This was the new me! The support I received from my family and friends gave me the confidence to walk out in the world with my head shining in the light.

Reactions to my baldness? The "cancer look" is easy to spot – people may be smiling, but their eyes are so sad. When I see this look, I turn quickly so they can see the tattoo on the back of my head. The dynamic changes immediately. "Did that hurt?" Good question! I explain that the tattoo on the back of my calf hurt more than the one on my head. I then explain that not only do I have a great tattoo on my head, but I am lucky to be VERY healthy; I just have no hair. It's OK. I explain alopecia and tell them my immune system has over-protected me and sent my hair a packin'. I take advantage of the conversation to tell them about my "15 minutes of fame" on Miami Ink. By the end of the conversation, we are all smiling – real smiles. Yay! Now, one more person knows about alopecia!

Indeed, there have been many "strange" looks – A bald woman with a tattoo on her head? Oh my! The positive responses far outnumber the bad. There was a small child in the supermarket whose mother couldn't move fast enough to cover the child's mouth before she asked innocently, "Where is your hair?" I smiled at them both and told her that some people have hair and some do not. I strongly believe in the importance of educating younger people, children in particular, that people are different for many reasons and that it's okay. I think this will lead to more acceptance of diversity as this becomes their world. At three, my youngest granddaughter, Nicole, had already accepted my "look" as just part of me. She has shared with me that if I ever wanted hair, that she would cut hers when she got older and glue it on my head so that we could be "hair buddies." If there really is a reason for everything, then my baldness is a blessing which has inspired me to reach out and try to help others who are not as fortunate as I am in terms of confidence, acceptance, and understanding. I have volunteered with the American Cancer Society to speak to women facing hair loss. I was not sure what kind of contribution I could make. It wasn't long before I realized the beauticians, doctors, and other people with hair could never share the secrets I have learned about tying a cotton bandana on my bald head and making it stay!

How do I wrap this up? Recent news has reported some medications for other illnesses or disorders have produced hair regrowth for people with alopecia. I often have dreams where my hair grows back, and of course it looks better than it ever did in real life. In spite of that, I always shave it back off before I wake up. Although I know many people would be happy to regrow their hair, I am fine.

After Joyce shared her story with Pam Fitros, for her book, Boldly Bald Women, she was also pleased that Pam chose her artwork for the cover. Pam has become one of her dearest friends – yet another wonderful person who would never have become part of her life if not for alopecia.

Darnell Wilburn

Mikaya

For many girls, age twelve is the meaning of a lot of new things. It's the end of the pre-teen era and usually the beginning of puberty. The onset of raging hormones, the curiosity about dating, boys and how to get their attention, along with physical changes in body structure. However, that's not how I remember it. I remember that year being the beginning of what would be the most trying time in my life, when I was diagnosed with alopecia.

Before my diagnosis, I would describe myself as a very creative, confident, secure, feisty, girly girl who loved the skin she was in. I was outgoing, yet shy at times. I still maintained confidence in even the most uncomfortable settings. I loved to dance and had recently discovered a love for modeling. I was feminine and loved my soft, wavy hair and enjoyed styling it, which I was very good at. I enjoyed makeup, nails, and dressing up. Everything you'd think a prissy girl would like, I loved! At one point during the year, I began to notice small clumps of hair coming out. I'd mentioned it to my mother, but we concluded it was normal shedding. We didn't worry too much about it, until one morning when I noticed my signature look, the full, bouncy afro puff ponytail I once cherished, had diminished to a thin, frail, barely there portion of hair on my head. After the initial shock of being diagnosed with alopecia, I was devastated. I was young and could not comprehend that my beautiful, long, wavy locks of hair would never come back. I was still optimistic that I would be a part of that small percentage doctors said could experience full hair restoration. Looking back, I believe I was in denial. As weeks went by and more hair disappeared, I held on to the last three strands of hair on my head for as long as possible. I could no longer deny my hair was GONE and I was BALD. After about a month, my optimism faded and turned into fear and disappointment.

There were many days and nights I cried in disbelief and had feelings of insignificance because of this new appearance I was being forced to deal with. I was quickly stripped of the confidence I had. The hopes I had of becoming a model, faded because I thought models were beautiful, with long hair and confidence. Everything I was not. All I wanted to do was fit in, but I stood out in the crowd. I gained attention but not the kind of attention a 12-year-old girl would want. At the time, I attended a private Christian school, where you'd think my situation would be handled easier than elsewhere, but kids were just that... kids. Kids can be cruel. I was isolated and felt like an outcast. The teasing, pointing, whispering and stares I endured from peers at school and strangers became unbearable. I felt ugly and like I would never be normal again. I didn't feel there was any reason for me to dream or even live anymore.

I attempted acupuncture and considered steroid treatments and some of the more promising products seen on numerous infomercials. Ultimately, I resorted to wearing wigs. I remember my first trip to the wig store with my mother like it was yesterday. It was one of the hardest, most awkward experiences along this journey. I remember looking at all the pieces that clearly weren't meant for a pre-teen girl. It was going to be impossible to find a wig I could wear. This made the acceptance process even more frustrating. Not only were the style options insufficient for me, but I was "blessed" with a tiny head, making the selection process even more difficult. I remember my mom being very patient with me. I finally picked out the best thing I could, which was a "Curly Sue" wig with a head band. It wasn't MY hair, but it made me feel like I was a part of society again.

Mikaya's Story Continues . . .

Only at home when the wig came off, did the reality of how I viewed myself hit me all over again. My mom noticed I became withdrawn and felt me slipping away. This is when she took action to fight for her daughter and what she saw in me. I didn't understand it then, but my mother began to breathe life back into a dying soul. I thought, then, that my mom was patronizing me for being bald. She forced me to look at myself in the mirror and say, "I'm beautiful," out loud over and over again. Sometimes, we'd stay in that mirror for hours at a time until the tears would stop rolling down my face. It didn't make much of a difference once the moment had passed away. Not until later in life, would I understand the self-proclamation and how it changed my outlook on my life, my esteem, my being.

Through the following years, I continued to wear wigs and experiment with different styles as it became a part of me. I'd spent countless amounts of money on them, including an insanely expensive customized lace front. I wanted so badly to just be free, but I was still holding on to what was most comfortable. I began pursuing modeling again, despite being told I could never model without hair of my own. Little did I know that it would become therapeutic for me and ultimately be one of the driving forces to push me further toward what I believe is my destiny. Modeling became one of my coping mechanisms. It gave me courage. It made me feel vulnerable, yet invincible all at the same time. All eyes were on me, for those brief moments while on the runway. But for once, it felt good to be the center of positive attention. When I stepped onto a runway, I felt alive again. I took the ultimate leap of faith, without my trainer knowing, and walked the runway bald for the very first time at a competition. I remember turning to my mom as I was putting makeup on for the runway competition, and saying "Mommy, I think it's time!" She looked at me with the most fearful, yet proud expression and said, "Are you sure?" She saw a look of determination and confidence on my face and knew I'd reached my liberation point. I was ready. My mother wasn't sure of the response I'd get from the competition, which sparked her fears, but she knew I was prepared. "Contestant number 245!" When I heard my number, my heart began to race. But as I took the first step onto the runway, all fear was gone. I received a standing ovation that night and took home first place! That was one of the first steps toward my ultimate liberation.

Seven years ago, I met the man who'd ultimately be my soulmate and immediately sparked a friendship with him. That friendship progressed into a more serious relationship, and after about two months our relationship matured to a point where I knew I couldn't go any longer without telling him about how I really looked. I just didn't know how. I knew the relationship was substantial enough and that I'd have to tell him about my baldness. I'd read an article about a lady who had alopecia and didn't tell her husband for years. I knew I couldn't do that, but I had no clue how I'd break the news of who I really was and what I really looked like. Do I just show up without hair? Do I just come out and tell him? I finally decided the easiest way would be for me to show him my modeling photos without a wig.

I was a nervous wreck, completely clueless of his reaction. Would he stay? Would he think I was unattractive and leave? I took the chance and told him I had something to show him. Heart racing and hands shaking, I handed him the photos. He looked and said, "Oh. This is all you had to show me?" I immediately said, "What do you mean is this all?" He was head over heels in love with the way I looked without a wig and expressed he'd rather me not wear one. I was relieved to finally know someone cared and was in love with me for who I was.

Three years later, we were married. Being happily married, I can honestly say it's an unbelievable feeling to know that he loves me for and beyond my bald.

Four years ago, I was put in contact with a photographer, and for the umpteenth time was challenged with the decision to be photographed with or without hair. The photographer asked me to send him a headshot without hair. After he received it, he called back excitedly saying how "dope" the look was and how it was so unique. From that moment on, I questioned myself less about being a bald model.

With the help and support of my husband, parents, family, and friends, I gave up the wigs and was finally at peace with being me. I'd finally come to a point in my life where I accepted it all. I was beautiful, and it was time to live the life I was given with my head held high.

I received amazing responses in the modeling industry. I even entered into *America's Next Top Model Competition* as a bald model and made it to the final cut before production. I was ready to flaunt the natural beauty God gave me and show the world that bald truly is beautiful. I'd reached my ultimate liberation!

I still felt compelled that there was more for me to learn, give, do, and see. I began to run into many young girls and women who suffered with low self-esteem and alienation due to their unique appearance, and who were inspired by my courage.

Three years ago, I had a conversation with my husband when he began asking questions about my experiences with alopecia. The questions began to probe into feelings and emotions I'd hidden for so long, and I felt a burden finally lift. Beyond that, it also caused me to realize that even though my personal liberation was reached, there had to be so many other young girls and women walking the same path I once struggled to walk. The thought of others experiencing the same feelings, trapped emotions, thoughts of unworthiness, emptiness, ugliness, loneliness, and depression presented yet another burden on my heart.

That was the night I conceived the first ideas about an organization I would form called, *My B.A.L.D. Is Beautiful, Inc.* I wanted to provide support to young girls and women in my community, help heal self-hate, low self-esteem, and the feeling of ugliness. I wanted to change the stigmas associated with being bald and teach young girls and women to re-define their beauty by their own standards, instead of society's standard.

Without support, I would not be here. I began writing the visions I had. It took planning and lots of research. I found there was no organization in my community that catered to uplifting young girls and women with alopecia, or any hair loss. I knew it was needed, and I couldn't hold off. It's now been two years since establishing *My B.A.L.D. Is Beautiful, Inc.* The organization has since reached, inspired, and encouraged girls and women as far as the U.K. Establishing *My B.A.L.D. Is Beautiful, Inc.* is my way of giving back to young girls and women who are struggling to accept themselves. I vowed to make it my duty to ensure that any girl or woman who has experienced or is experiencing the trauma of hair loss will have support and know their worth. I'm thankful I listened to my heart.

Mikaya works diligently with My B.A.L.D. Is Beautiful, Inc., supporting the community of women and girls affected by hair loss throughout the world. Passionate about the cause of education, awareness, support, and inspiration of women and girls with hair loss, Mikaya's ultimate goal is to ensure that not one girl or woman has to walk the hair loss journey alone, without sufficient support. She has made it her life's work to continue to find ways to execute that mission. She's also enjoying the wonders of motherhood, raising four beautiful children and supporting her husband, Kevin, who travels as an author, life coach, and motivational speaker, enriching the lives of today's youth.

Dean

It was a hot day, and when I ran some water through my hair, followed by rubbing my hands through it, they were covered with more hair than usual. I didn't say anything for a day or two to anyone, but when it didn't stop falling out, I consulted with mum. We followed up by going to see a specialist. When I was first diagnosed with alopecia by the dermatologist, he pretty much just said, "You have alopecia. You can try steroid injections in the scalp. Otherwise, there isn't much else you can do."

When I went home, the first thing I did was get on the internet and research more. My hair loss was so rapid that the hair on my head had totally disappeared within three weeks, and the remainder of my body hair took another two months from onset.

From what I could find online, it was clear what type of alopecia I had and that there was no clear treatment known to work.

I had just started dating my now wife, Erin. She was my rock from the beginning. We were living in different states at the time, and Facetime wasn't around then. So, a photo when I first started losing my hair, made her realise what was happening. She came over when I lost all the hair on my head but still had my eyebrows and lashes. I started to lose confidence in myself and wasn't sure how she would react. She was nothing but supportive.

I was told the most common cause of alopecia is stress. So, of course everyone kept asking, "Are you stressed?" Everyone has stress in their lives, but I personally didn't believe it was stress related. While I was still going through the period of not knowing whether my hair would grow back or not, I was still in my first year of V8 supercar racing as a full-time driver. I wasn't sure how to deal with my condition to the public, so I tried to hide it for a while by saying I shaved my head to raise funds for charity.

My results in racing began to show my loss in confidence. Once all my hair was completely gone, it was harder to hide the truth any longer. I then opted for a professional wig. The wig really did nothing for my confidence, and I didn't want to hide behind it. I soon made the decision to stop wearing it and embrace my appearance. After I stopped worrying about what others thought and concentrated on my job, my results and confidence improved. The only issue with not having hair in the race car was that sweat would not be caught by my eyebrows and would sometimes drip straight into my eye. Other than that, it had no other effects.

My new look soon became my trademark. I was more noticeable than before. I had a couple of parents come up to me at race meetings asking if I had alopecia. They told me their sons had the same condition, and they weren't very confident, were picked on at school… This made me realise I could try and help these children with the condition and show them they were still the same person, and it wouldn't stop them from doing what they wanted in life. I know how difficult it was to go through alopecia, even at the age of twenty-two, and I can only imagine how hard it must be for children to go through the same thing. I have been lucky enough to have positive effects on some children I've met. When their parents contact me, I encourage them to bring kids out to a race meeting to ask me any questions they want. One little boy, who always used to wear a bandana, made his mum cry when he removed it after talking with me at a meeting. He embraced his look, and his parents couldn't be happier.

One of the mothers made me laugh when she saw how stunning my wife was and remarked that, "Even with alopecia, you could still have someone as beautiful as her."

One of the positives of having alopecia as a male is not having to shave facial hair. My wife also hates the fact that my legs are smoother than hers.

My alopecia hasn't changed who I am. If anything, it has made me more noticeable.

I am a healthy, happy person, and a husband and father of two boys, who enjoys life. I don't let my condition change what I want to do and achieve in life.

Dean Canto is a multiple-championship winning Australian motor racing driver. He was the inaugural winner of the second-tier V8 Supercar development series in 2000, and the first to become a multiple-champion five years later. When not driving in endurance races, Dean runs "Ultimate Stunt Driving" performance driving school in Sydney. Dean recently competed at the Bathurst 12 Hour where he finished 5th, and will continue racing throughout 2015 in The Australian GT Championship. www.canto.com.au

Sarah

I first noticed my alopecia two years ago. I usually wore my hair in pigtails, and one day at a theme park, I noticed my first patch. It's kind of funny if you think about it…one of the most entertaining places in California is where I developed a disorder that would affect my entire life. Over the next few weeks, the small patch started getting bigger until finally the entire bottom half of my head was bald. My mother and I went to the doctor and were told my hair was falling out because I was wearing too tight of ponytails. We weren't really sure what to say, and a few more weeks went by until I barely had any hair left. I was still in denial at this point and wasn't sure how long it would take to go completely bald. In the meantime, my eyebrows slowly started falling out, and then my bottom eyelashes.

The day finally came when I realized I would be entirely bald. I don't know why it took me so long, but I remember sitting on my bed and doing research on this weird disease called alopecia. I grabbed a pair of scissors, walked into the bathroom and started cutting my hair. I cried and realized I couldn't get to it all without help. When I walked into my mom's office, she looked at me, saw how puffy and red my eyes were, and the clusters of hair in my hand. She grabbed a razor and shaved off what was left. It was so surreal. After that, I just went straight to bed. I still remember how my head felt while I lay on the pillow. We didn't say anything. Just a hug and a kiss, and I went to sleep.

At some point during the night, I woke up to use the bathroom. Still a bit groggy, I turned on the light, looked in the mirror and saw a bald person standing there, and I got scared. It took me a moment to realize it was me.

While 75% of my head was bald, I could get away with wearing a hat that made me look semi-normal. I dealt with constant questions, staring, and pointing. It was difficult, and my mom and I finally went to the wig store. I could barely hold myself together on deciding which wig to choose. The experience was overwhelming, but I finally decided on a medium length brown one.

The first time I wore the wig to school was exhausting. I was constantly wondering if someone would pull it off. Would someone notice how I went from incredibly short hair under a hat, to thick hair under a wig? Through all this time, my best friend Beverly stood by my side. We are like sisters, even though we haven't known each other long. I remember the first time she came to my house. When she rang the doorbell and I ran to answer it, I was bald. She took one look and gave me a huge hug. Beverly is a true friend, and I would not be able to get by without her support.

I think people did notice my change in hair but didn't want to say anything. The day arrived when I was completely bald. Not one hair left on my body. My mother had ordered false eyebrows that were human hair glued onto a silicone base. All you had to do was put false eyelash glue on the back and glue them where they should go. As time went by and I learned to perfect wearing makeup and false eyebrows, lashes, and wigs – I got more confident.

A few months later, as Beverly and I sat in one of our favorite teacher's classrooms during lunch, a seventh grader came by, looked at me, and pulled my wig right off my head. I was completely shocked and started crying. She looked so embarrassed. The entire ordeal felt like it was in slow-motion. Middle school was really tough, even though I discovered who I was through it all.

I'm about to enter high school. I've now made the decision to tattoo my eyebrows and not wear wigs anymore. I'm just so tired of hiding. I don't know what the future holds for me. I'm pretty sure it's going to be a bumpy ride, but I think I'm prepared.

Sarah is a 9th grade student living in California. She followed through on her desire to get her eyebrows tattooed and claims it is the best decision she ever made. She attends school without her wig and is happy with who she is.

2 point 8 Studios

Angelica

I was diagnosed with alopecia when I was twelve years old, after noticing my first spot at age eleven. We were all devastated. My mother told me to shave it off because I was going to lose it anyway, but she still supported my decision when I continued with the treatments. I had regular injections and three different steroids on top of my asthma medication and iron supplement. My alopecia became a distraction for me. My grades started to drop, and I stopped doing the things I enjoyed, like playing softball and playing percussion, so I could focus on overcoming my alopecia.

After overcoming my alopecia, I became more involved with friends and social events. A friend of mine asked me to take a cosmetology class with her during our junior year in high school. I took off my wig in front of everyone and educated them about alopecia. Since that day, I continued teaching my classmates about other things like nails and coloring. I grew fond of what cosmetology offered and spent the rest of high school, including summers, working toward my license. I earned my Barber/Cosmetology license two months after graduating high school. My plans were to work in a high-end salon and continue my education. I attended Utah State University, majoring in business. I decided to change majors because I knew I wanted to be in the fashion industry. I continued working and living everyday life. When I attended my grandmother's 80th birthday, a friend of hers took a photo of me and sent it off to a pageant director. I had no idea what was in store for me next.

A few weeks later, I received a call asking me to join Miss Philippines (Earth) USA 2014. I contemplated for weeks and weeks, not knowing if I wanted to participate in the pageant. After a lot of debate, I finally jumped in. When I had pageant pictures taken, it was only the second time I was bald in front of a camera. I sent both photos of me, bald and with a wig, to the pageant director and called him the next day to ask if it would be okay to participate without my wig. He enthusiastically said, "Yes. Of course." I soon realized he thought I was talking about hair extensions. He soon saw my photos and called me, informing me that he had misunderstood, asking if I was comfortable with the media storm that would happen if I won. I immediately confirmed I wanted to be an advocate for mother earth and relayed to him that just by being myself, I could also spread awareness of alopecia.

The next thing I knew, I was flying to San Francisco to meet with the director. He wanted to make sure I was comfortable joining my first pageant, bald. Pageant day came. I had no idea what I was doing. I followed directions and basically played follow the leader. I analyzed the other girls' walk and how they spoke to the crowd. I studied the questions and practiced my answers, but by the time it was my turn I only remembered three words. I couldn't even remember what I said. I answered to the best of my ability and soon discovered the crowd loved my answers. As everything raced by, I found myself given the title of, "Miss Philippines WATER USA 2014!" I had won one of the five major titles, allowing me to proceed to regionals. Miss Philippines EARTH 2014, was to be held in the Philippines. If I were to win the title, I could compete in Miss Earth 2014.

I spent the entire month of February fundraising for my trip to train and compete in the Philippines, crowdfunding, having garage sales, and selling homemade cinnamon rolls to raise enough money to go. Two days before I left, the pageant director informed me that I would not be able to compete due to "complications" and the possibility of "taking too much attention away from the pageant." Sadly, I was unable to compete in the Miss Philippines Earth pageant, but it opened me up to more possibilities. I considered canceling everything, but in the end decided to keep my plans in order to train with Kagandahang Flores (KF Team). I was able to train with all the Miss Philippines Earth candidates. It was mentally and physically challenging. I felt like I was back in junior high, so out of place. I felt that some of the girls wanted me to feel that way. I still tried to own it and stay confident. I kept my head up and kept moving forward.

I never entered a "beauty pageant," but most pageants still focus on hair, body shape, waist size, appearance, and your platform. They really want you to have the whole package, body and brains. Honestly, I think if you're truly dedicated, you have to make yourself credible in the pageant world. I believe all that matters is being humble, confident, dedicated, and true to you.

I believe everything happens for a reason, meaning if something doesn't go your way, then there's something even bigger and greater coming your way. I would say, "Don't dread on what could have been, and be excited for what's in store." There are so many opportunities out there, but it's all about timing. The right opportunity often happens, but wrong timing.

Angelica recently placed 10th in the Miss United Nations USA 2014 pageant in Utah, and is now competing in The Miss Herriman Scholarship Pageant 2015 for the Miss America preliminaries. She would like to continue to pursue high fashion modeling, being a public speaker for alopecia awareness, being a multi-business owner, fashion designer and much more. "I am still young. So, I still have a lot to learn about what I want to do."

Lessons Learned

"If you don't get lost, there's a chance you may never be found."
Author Unknown

"Thank you alopecia!" is a common phrase of gratitude within many of these stories. "Thank you for the opportunity to grow and to meet others who truly understand." "Thank you for helping me realize I am more than just my hair." Our internal and external struggles translate into discovering qualities about ourselves we may never have learned without our experience with alopecia. Moving beyond these struggles, and remembering what they teach us, is essential in helping us to grow in all aspects of our lives.

"I often wonder if I would have learned as many valuable lessons about surrender . . ." - **Laura**

"What I have come to learn after all these years, is that my life with alopecia prepared me for who I believe I was meant to be . . ." - **Melissa**

"Somehow this builds character – To fall down and get back up." - **DK Wright**

"I realize now, that in order to create music, you need to first become in tune with yourself." - **Paul**

"I have a drive that I didn't have before . . ." - **Emma**

"I am beautiful and authentically deserving of that cup of love . . ." - **Heather**

Laura

I had always prided myself on having long, thick, lustrous hair which flowed down to my waist when I was young. Just like many other little girls, my childhood was filled with blonde Barbie dolls and stories of Rapunzel. I studied classical ballet from the time I was eight years old and eventually moved to New York City at seventeen to pursue my career in dance. The required hairdo during those years, was a tightly pulled back bun piled high on top of the head. Later, when I left classical ballet to join a contemporary dance company, long, loose hair was often a prop or accessory in many of our numbers.

It symbolized wild abandon and freedom. Women, in general, are constantly fed images and ideas in our society that emphasize the importance of our looks. Shiny, flowing hair equals femininity, youth, and beauty and is something to strive for. Having come from a career where I was constantly being seen by the public made it especially difficult when my hair began falling out.

I noticed my first bald spot in the late summer of 2008. I woke up one morning, rolled over in bed and

Laura's Story Continues . . .

153

rested my head on my arm. My fingers felt a patch of perfectly smooth skin where my hair should be. I was surprised and a little confused, but didn't give it much consideration. I remember jokingly thinking, "Maybe aliens visited me last night and that's where they inserted their probe to analyze my brain!" Sometime later, while getting a trim, my hairdresser noticed it too. That's when I first heard the word alopecia. Little did I know at the time how significant that one word would become and how it would be part of my vocabulary nearly every day. My hairdresser told me a few cortisone injections would take care of it, but why should I bother? I had so much long, thick hair that a bald spot about the size of a quarter wouldn't be noticeable at all. Several months later, I discovered a few more bald patches and began to get a little concerned. I had to find ways to style my hair creatively so no one would notice these bare spots.

Of course, I questioned why this was happening, feared that my health was in jeopardy or that I had some rare, life-threatening disease. Part of me felt extremely betrayed. I had been practicing and teaching yoga for over five years. I led a healthy lifestyle, maintained a good diet, got plenty of sleep, fresh air, and exercise. I had been in a verbally abusive relationship filled with stress, anger, and conflict since 2004, but didn't really think there was any connection between that and my hair falling out. Heck, I had survived a difficult divorce in 2003, leaving me as a single mom with two young kids to care for. I thought if I could weather that, anything should be a breeze in comparison.

Over the next several months, my hair loss began to progress more rapidly. I became filled with worry, confusion, anger, and shame. I was looking for someone or something to blame for this scary, frustrating process. Oftentimes, that someone was myself. I clearly remember one morning while showering, I sobbed hysterically while holding piles of hair in each hand, thinking I must be dying, that my body was falling apart before my very eyes. And

because my mindset was one of loss, grief, and illness, that was exactly how I felt. I was exhausted and weak, not only from the stress of losing my hair but also because that's what I was telling myself. My thinking was filled with negativity. Through the process of learning to live with and eventually accept and celebrate alopecia, I would come to know and appreciate the power of the mind and its intimate relationship with the body. But I wasn't there yet... I was still in panic mode. I had to find answers. I had to educate myself about this horrible curse of a condition. I had to fight and find a cure.

In the spring of 2009, I made an appointment with my doctor to see if he could figure out what was going on and hopefully offer a solution. Unfortunately, I was wrong. He made an official diagnosis of alopecia areata and basically told me there was nothing he could do for me. He explained that this condition is caused by the immune system mistakenly attacking the body's own cells, that it is completely random, can strike anyone at any time, and has no known cause or cure. He basically sent me on my way with no real answers. I felt there had to be something more that could be done. I sought out a second opinion from a dermatologist who also confirmed the diagnosis. He said we could try treating the bald spots with cortisone injections and Rogaine, and so began a full on war with my hair.

I endured painful injections to my scalp once a month, slathered my head every morning and night with toxic chemicals, began taking large doses of vitamins, and drinking protein shakes in the hopes of strengthening my body. I spent countless hours on my computer, researching and learning all I could about alopecia and looking for different cures. After a couple months, my dermatologist decided to supplement my regimen with weekly UVB laser treatments (essentially burning my scalp) to see if that would increase the speed of my hair growth. I had a few sprouts of hair growing back where I had received the cortisone injections but still had new spots appearing elsewhere. All of this only added to my feelings of hopelessness.

After about six months of these painful, expensive, and invasive procedures, I began to think there must be a gentler way to treat this. At the time, I was still determined to "win" and grow all of my hair back. Through an online search, I discovered an Ayurvedic doctor in India who claimed to have had much success in treating people with alopecia. Ayurveda is a 5,000 year old system of natural healing that has origins in the Vedic culture of India. It seeks to address a person as a whole and bring one's body, mind, and spirit into balance rather than just treating specific symptoms. His treatment consisted of herbal oils to rub into the scalp daily, as well as weekly mud pack applications. This idea resonated more closely with my beliefs, so I ordered his products. I rubbed the herbal oils into my head every night while mentally stating affirmations of health. I sat with henna paste on my head for an hour each week, while focusing my thoughts on healing and visualizing my hair growing back. By this time, I had very little hair left. Perhaps 60% had fallen out, and I was wearing a partial integration wig every day to disguise that fact. I never left home without putting my wig on first. No one, except my family, was aware that anything was going on.

In November 2009, I was invited to teach yoga at a sports retreat in Turks and Caicos. I was excited about this opportunity but also nervous. One of my first thoughts was, "How am I going to disguise my hair loss?" I wanted to be able to enjoy the tropical climate and warm weather, which meant swimming in the ocean, boating, snorkeling... all activities I feared would make my wig fall off. I accepted the offer and away I went, making sure to pack my herbal hair remedies so I could continue treatment while away from home. The first few days of the retreat went without a hitch. I wore my wig when I taught yoga and made sure to only wade in the water up to my waist to avoid the chance of my wig falling off. My boyfriend and I decided to go snorkeling one day, away from the crowds playing volleyball on the beach. Even though we found a secluded location, I was still hesitant to take my wig off. I had the brilliant idea of braiding the wig into my few strands of remaining hair to keep it securely in place. Boy was that a mistake! The salt water left the wig and my hair tangled into a huge, wet rat's nest. After we returned from snorkeling, I tried to comb the knots out of the wig in order to separate it from my own hair. Three hours and almost a full bottle of conditioner later, the wig and my hair were still a jumbled mess. I was crying, desperate, knowing we had to show up for dinner very soon. So, I painfully ripped the wig off of my head, leaving my remaining hair more sparse and scraggly than ever before. I felt like I looked sick, and there was no way I was going to be seen in public like this. Knowing that hiding in my room was not an option, I tied a bandana around my head before we proceeded to the dining room. Throughout dinner, I was paranoid that everyone would be staring at me, wondering what was wrong. I held back tears of embarrassment as I ate. Of course, no one questioned me or stared, but I was extremely uncomfortable without the security of my wig. As the remaining days of the retreat continued, with my wig now in useless shambles, I had no choice but to continue wearing the bandana. I was still worried what people were thinking. They must be judging me in their minds, making assumptions that I was sick or had cancer. But no one ever asked or commented.

Upon returning home from the retreat and looking at myself in the mirror, I remember saying to my boyfriend, "I'm done. Cut it off." As he chopped off the last remaining strands of hair and I watched them fall to the floor, tears were streaming down my face. I forced myself to look at my reflection, knowing I was surrendering the battle, admitting defeat. There was no other choice. My body was just going to do whatever it wanted to, and there was nothing I could do to control or stop it. Letting go of something that you've been attached to and identified as part

Laura's Story Continues . . .

155

of yourself your entire life is not easy. I was saying goodbye to ME, to the person who I had been. I felt like I was losing my identity, my femininity. Although I didn't realize it at the time, this act of surrender in cutting of my remaining hair was actually the first step in finding acceptance and peace in living with alopecia.

I had to resume my yoga teaching schedule the next day. There was no way I was going to show up in front of my students wearing a bandana, having them think I was sick or having to reveal my struggle with alopecia. I spent the entire day trying to find a wig shop that was open on a Sunday (which was no easy task). I drove miles away and was horrified at walking into the wig shop. I felt embarrassed and humiliated as I tried on wig after wig, trying to find the closest match to what my own hair had been. When I finally found one I thought would fool everyone, I made my way to class, nervous and scared. I tied a scarf around the wig to make certain it wouldn't fall off while I was demonstrating yoga poses. Some of them actually gave me compliments on the shininess and bounce of my hair, thinking I had just had it done! I guess my disguise worked. Although this off-the-rack wig was passable, I wanted something that looked more like the person I was used to seeing in the mirror. I found a local shop that worked with cancer patients and made an appointment for a consultation. Finally satisfied with a piece that was very similar to my old hair in color, length, and texture, I felt that if I could at least look like myself, then maybe I would feel like myself.

I used to think I was a fairly confident person. I knew that I was considered an attractive woman by the standards of society and maybe had put too much emphasis on my looks. Now that I was losing my hair, I felt self-conscious, ashamed, and essentially worthless because I didn't measure up to what I thought was beautiful. I knew that the body was impermanent, that life was fleeting, and our inner qualities were more important than our looks, but I could barely stand to see myself in the mirror at this point. At least I could hide behind my wig.

No one was any wiser until one horrific day. While teaching a yoga class, my wig partially came off. I was wearing a sweatshirt over my tank top, and through the course of teaching I began to get warm. As I pulled my sweatshirt off, my wig started to come off with it! Flustered, I scrambled to get the wig back on, hoping and praying no one noticed. With my heart nearly pounding out of my chest, I continued the class. When I got home that evening, I took the incident as a sign to stop hiding. I had to start accepting I was now bald and possibly could be for the rest of my life. I had to start being honest with others and share what was happening to me.

One of the first people I shared my story with was a dear friend whom I hadn't seen in a while. I arrived at her house wearing my wig and after we greeted each other with a hug, she began to tell me of a dream she recently had. In her dream, I was completely bald, yet completely happy with myself and my life. Before I could say anything in response, I began shaking and crying. Without any words, my hands trembling, I reached up and took off my wig. She gasped in surprise and began to cry with me. But these weren't tears of sorrow. They were tears of relief, recognition, and gratitude of finally being able to let my guard down, of finally letting someone else know of the struggle and loss I was going through. We shared feelings of awe and astonishment at the clarity of her dream. Although I was not completely happy, I was definitely completely bald. Moments after our exchange, my friend's roommate came outside to where we were talking to show us a monarch butterfly that had just emerged from its cocoon. Its wings were still wet, and it couldn't yet fly, so it perched on our fingers. The significance and symbolism of my friend's dream, revealing myself to her, and the butterfly emerging, all simultaneously impacted me. This too was a sign that I was transforming, becoming something new and in the process, shedding something of my old self. I wasn't quite ready to reveal myself to the entire world and wear my baldness proudly, but I was starting to shift my thinking. Rather than spending so much time obsessing over my appearance and how to make my hair grow back, I began to focus more on other things such as the spiritual lessons of my yoga practice, quality time with my family and kids and the joy that brought me, pursuing my hobbies and interests, and appreciating the simple pleasures in life. Another friend had once told me that one of the reasons monks shave their heads is to release all bad memories. Perhaps in losing my hair, the universe was telling me to let go of my past, to forgive myself for any mistakes or wrongdoings, and to allow the emerging of whatever newness was to come.

While I still wasn't quite confident with my new hairless look, it was becoming more familiar every day. By this time, my eyelashes, eyebrows, and body hair had all fallen out as my condition progressed from alopecia areata to alopecia universalis. But I called a truce with my body, stopped all treatments for my alopecia, and decided to start loving and accepting myself the way I was now. I still wore my wig every day, but I decided to be adventurous and try some new looks.

Since I now had a clean slate, I could create any look I wanted. I had been a performer for most of my life. So, wearing a wig as part of a costume wasn't foreign to me. Wearing one on a daily basis to hide my baldness was a completely different thing! With more courage this time, I made my way to a local wig store and tried on several fun new styles and colors of hair. I ended up purchasing two new wigs: a long, platinum blonde one and a short, tapered burgundy bob cut with bangs. Although I didn't wear these right away, I would soon be going to a Burning Man type campout event where costumes, wigs, alter egos, and outrageous characters were warmly welcomed. I brought my two new wigs with me, and it was actually lots of fun showing off these new styles! Friends would see me but would take a moment to recognize me. It was very entertaining to see the look in their eyes change when they realized who I was. Most of them thought I was just playing with new looks, but with my campmates I revealed what was underneath.

I usually wore a scarf or bandana while relaxing at camp because it was a strange phenomenon to be seen without anything on my head. I actually felt more naked than if I had no clothes on. But another phenomenon also occurred: I began to trust and open up. I began to tell others about my alopecia. And as I revealed my "flaw," that I was ashamed of and felt I had to hide, others did the same with me. It was as if we were giving each other permission to be imperfect, to be human, to be scarred but whole and lovable anyway. This process of sharing was cathartic, humbling, and healing.

When I returned home from this trip, I decided to be bold and wear my new fun, flirty, red bob wig when I taught my next yoga class. My students were surprised and delighted with such a drastic change in my appearance and complimented me on my new look. I briefly explained there was a story behind it and that I would tell them about it after class. As I sat with my students, telling them of the struggle I had been going through, I felt vulnerable and humble, yet also more real than I had been in a long time. I received sympathy and kudos for being able to share something so personal and in doing so, I found strength. This bold new look became a favorite of mine, and I soon started wearing my short, sassy red wig every day rather than my "normal" wig that looked like my old hair. Sometimes, I would receive compliments, and a few people questioned where I got my hair done. I used this as an opportunity to educate people about alopecia. I also told them I was wearing a wig and why. The more I opened up and shared, the more confidence I found. I had my eyebrows tattooed on permanently in June 2010, and the reflection looking back at me in the mirror wasn't quite so foreign, so alien. I was bald, but otherwise felt healthy and strong. I began to affirm this to myself every day; "I am healthy." "I am strong," and eventually (timidly at first), "I am beautiful," and even "I love you."

Laura's Story Continues . . .

Finding comfort, solace, and refuge in my yoga practice throughout the years definitely helped me move through the process of losing my hair. In September 2010, I attended a three day yoga and music festival in Joshua Tree, CA. Knowing I felt at home and accepted within the yoga community, I dared myself to be seen without my wig. Most of the time, while out in the hot desert sun, I wore a scarf or bandana. Yet sometimes, I would go completely bald. I felt naked, in a strange sort of way, but also very liberated. I was curious if people would ask about my baldness since it is rare to see a woman without hair. Mostly, I received compliments on my unique look, and when the occasional person did ask, I would tell them about alopecia and my experience. While browsing around the marketplace one day, I came across a booth offering Henna tattoos. I struck up a conversation with the lovely artist. She told me that she often dreamt of bald, blue, larger-than-life Goddesses soaring in the Heavens and that she would be honored to paint my head. I sat for hours while her diligent hands crafted the most beautiful, intricate lotus design gracing my crown. Passersby would stop and admire her art work. Throughout this process of being adorned so lovingly, I felt as if I were truly accepting, embracing, and honoring myself as I was for the first time, making peace with the fact that I was now bald and may never have hair again. When I saw the completed piece in the mirror, tears of joy began streaming down my face. I felt like a Goddess! I carried that glowing confidence with me through the remaining days of the festival. People would sometimes stop and ask for my photo, and I happily obliged. Here I was completely bald, surrounded by strangers and allowing them not only to see me but to capture the moment for eternity with a photograph. Reflecting back to the summer of 2008, when I found my first bald spot, to where I was now made me appreciate how much I had overcome. But I still wasn't quite ready to reveal myself to the world at large and go about my day to day existence bald. I still continued wearing wigs when I went to work teaching my yoga classes.

In January 2011, I ventured onto a path that would alter my life and career in a very exciting way. I began taking classes in aerial arts. I had been completely fascinated by the aerialists soaring high above the crowd on a couple of occasions when I had watched Cirque Du Soleil performances. When I received a coupon for discounted classes at Aerial Revolution, I thought it would be something fun to do. I was hooked from my very first lesson! My background in ballet and yoga gave me a foundation of strength and flexibility that allowed me to excel quickly in this newfound expression of movement. I wore my wig to aerial classes, and it managed to stay on fairly securely even while turning upside down. That is, until I tried my first big head over heels flip. I had climbed up on the fabric and wrapped myself for this new move I was learning. I had to dive forward to rotate around completely and knew my wig was going to fall off. Nervous and excited, I deliberated for a moment about whether or not I should execute the trick and risk embarrassing myself, or if I should just unwrap the fabric and climb down. My passion for mastering aerial arts outweighed my modesty. I seized the moment, throwing caution and dignity to the wind. My wig indeed flew off my head, but it was exhilarating to flip around in the air. After coming back down to the ground, I think I mumbled something like, "Well, there goes my hair," a bit embarrassed, yet proud of my accomplishment. Soon, I began showing up to classes wearing just a bandana, focusing my attention on learning as much as I could rather than worrying about what the instructor or other students thought of my baldness. After six months or so, I participated in my first aerial performance (gluing my wig on this time!). I had a unique grace, athleticism, and musicality that made me stand out. I knew then that this is what I wanted to dedicate my life to. I continued teaching yoga but spent more and more time training at Aerial Revolution, eventually teaching aerial classes there and accepting every opportunity I had to perform. My aerial performing would later lead to the most amazing opportunity to tell my story, to be seen by the world and inspire millions of people, the details of which I will share in a moment.

Part of my yoga teaching included working one on one with private clients in their homes. A friend who I was instructing, on occasion, was a photographer. Because I felt comfortable around her, I would take my wig off during our sessions together, putting it back on before I left. One day, she told me she would love to photograph me without my wig, capturing the unique beauty of this hairless look. I graciously accepted her offer. I was shy at first during the photo shoot, feeling so exposed but eventually became more comfortable. It was a few weeks before I had a chance to see the pictures she captured. During that time, I went on vacation for a few days to a secluded location with some friends. Because we were removed from civilization and other people, I let myself go bald while we swam among streams and waterfalls and soaked in natural hot springs. Being in and out of the water so much, I was careless about reapplying sunscreen to the sensitive skin on my scalp, and I returned home with a severe sunburn on my head. My entire scalp was one huge blister. This made it impossible to wear a wig, since anything that touched my head would cause pain. I'm sure at some point I would have had the courage to leave my wig at home while I taught yoga and went about my day. Now, that decision was made for me. With such a terrible burn on my head, the only thing I could cover it with and not be in pain was a scarf. So, I tenderly wrapped my head, walked out the door, and that was essentially the end of my wearing wigs on a daily basis. Leaving the security of my wig at home was not nearly as traumatic as I had anticipated. I thought everyone would be staring, whispering behind my back, thinking I had cancer. But just as I had experienced in Turks and Caicos several months prior and just as when my wig flew off during aerial training, no one said a word or questioned me. I was afraid of thoughts and opinions from others, but in reality, I was making a bigger deal of being bald than anyone else was. It was my own thoughts and opinions of myself that were cruel,

harsh, and judgmental. When I finally had a chance to get together with my photographer friend to see the photos from our session, I was blown away. She captured me so beautifully that I was moved to tears at seeing myself. I began to realize there was no need to hide anymore. I saw the essence of my spirit shining through my eyes, the grace of my long neck, the lovely curve of my cheekbones. I knew that being real and vulnerable was more captivating than any wig I could hide behind or any persona I could put on. So, I saved my expanding collection of wigs only for performances and began wearing colorful scarves or bandanas instead.

It was now August 2011. My growing strength, confidence, and self-worth gave me the courage to finally end the abusive relationship I had been involved in. It was scary being on my own, knowing that eventually I would want to date again and wondering who would be attracted to a woman with no hair. By now, I was completely comfortable just wearing a bandana on my head throughout the day and while working. I was thinking less and less of my alopecia and just living my life, pursuing my passions. I was in service to others through my yoga teaching, helping people improve their lives. Aerial and dance performing gave me the freedom to express my spirit through moving art. I was happy with who I was, the way I interacted with others, and felt confident in the gifts I was sharing with the world. Having alopecia became insignificant. It was simply one facet of who I was. Life was flowing wonderfully, and I was proud of how much I had grown and learned from overcoming the challenge of losing my hair. In April 2012, I felt ready to explore dating once again. On a whim of curiosity, I signed up with an online dating site to expand my field of meeting new people. In my experience, it seemed that people made certain assumptions about bald women, thinking they were either rebellious, tough and edgy, or worse, undergoing chemotherapy treatment for cancer. I didn't want to give the wrong impression by posting bald pictures

Laura's Story Continues . . .

159

of myself on this dating site or have to go into too much detail explaining about alopecia. So, I used only photos in which I was wearing a wig, even though I felt like a bit of a phony. I knew that when the time came and if I met the right person, I would be fully honest and reveal my condition to them. Anyone who was worthy of my love and devotion would accept me completely as I was, hair or no hair. After a few casual dates with men who sparked my curiosity, there was one in particular who I felt a special connection with. The feeling was mutual, and we agreed to meet for a second date. I wanted everything out in the open from the beginning. So, it was on this second date that I told him I had alopecia and was wearing a wig. He was completely nonchalant about it, and I would later learn that this brave honesty is one of the things that made this amazing man fall in love with me. As our relationship deepened over the next few weeks, I had enough trust to let him see me bald, completely exposed and vulnerable. He graced my bare head with the most tender loving touch and kisses that let me know he admired my strength, and saw beyond the superficial confines of beauty and into the depths of my heart and soul. Over the course of the next several months, our love grew stronger and deeper, and we both knew we had truly found our soul mate. From that love, something miraculous occurred.

I noticed a small patch of hair growing on my head in March 2013! I was aware that alopecia can be cyclical, and one can experience many episodes of hair loss and regrowth. But I do not think it is merely a coincidence that my hair began growing back shortly after I had completely surrendered my struggle, learned to fully love myself unconditionally, and to find that love reflected through another. I truly believe in the healing power of our thoughts, emotions, and the environment we are surrounded by. I am by no means saying this is true for everyone with alopecia, or that they are at fault for losing their hair. But perhaps I was and am more sensitive to subtle energies and needed this important lesson from the universe to teach me certain things. Nearly five years prior, my hair fell out when my life was filled with stress, conflict, anger, fear, guilt, and shame. I think my body had had enough and was shutting down to protect itself and to send me a loud and clear message. Now that I had found peace, happiness, gratitude, and love, my body was beginning to heal. This small patch of hair growth spread further across my head, and to this day I have about 70% regrowth. And what is completely ironic now is that I choose to shave my head for certain performances and art modeling projects. But it is exactly that: a choice. I have learned through my experience with alopecia that we don't get to choose what happens to us, but we DO get to choose how we feel. For a long time, I was choosing victimhood, choosing to feel ashamed or embarrassed about my condition, choosing to wear wigs to make myself fit in and feel like everyone else. Now, I was choosing to live bravely, to feel proud of my accomplishments and what I believe in. I was choosing to love myself and feel good about who I am both on the inside and outside. It doesn't matter if I am completely bald, have a week's worth of stubble on my head, or wear a colorful scarf or a fun wig. I know that I am fundamentally a strong, valuable, unique, amazing, kind, and loving person and that will never change no matter what I might look like.

For a couple of years, I had wanted to be able to inspire others by sharing what I have learned through my experience in living with alopecia, but didn't quite know what the best platform was for getting my message out there. The most amazing opportunity for sharing and being seen came to me in January 2014, when I received a phone call from a casting agent from *America's Got Talent*, a major network television show in the U.S. Contestants compete during multiple elimination rounds for the chance to win a 1 million dollar prize and have their own featured show in Las Vegas. The casting agent told me that she presented one of my YouTube aerial performance videos to the executive directors of the show, that they loved what

I did and asked if I was interested in auditioning for season 9. I thought, "What have I got to lose?" and jumped at the opportunity. I knew this would be a chance for me to possibly be seen on TV, to show my talent in aerial arts to the world and also to share my message of hope and inspiration. Over the next couple of months, I prepared a routine to perform during my audition. The audition day finally arrived, and I was nervous, yet very excited. There were cameras everywhere backstage, capturing behind the scenes moments and interviews. After hours of waiting, I was finally called up to present my routine. It was an incredibly surreal feeling walking out onto the stage, seeing the celebrity judges and the 3,000 people in the audience, knowing all eyes were focused on me and every word and movement was being filmed. It was reassuring to know that my boyfriend, mom, and sister were there cheering me on. I introduced myself to the judges, then proceeded to climb up my fabric. As soon as my music started, I became lost in the moment and poured my heart into my performance. After my routine was finished, I looked out into the audience and saw nearly everyone standing on their feet. I was amazed and almost moved to tears. All of the celebrity judges loved my routine, and I was headed into the next round of the competition! Over the next month, as auditions wrapped up in other cities, I was contacted by an associate producer asking for some family photos. This indicated they were going to feature me on the show and share my story of triumph over difficulty. When the air date of my show arrived, I gathered with my entire family to watch. My segment was saved for very last in the episode. I was elated with the final edit of how my segment was put together. I had worn my wig during my audition routine but took it off backstage while I was being interviewed. This clip of me revealing the baldness under my wig had just been seen by millions of people all over the world! I was overwhelmed with pride to be able to represent all of those with alopecia who had gone through the same struggle I had. Moments after my audition aired, I was inundated with fan mail, messages from people far and wide congratulating me for my bravery and thanking me for inspiring them with hope. Through leading by example, showing how to overcome adversity with grace, to persevere and pursue my dreams, others were able to find that same strength and determination within themselves. This was one of the greatest accomplishments of my life and still fills me with pride.

Looking back to 2008, I realize how much strength, wisdom, compassion, and spiritual growth I have gained from living with alopecia. I often wonder if I would have learned as many valuable lessons about surrender, acceptance, and self-love if alopecia had not affected me. Would I be the same person I am today? Approximately 1 in 100 people develop alopecia, and I believe we are chosen for a higher reason: to help ourselves and others see beyond appearances, identity, and ego, and to realize that underneath, we all have the same desires to feel unconditionally accepted, loved, appreciated, and valued. I have realized that life is not about status, income, possessions, or looks: the things we SHOW to the world. Rather, it is about caring for each other, reaching out to help those who may be suffering, rising above our own challenges, and allowing the creative expression of our spirit to flow freely: the things we SHARE with the world. It is my greatest hope that by simply living my life and doing the things I am most passionate about, others will see me as an example and discover their own beautiful brilliance, allowing that light to shine for the entire world to see.

Laura had the honor of competing in the inaugural U.S. Aerial Championships in New York City earlier this year. She was also invited to perform in Costa Rica at Envision Music Festival in March. Laura is currently busy at work, collaborating on the creation of a production to be performed in San Diego at the International Fringe Festival this summer.

Melissa

understand

someone to catch my falling tears
that is all i ask.
understanding me

someone to help me breathe
when all i do is gasp.
understanding me

someone to feel what i feel
and know i hurt.
understanding me

someone who understands the confusion and pain,
realizes the meaning of love...
and gives it to me.

Not long ago, I again came upon this poem I had written in high school; a time when book reports and term papers were hand-written in runny ink on a pad of grey-ish pulpy paper with faint blue lines, then typed on a heavy typewriter that sat upon a dingy brown metal cart with squeaky wheels. Tethered to the wall, it droned with an eerily calming electrical life force. I loved the feeling of that soothing vibration as it passed through my hands and into my body, like a tangible "ohm." I remember the swift, delicate action of the keys under my fingertips and the quick response of the font ball. The imperfections of the outline of each letter and number slapped onto the paper seemingly faster than the eye could see, decorating the chosen mashed pulp like a delicate hand-crocheted doily atop an antique dresser. The accepted non-symmetry, the miniscule nick in a hand-carved beauty. The

162

subtle shift in pigment. The over-sanding that reveals another layer of imperfections. It all amazes me.

There is something so beautiful in imperfection.

It took a lot of time and life experience to realize that in my childhood and adolescence living with alopecia, I subconsciously put myself through the most abusive form of criticism and psychological self-destruction I know: PERFECTION. It was a strange paradox of perfection and non-perfection that collided inside me. I was trying to achieve the perfect form of non-perfection in everything. Basically, perfecting my less-than-perfect appearance by dressing differently, thinking differently, and being different in any way I could. I was an imperfectionist – fighting the good fight to find my own individual perfection through my intended path of imperfection. I still am an imperfectionist – I've just become more efficient with where and how I spend my energy.

As a creative, I embrace all of my imperfections because they are the means by which I see and experience the connections between my deepest and innermost inklings of intuition, and the fruition of my life and work. Without that connection, I don't believe I could truly embrace what I create. It is this very connection that makes the height of my creative ecstasy a phenomenal ride. At that peak, I see the possibilities, and the images in my mind come to life. Like watching my future before it even happens. For me, the craft is then in the work. Working with my medium until it all comes to life. I don't believe this process would have revealed itself to me had I not been able to let go of the extreme superficial focus I had on my outward appearance.

Had it not been for this release and the unfolding of some very specific and poignant moments in my life, I would not be where I am today. Had I been blinded by many more of those unnecessarily all-consuming and pointless worries, I would have missed the beautiful and amazing ride that is my life. Today, I am more humble, and choose to live with little expectation. At times, I don't think I completely understand and realize where I am, what I've achieved, and how much of an impact I make and have made on others in my lifetime. Perhaps it's the residual doubt lingering. Or maybe I've finally allowed myself to just "be." People tell me I am important. That I have brought joy and change into their lives, and that I am a role model for them, providing hope and the glimmer of possibility that exists for them. For me, there exists a handful of very important people that have done the same and I will never let them forget it. What I have come to learn after all these years, is that my life with alopecia prepared me for who I believe I was meant to be, but would have never known had I not gone through what I did. What I have learned is that in order to become selfless and help others, we need to first understand ourselves wholly.

I could have taken this time, this paper, this ink, and my breath to tell you my life story and experiences having alopecia, but lately I feel that it is best not to recant or wallow, rather get to the gist. What I realize now, so many years past, is that I wrote this poem not as a cry for the love and understanding that might be found in or from someone else, but as a plea for the love and understanding of MYSELF those many years ago. I just didn't realize it then. Stay present. Be open and find yourself.

Melissa is the creative mind, body, and Artistic Director of her pick-up company REXDANCE, and a faculty member in the School of Film, Dance and Theatre at Arizona State University. She is also the Director of the Capoeira for Kids program at Grupo Axé Capoeira AZ, and has been training for many years under the tutelage of Professor Camara and world-renown founder, Mestre Barrão. www.axecapoeira-az.com

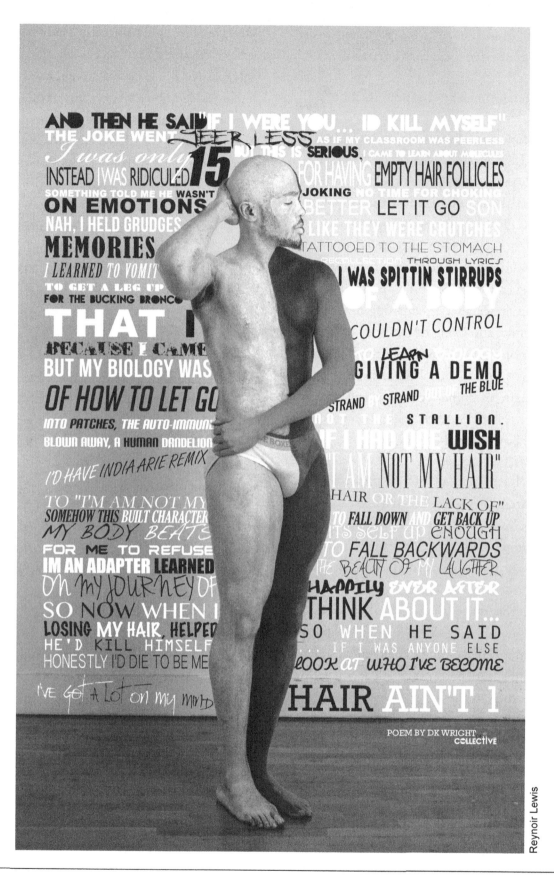

AND THEN HE SAID "IF I WERE YOU... I'D KILL MYSELF"
THE JOKE WENT PEERLESS AS IF MY CLASSROOM WAS PEERLESS
I was only **15** BUT THIS IS SERIOUS, I CAME TO LEARN ABOUT MOLECULES
INSTEAD I WAS RIDICULED FOR HAVING EMPTY HAIR FOLLICLES
SOMETHING TOLD ME HE WASN'T JOKING NO TIME FOR CHOKING
ON EMOTIONS BETTER LET IT GO SON
NAH, I HELD GRUDGES LIKE THEY WERE CRUTCHES
MEMORIES TATTOOED TO THE STOMACH
I LEARNED TO VOMIT RECOLLECTION THROUGH LYRICS
TO GET A LEG UP I WAS SPITTIN STIRRUPS
FOR THE BUCKING BRONCO OF A BODY
THAT I COULDN'T CONTROL
BECAUSE I CAME LEARN
BUT MY BIOLOGY WAS GIVING A DEMO
OF HOW TO LET GO STRAND STRAND THE BLUE
INTO PATCHES, THE AUTO-IMMUNE STALLION.
BLOWN AWAY, A HUMAN DANDELION IF I HAD ONE WISH
I'D HAVE INDIA ARIE REMIX "I AM NOT MY HAIR"
TO "I'M AM NOT MY HAIR OR THE LACK OF"
SOMEHOW THIS BUILT CHARACTER TO FALL DOWN AND GET BACK UP
MY BODY BEATS ITS SELF UP ENOUGH
FOR ME TO REFUSE TO FALL BACKWARDS
IM AN ADAPTER LEARNED THE BEAUTY OF MY LAUGHTER
ON MY JOURNEY OF HAPPILY EVER AFTER
SO NOW WHEN I THINK ABOUT IT...
LOSING MY HAIR, HELPED SO WHEN HE SAID
HE'D KILL HIMSELF ... IF I WAS ANYONE ELSE
HONESTLY I'D DIE TO BE ME LOOK AT WHO I'VE BECOME
i've got a lot on my mind HAIR AIN'T 1

POEM BY DK WRIGHT
COLLECTIVE

Reynoir Lewis

DK Wright is an artist in every sense of the word poetically, professionally, and personally. Currently the Digital Media Manager with Urban Word NYC, he is a youth mentor, writer, and 2014 recipient of the Innovator of Change award. DK is motivated by challenges and self-accountability, and measures his life success in a similar fashion to his poetry: whether or not he deems it worthy enough to share with others. His advice to all young adults he mentors is to, "Be flexible. What doesn't bend will surely break."

DK Wright

And then he said
"If I were you…I'd kill myself"

The joke went jeerless
As if my classroom was peerless
I was only 15, but this is serious
I came to learn about molecules
Instead I was ridiculed
For having empty hair follicles
Something told me he wasn't joking
No time for choking
On emotions
Better let it go son,

Nah, I held grudges
Like they were crutches
Memories tattooed
To the stomach
I learned to vomit
Recollection through lyrics
To get a leg up
I was spittin stirrups
For the bucking bronco
Of a body that I couldn't control
Because I came to learn biology
But my biology was giving a demo
Of how to let it go
Strand by strand, out of the blue
Into Patches, the auto-immune
Not the stallion.

Blown away, a human dandelion
If I had one wish
I'd have India Arie remix
"I am not my hair"
To "I am not my hair, or lack of"
Somehow this built character
To fall down and get back up
My body beats itself up enough
For me to refuse to fall backwards
I'm an adapter
Learned the beauty of my laughter
On my journey of happily ever after
So now when I think about it…
Losing my hair, helped
So when he said he'd kill himself
…if I was anyone else,
Honestly
I'd die to be me
Look at who've I've become
I've got a lot on my mind, hair ain't 1

Brian Gonzalez

Paul

My alopecia story began at the end of eighth-grade, when my doctor told me that I suddenly carried tuberculosis. During my yearly physical, I failed the tuberculosis skin test, but luckily I was only carrying the infection. I did not suffer from any symptoms and was not contagious. To get rid of tuberculosis, my doctor prescribed medicine to take daily for a few years. Despite carrying the disease, I generally had a healthy and active adolescence. Except for one thing - I started losing my hair. No one made the connection between my hair loss and the medicine until I became quite bald.

When I was younger, I fussed a lot about my hair and spent a large part of my morning routine styling it. In junior high, I loved spiking my hair, and by the beginning of high school I sported gnarly liberty spikes. When I started noticeably balding, my mother

thought I was losing hair because I cared about it too much. She thought if I let go and didn't worry about how I styled it, it would return to its original fullness. At the time, I cared too much about my appearance to quit spiking my hair. I had dreams of becoming a rock star, and I really couldn't have normal, non-spiked hair as a rock star.

My classmates started noticing my hair loss before I did. While walking down the hallway, my self-esteem disintegrated when someone would yell, "Hey, you've got a bald spot." "You're going bald!" At first, I thought they were just teasing because you can see some scalp through spiked hair. I soon had to acknowledge that I had areas on my head that appeared thinner than the rest: spiked, combed, or untouched. By the end of ninth-grade, I started to put my hair into liberty spikes, mostly because I thought it looked awesome but also

because I thought I could meticulously arrange my spikes to cover up some areas of thinning. My father, my maternal grandfather, and many of my uncles had male-pattern baldness. In junior high, the prospect of losing my hair to male-pattern baldness terrified me, and I wanted to desperately rebel against heredity.

By tenth-grade, I started to become obsessed and depressed by my hair loss. More classmates, and surprisingly their parents, started pointing it out. While doing homework, I would get distracted by the hair falling on my assignments. Sometimes, I would run my hands through my head to see if I could just shake all the hair off and find an end. Instead of finishing my homework, I would end up with a little mound of fallen hair. I looked at my head in the mirror for hours, hoping that I was imagining things. I avoided being photographed as much as possible and sometimes used photoshop to cover up my bald spots. In public, I hoped others wouldn't look at my head at a certain angle, and I tried to avoid being under bright lights. I played in a rock band, the school orchestra, and jazz band, and bright lights were impossible to avoid. The worst blow to my self-esteem came after concerts, when someone would tell me that I was going bald, instead of commenting on the music. Rock stars cannot be bald.

Eventually, my parents started to take action. I tried Rogaine, a higher prescription of Minoxidil, saw palmetto, black sesame, a variety of holistic and herbal treatments, acupuncture, laser combs, and tapping my scalp over and over again with a brush. Supposedly, tapping my head would stimulate and strengthen my hair follicles. As you probably guessed, none of these treatments worked.

The summer before my senior year in high school, I lost so much hair I had no more ways to hide it. I had no way to spike or comb over my baldness, and I became so depressed that my father finally took me to a well-known hair restoration clinic geared towards middle-aged men. At the clinic, my father paid a large sum of money to have my head shaved and have a hair system glued onto my head. Finally, I had hope that I could experience my senior year without worrying. Although the clinic treated people with alopecia, they never mentioned the word to me. Around this time, my doctor finally admitted the medicine for tuberculosis may have caused my baldness, but strangely did not mention the word alopecia. Despite my veneer, I felt weird and alone. I thought I had some unique situation that no one understood.

To my surprise, no one during my senior year seemed to notice I suddenly had thick hair. The hair restoration company stuck the hair system onto my scalp with such strong adhesive that it was supposed to be able to withstand the wind and water. Apparently, it also fooled some of my extended family. I thought I could finally enjoy my last year in high school without worrying about my hair.

Nevertheless, the hair system brought new anxieties. My family could not afford the monthly payments. First, my father paid for the service and when the bills became burdensome, he passed the bills off to my mother who totally disagreed with the product. The company also really lacked in quality control and customer service. Every month, I needed to get my hairpiece replaced and my scalp cleaned. A new hair system came with very long hair. After they glued it to your head, the company gave you a haircut and a supply of special shampoos and adhesive strips for daily maintenance. I often received terrible haircuts and hair color that did not match my natural color. Almost every month, I left the hair restoration clinic wearing a hat and rushed home hoping no one would see me. Then, my mother would fix up my hair, dye it, and cut it to look more natural. For the first two weeks, the hair system held up well after some adjustments but would then deteriorate to a gross level before I needed to replace it. The adhesive broke down and became gunky on my scalp, causing the hair system to detach from my

Paul's Story Continues . . .

167

head. Now, I began to worry that before I could get my monthly replacement, the hair system would fall off my head and reveal a messy weird scalp in front of my friends.

Going to college with a hair system also made me feel nervous. I went to college in North Carolina, far away from the safety of my home in New York. College meant I would be immersed in campus life and in constant contact with strangers. I tried to have a normal freshmen year, except I was ever vigilant about my head. What if I had a problem with my hair system in the middle of class? What if at a party, someone accidently touched my head and revealed something unnatural? What if someone got too close to me and saw the seams of the disguise I was wearing. Meanwhile, my parents continued to bicker over the bills.

One night, the summer after my freshmen year, I came to an impasse. I had an appointment with the hair restoration clinic the next morning, but I was extremely disappointed with their treatment of me. Just the previous month, they gave me a light brown hair system when my natural hair was black. When I complained, the company branch manager told me that he couldn't tell the difference, and the system would settle into a color with a few washes. I could no longer tolerate such terrible customer service for such a high price.

That night, I contemplated my present life and how I wanted to live in the future. I felt it was time to come out of hiding. I logged onto my computer and spent the entire night researching how to shave my head. I also researched baldness and discovered alopecia. I found some helpful sites and support groups. Until that point in my life, no one had ever suggested I could have alopecia. None of my doctors uttered the word "alopecia." More importantly, they never told me I was not alone to be losing my hair so young. I did not sleep that night because I had made an

important decision about my life. I could not wait to act upon it.

The next morning, I waited until my mother left for work. I called a close friend, told her I was about to change my life and needed a witness. She knew I wore a hair system but never knew what was underneath. When she came over, I ripped off my hair system and shaved off whatever bits and pieces of hair I still had left on my scalp. After shaving my head, I simultaneously felt like a new person and more like myself. I felt a huge burden lift from my shoulders, and I felt extremely happy and relieved.

Even though I felt comfortable shaving my head bald, I initially felt uneasy about telling others about alopecia. Many of my friends and family were understandably shocked when they first saw me. Some family members told me to give my head one good shave and then perhaps it would grow back fuller. With the exception of one close friend, I told most of my other friends that I simply shaved my head because I wanted to. Baldness was my fashion choice. Thankfully, many of them accepted that answer and did not pry any further. Sadly, others grew distant from me. Unfortunately, before I shaved my head, Britney Spears had a public mental breakdown. Some people thought I was recovering from a tough freshmen year in college and had experienced something similar.

After I returned to college with my head shaved, I started noticing that I sometimes had less hair or bald spots on other parts of my body. I was really confused and couldn't figure out why I was losing this hair. Sometimes, I would wake up in the morning and look in the mirror to find that part of my eyebrow was missing. This new development frustrated me but also finally helped prove to my parents that I had alopecia. Still, my mother wanted one last attempt to salvage my hair by sending me to another hair restoration specialist. I felt comfortable being bald at this point, but I wanted to indulge my mother's last effort. During my consultation, the nurse at the clinic looked at my eyebrows and finally said the words I needed to hear, "You have alopecia areata." Hallelujah! A medical professional had finally confirmed my suspicions.

That was then, and this is now. I am now an active composer who feels open and comfortable with himself and the people around him. Acceptance came after a few steps, but now I feel happier than ever. I waited until I finished college to start telling others I had alopecia when they asked. After college, I finally joined one of the alopecia support networks I found on the night I shaved my head. With acceptance and inner calm, I found that I grew as a musician and found more inspiration for my compositions. As I've come to accept myself, I've also come to accept and appreciate others.

For as long as I can remember, I've always fantasized about making music and admired great creators of music. My parents started sending me to piano and violin lessons when I was five. I received my first guitar at thirteen, and I finally felt I could create music of my own. The guitar allowed me to explore different expressions of music. In school, I performed with the orchestra and jazz ensemble, and on the weekends I jammed with my rock band and jazz quartet. I felt the happiest about music when I wrote songs for my band. However, unlike other musicians after high school, I did not apply to any music schools or conservatories. Instead, I decided to attend a liberal arts college and pursue other academic interests.

I struggled during my first two years in college with music. I tried writing songs, but I felt blocked. Whenever I sat down with my guitar, nothing came out as I strummed, and whatever I thought was mildly creative never stuck around. Looking back, I believe this block came from my stresses and inner conflicts. I realize now, that in order to create music, you need to first become in tune with yourself. In high school, comments about my thinning hair and bald scalp shining on stage sunk in and caused some of my writer's block. I thought I would never look like a musician, so I should not be a musician. Like many other musicians, I felt a lot of initial hesitation to fully commit to music. In a strange way, shaving my head symbolized acceptance: not acceptance of my situation, but acceptance of myself. After this acceptance, I began my formal training in composition during junior year in college. Once I finished writing my first piece of classical music, I gladly welcomed that incredible joy of music back into my life.

Alopecia can be a frightening experience. The journey into acceptance and empowerment is as unique as each individual, but there are still some common experiences. If you've just discovered you are losing your hair, at whatever age, please do not feel alone. No matter what happens with your hair, you will continue to grow. Shine on!

Paul currently lives in the Boston area and composes music. In the near future, he hopes to be in a doctoral program, somewhere warm, to advance his studies in music composition. For now, he grabs whatever opportunity to write music that he can, whether it's for children's orchestra, solo classical piano, or parody rap songs.

Katrin Unge

"We set our own limits to what we can achieve. Let the limits disappear, and let our personality shine over the world. Never give up on yourself or your dreams, regardless of what they might be.

Life can be cruel, but it can also be beautiful if we let it."

Emma

My name is Emma. I am twenty-five years old, live in Sweden, and I have alopecia areata.

June 25, 2012, was the day I discovered my first bald spot on the side of my head. Since I am a hairdresser, hair was a very important part of my life. The fear of looking at myself in the mirror and seeing chunks of hair gone, without my noticing, was an unforgettable feeling. The heart beats a few extra beats and thoughts bounce around like a hurricane. Taking a small hand mirror and directing it toward the side of my head, I could see straight into the pale skull where there should have been hair. I felt nauseous and was a little scared to tell my partner what I was looking at. A few seconds went by, and I said in a panicked voice, "I'm losing my hair. I'm losing my hair!" I heard him laugh a bit and call back with a joking voice, "Are you going bald on me now?" I realized he was joking with me

and probably thought I lost a couple of hairs and was exaggerating. I felt the tears begin to push forward and with shaking hands, showed him. He responded with equal shock. Neither of us knew what was going on. We were like two question marks who just stood there in the bathroom looking at each other. It was as if time just stopped.

That first night, I had difficulty sleeping. To just lay my head on the pillow felt like a big challenge. I had already got into all the "What if?" thoughts. "What if I move my head in my sleep and the hair falls off?" "What if I wake up and everything is gone?" I quickly realized that I was making it worse for myself to think of different scenarios. Thoughts become reality if you believe in them enough. So, I decided to calm down, stop thinking, and go to the doctor the next morning.

The doctor took all possible samples of my blood, and to my surprise everything was normal. They could not find a steady basis to why the hair had fallen out. They told me the disease is called alopecia. Everyone is susceptible, and there are various factors why it occurs, but there is not much research on it. According to my doctor, it was stress and anxiety that triggered my hair loss, and the only thing I could do was to take sick leave from work, take it easy, and hope for better times.

I had just started a new job working at a hair salon. To take sick leave now, after such a short period of time, was probably not the best thing to do, but my well-being was more important. I went on sick leave for a month and became unemployed after that, which did not help with all the stress.

Time passed, and I slowly lost more hair every month. I was panicked every second of every day. I could feel that I was falling apart, just disappearing. My hair was such a big part of my personality. I loved experimenting with different hairstyles and hair colors. I could feel I was starting to lose myself, which of course was very nerve-racking. When I could no longer hide my spots with my own hair, I decided to buy a wig that I liked very much. I was very afraid of what people would think when I suddenly had new color, new hair quality, and it had all of a sudden grown five inches in a day. I had the choice to either let everything be and let people see my blotchy head, or I could put on the wig and try to be happy. I had a hard time just going to the grocery store. My stomach turned upside down, and thoughts of everyone looking at me scared the life out of me. I felt so small, and that I no longer fit in anywhere. I was especially afraid my partner would be ashamed of me, and that my friends would no longer want to be seen in public with me. All fears just flew into my head, and I did not know how to stop them. The wig I bought was a shoulder length black one with crooked bangs. Since it was synthetic hair, I could not wash it with regular shampoo or conditioner. On top of that, I had a lot of bills to pay, and to prioritize beauty products for my wig was mighty low on that list. I applied for a job as a hairdresser, which was a challenge, but I did it. My first interview did not give me any confidence at all. There was something "not quite right" with my hair. "Something looked odd," according to the person I had interviewed with. I told her my situation and that my hair had nothing to do with my skills of cutting hair. I had been training like everyone else. According to them, I could not work there because she was afraid the customers coming into the salon would look directly at me and make the judgment they did not want me to cut their hair. In other words, "bad for business." My heart took a beating. I had such a bad experience in the interview, that I decided not to work as a hairdresser. I decided to wait until my hair grew back and in the meantime be a hairdresser at my own leisure.

I began working as a kindergarten teacher instead. Being with happy and positive kids, who haven't learned how to judge people, was very rewarding. Children have a completely different view compared to adults. They do not care about how you look. If you are you kind and funny, you become accepted at once. No questions asked.

December was approaching, and I felt relief with being able to wear a hat with my new hair.

Now, the shock started to calm down, but the stress still felt difficult to control. I had so much to think about. In addition to losing hair and losing my job, it was a difficult time for my family. My dad had been an alcoholic for as long as I can remember. He had periods when he drank to excess but always managed to end up on his feet. He had another episode, but this one turned out different. We have had very difficult moments in the family, but we were generally still a happy family who loved each other. Dad's deep depression began around the same time I started to have hair trouble. I got calls from my dad's boss at work a few times. They did not know where he was. He did not answer the phone and would be gone for

Emma's Story Continues . . .

days without talking to anyone. It started to feel like I was responsible for him. He started pulling away, and I sensed something very early. I have always been close to my dad. It was always me and him in some way, and we could easily understand each other. This time was different. It was hard to deal with, and accepting it felt like I was losing my dad and my best friend. I always had something to stress over, and in retrospect, I of course wish I'd handled my emotions and thoughts differently. Now, I can only accept and learn from it, and do differently next time an obstacle comes my way.

In December, I had lost almost half of my hair. After a few weeks, my wig began to irritate my scalp and itched all the time. So, I decided to buy a Buff instead. Easier to handle, easy to put on, and no extra accessories that I needed, compared to a wig. It was perfect for me. I immediately felt happier, more energetic, and free to move my head around. It was a relief to finally find what I felt most comfortable in. It was still difficult to meet with friends, but I was at least on the right track.

When something changes in our life, big or small doesn't matter anymore. Every event we suffer from helps us develop, either good or bad. It's just up to us to decide how we handle it. For me, that was really difficult to control.

Christmas came and went. I was still feeling better mentally. My mind was not as negative, and I started to accept the situation I was in. My life began to feel like a life again until February 14, 2013, when my father took his own life! My mind totally collapsed. It was so hard on me that I lost control of my emotions and my body. It felt like I was in a horror movie, a dark fantasy world that I hoped to wake up from. I lost all my hair. All I had struggled to avoid, came like a wave over me and my life. It took a while before I came to the realization that I could not keep doing this to myself anymore. I had to wake up, take hold of the situation, and accept that this is my life. This had

happened, whether I liked it or not. Obviously, things happen in life that I had no control over, and this was one of them. Events will happen, and my world will change. It is only up to me to learn how to handle it in a way that gives me strength to continue my journey through life with those experiences. It is a work in progress, and is definitely easier said than done.

When I came back to the reality of what I had experienced regarding my dad and my hair loss, I wondered what I wanted to do in my life? I certainly did not want to regret the things I never took the chance to do. Dad's suicide brought up emotions in me that I had never really thought of before, at least not as deeply. We all have one life that we know of, and we have to take care of it. I had struggled for years trying to help dad out of everything he went through. I was always there for him and never gave up. There is always hope if you believe in it enough. Unfortunately, my dad did not believe, and he took the easy way out.

A family either grows stronger after a tragedy or it totally collapses. My family collapsed. I had to start thinking about myself and my health. I never believed that stress can destroy the mind and body on such a deep level as it had with me. I was constantly told, "There are those who have it worse," "You are exaggerating," "It's just hair," and "Stop feeling the way you are feeling." I wanted support. I did not want anyone telling me how I should handle the situation. I just wanted someone who would listen to me, feel with me. My partner gave me great support. He was, and is my rock…my anchor that keeps me grounded. Although he makes me feel beautiful and strong every day, I know he will never really understand what I'm going through.

I ask myself constantly, "Why do I need hair?" No matter how much I think, I always end up with the same answer, that "it's normal," which is not a concrete answer for me. We are so engrossed in looking like everyone else that words like "change" and "different" scare us, and we take a step back. I needed to overcome this immediately, but it's easier said than done.

Dreaming is something I think people do not appreciate enough. I learned early that dreams are like wishes, something you only do when you're little. If you dream big, it's not realistic. Always think logically. I had forgotten about my dreams and didn't create new ones. Big and small dreams are important in order to see hope and light at the end of the tunnel, and to have something to look forward to. Everyone can dream, but it's another to make the dream a reality. I've thought a lot about how the people around me have influenced my way of looking at my dreams and what goals I have in life. I want to inspire and help others. If I really have the "why?" in front of me, it can become a reality. I decided to stop being negative and stop being the person others wanted me to be. Now was the time to pursue the life I wanted. Fear had to disappear from my dictionary.

I have always known that I wanted to help people, which must be why I am a personal assistant, teaching assistant, nanny, and a hairdresser. All these professions are about helping people in some way. I wanted to do something more. More than just an eight to five job. Three months after my father died, my partner and I decided to attend a business presentation we had long thought of doing but never really had the will or strength to do. We wanted to have a big change in our lives. After ten minutes in the presentation, it was getting hard to sit still. My partner and I looked at each other, without saying a word. We knew this was a start of something big. This was what I had long been looking for. To help people live a healthy and stress free life. I know that I couldn't help my dad get better, but I had the opportunity to help those who wanted to be helped, who wanted a change

in their lives to something better. We started our own business that night. I could feel the happiness I had been longing for, return. I was going to do this no matter what. I had to visualize that everything would fall in line eventually.

I discovered it was challenging to run a business that is mostly about beauty and health. In the beginning, I did not feel so healthy because I had no hair, but my partner made me realize hair doesn't matter. It's such a little part of who I am. In a way, it was a good thing I didn't have hair. I would have more empathy when talking about my business and how important health is, and how stress can affect the mind and body in such a negative way.

This is my "coming out" story. Not many people know I have alopecia, only my closest friends and family. It's been hard and embarrassing to tell people. I was very shy and drawn back, and my self-esteem was on the bottom of the ocean. But that's behind me. It's time to embrace this and help people who have a hard time in life, no matter what they are going through. Be different. Be proud. Look at yourself in the mirror every day and smile. Don't forget that fear is an illusion that you create for yourself. Only you can change it.

I now have a different view of the world around me, and I have learned a lot about myself these past two years. I have a drive that I didn't have before, to do something great and meaningful with my life with or without hair. I wake up every morning, thinking that it is a new day with new opportunities. I still have bad days. It's like a roller coaster, but this time I have taken control over what bump I ride on and how far I'll fall.

Today, Emma works with her partner in their company, helping people better their health or even trying to stabilize their income. One of her core projects is humanitarian initiatives where she searches for people who want to help make a difference by donating nutritious food packages to starving children in Malawi.

Heather
Cup of Worthiness

I am a bald woman. I am creative, loving, and I. Am. Worthy. I have finally accepted a cup of tea. I was eighteen when I accepted my first cup of tea from my therapist. For two years, at each session, my therapist offered me tea, and I always politely declined. In my head, I wondered why I would make someone waste five minutes making a cup of tea for me? It wasn't worth the time and neither was I.

This was the narrative I believed in for a long time. Although my therapeutic process wasn't always just about my hair loss to alopecia areata, it was a marker of what I thought I didn't deserve. Once my hair was gone, I believed I did not deserve basic human rights, attention, or even a cup of tea. There was something translatable from the initial hair loss that society (whether that be media, social expectations or bullying) reminded me that I was something less than.

I stepped aside at times because some told me to, because hairless, I may have been seen as a liability and unworthy to go ahead in life's successes. I stepped aside and denied myself happiness for a while because without my hair I felt worthless. Hair loss causes a reboot to self no matter how you look at it. My hair loss was a transformation from something being taken away, to something that built me up higher, aware, gaining, and more in love with life than I ever would have imagined.

My process of getting back up, my resiliency, all began with a theory I call "my pit theory." When I initially lost my hair, I felt disembodied and paralyzed. I was in an altered state where I felt my life was consumed with hazy depression. After a year, I began to wake up from my depressive slumber. I realized on my "hair loss" anniversary that I was stunned and had

174

been emotionally asleep to my life. I had a couple of choices. One - remain sitting in my "pit" of grief and let depression win me over, or two - attempt to get up from my pain and suffering. At that moment, I was given a ladder to rise above the emotional pit I was in for too long. The ladder represented my support network, creativity, and dreams for the future. I chose to climb the ladder because the other options were never going to allow change or transformation. My resilient core kicked in, and I wanted to begin my life again, even if it was about rebuilding from foundation up. I wanted to reboot and have another chance.

I soon discovered my new self and life were tiring and challenging. I was confronted with realities that were going to question my worthiness, social interactions, and disclosure about alopecia areata. I learned new lessons about love, loss, and life during my twenties. In my undergrad, I became fascinated with how visual images produce meanings of hair, womanhood, and identity. My interest soon shifted away from my major of producing further scholarly literature around Art History. It transitioned into creating a project where I was able to process my identity, which allowed me to understand cultural and social contexts of my experience with alopecia areata.

Looking back now, a few months after graduating with my Masters, I realize the importance of my process. The journey through grief and loss, and coming out the other side gaining experience. In graduate school, I studied Art Therapy and Marriage and Family Therapy. Art therapy is a process to understand identity and can be used as a healing tool in mental health. In my undergraduate career, I wanted to connect the visual language and meaning of hair, but in graduate school, I was ready to ask: What got me back up after the loss? What made me believe in life again?

In December 2013, I finished the final edits to my thesis on resiliency and the use of Art Therapy in the alopecia areata population. In the summer of 2012, I was given the opportunity to gather data at the National Alopecia Areata Conference in Washington D.C. around the topic of Art Therapy, resiliency and the alopecia areata population. I discovered truths and definitions of resiliency were not just felt and experienced in the alopecia areata community, but could be used as motivation for others experiencing personal traumas and coping skills. I heard and witnessed the personal narratives of resiliency from my fellow community. I was inspired, and it was confirmed that tapping into one's characteristics of resiliency and expression is important and can help us get out of the emotional pit of hair loss. We can be our better selves. We can get back up and inspire others. We may have lost something when those strands slipped away, but what can be gained is powerful.

My hair loss is now thirteen plus years in, and I hold only a faint memory of feeling like I didn't deserve much of anything. I hold it away from myself, but always as a reminder of the transformational distance I have made and will continue to make in the future.

I hold the memory of loss, just as I hold my cup of tea resting against my belly. It's memory is resting and present; however, it's in a vessel of my resiliency. And as I sip loss, I digest the things I have gained. I accept that cup of tea. I accept the cup of life. I am worthy. Times have changed, and with many accepted cups of tea under my belt, I continue to learn how to ask for things. I am beautiful and authentically deserving of that cup of love, cup of humbleness, cup of compassion, and cup of life.

Heather continues to work on her Marriage and Family therapy intern hours and has a case manager position in the Bay Area. She is also working with probation youth and continuing to gain Art Therapy experience to become licensed. She has been getting back into crocheting, gardening, and continues to paint as self-care.

Helping Others

"Never worry about numbers. Help one person at a time, and always start with the person nearest you."
Mother Teresa

Once we use the resources around us to enable us to thrive, we soon find we are driven to help others in a similar fashion. Reaching out, in whatever capacity we can, helps contribute to a new cycle of giving in appreciation for what we have learned. Some become doctors or therapists, and others become advocates for raising awareness. There are also those who find a direct need in the alopecia community and succeed in taking it on.

"I created an international support and awareness event called "International Alopecia Day" - **Mary**

"As time passed though, it has become clear my experience with alopecia areata has been the driving force in my career." - **Carolyn**

"If bald was to be in my future, then a fashionable solution was too…the beaubeau scarf was born." - **Susan**

"I left the store with a new mission – to inform. To educate. …The result was: Boldly Bald Women." - **Pam**

"I helped MC a Locks of Love event…Fifty girls donated their hair to make wigs for children who suffer from hair loss." - **Kiah**

"I never really understood the phrase, "giving back" until I started contributing to this event…" - **Mat**

"…I created an anti-bullying organization called "Cam's Dare To Be Different." …I empower, inspire, and educate." - **Camille**

"Alopecia World was born, and became that vehicle." - **Cheryl**

Mary

I had waist-length hair in my teens, big permed hair in the '80s, and a nice short cut after that. I didn't even know alopecia areata existed until the first bald spots appeared when I was in my late forties. For about seven years, I continued having occasional small bald spots that were always hidden by my thick hair and always grew back following cortisone shots. In 2007, the bald spots began to appear more often and then to merge together. In January 2008, I shaved my head when the bare spots got too large to hide. I felt much better after shaving, especially since I didn't have to get sad every day as I picked up more hair off the floor or saw the bald spots getting larger in the mirror. I lost my eyebrows and all the rest of my body hair a couple of months later – alopecia universalis at age fifty-five. I decided to get permanent makeup (tattoo) eyebrows and eyeliner, which I prefer to applying makeup every day.

In March 2008, I was one of eight bald women with alopecia areata who taped an episode of "Shear Genius," the hair-stylist competition/reality show on Bravo television. It was broadcast in the summer of 2008, Episode 5, entitled, *It looks like a helmet.* The wigs were huge, heavy, and had way too much hair, and most of the stylists didn't know how to cut them. The best part was meeting the other women, especially since it was taped only two months after I shaved my head.

I began going out in public bald only a few months after shaving. I took "baby steps" to more and more places, keeping track of each new milestone in a journal: first time to the mailbox, first time to the grocery store, etc. I went from feeling like everyone was staring at me, to feeling like I didn't care if they were. After eight or so months of trying to wear a variety of wigs, I gave up on them completely because they were too hot for me. I was amazed at how liberating it felt not to have to worry about anyone else seeing my bald head or knowing I have hair loss. This is simply who I am now. I've found that the less concerned I am about my bald head, the less other people seem to notice or react to it.

For me, the decision to be publicly bald came down to a choice between suffering physically (being miserable and hot) or suffering emotionally/mentally (being stared at and feeling self-conscious). I chose to be free of the discomfort that I couldn't get used to - physical discomfort. I've become so used to being "out" as a bald woman, that I don't feel self-conscious anymore. I wore and still wear scarves, knit caps, and sunhats as needed for warmth or sun protection. But the moment I get warm, whatever is on my head comes off, the same way a coat or sweater would.

In August 2008, I created my first video about hair loss and uploaded it to YouTube, "Alternatives to Wearing a Wig." I demonstrated how I tie the scarves I wear, and also expressed my evolving preference for simply going out bald. I found that trying to help other women who are struggling with their hair loss has helped me deal with mine.

In 2010, I created an international support and awareness event called, *International Alopecia Day.* On *International Alopecia Day*, people all over the world take photos of themselves, send them to me, and I assemble a video slide show. In some locations, people have awareness events. In others, a social gathering. I encourage participants to hold a sign stating where they live. *International Alopecia Day* now takes place on the first Saturday in August every year. In 2014, there were over thirty-one countries represented. This was a big increase over previous years. My most recent alopecia undertaking is called, "The Bald Mannequin Project," where I encourage women (and men and children) to take photos of themselves at shops that have bald mannequins. In a world where

Steve Gould

Mary

I had waist-length hair in my teens, big permed hair in the '80s, and a nice short cut after that. I didn't even know alopecia areata existed until the first bald spots appeared when I was in my late forties. For about seven years, I continued having occasional small bald spots that were always hidden by my thick hair and always grew back following cortisone shots. In 2007, the bald spots began to appear more often and then to merge together. In January 2008, I shaved my head when the bare spots got too large to hide. I felt much better after shaving, especially since I didn't have to get sad every day as I picked up more hair off the floor or saw the bald spots getting larger in the mirror. I lost my eyebrows and all the rest of my body hair a couple of months later – alopecia universalis at age fifty-five. I decided to get permanent makeup (tattoo) eyebrows and eyeliner, which I prefer to applying makeup every day.

In March 2008, I was one of eight bald women with alopecia areata who taped an episode of "Shear Genius," the hair-stylist competition/reality show on Bravo television. It was broadcast in the summer of 2008, Episode 5, entitled, *It looks like a helmet.* The wigs were huge, heavy, and had way too much hair, and most of the stylists didn't know how to cut them. The best part was meeting the other women, especially since it was taped only two months after I shaved my head.

I began going out in public bald only a few months after shaving. I took "baby steps" to more and more places, keeping track of each new milestone in a journal: first time to the mailbox, first time to the grocery store, etc. I went from feeling like everyone was staring at me, to feeling like I didn't care if they were. After eight or so months of trying to wear a variety of wigs, I gave up on them completely because they were too hot for me. I was amazed at how liberating it felt not to have to worry about anyone else seeing my bald head or knowing I have hair loss. This is simply who I am now. I've found that the less concerned I am about my bald head, the less other people seem to notice or react to it.

For me, the decision to be publicly bald came down to a choice between suffering physically (being miserable and hot) or suffering emotionally/mentally (being stared at and feeling self-conscious). I chose to be free of the discomfort that I couldn't get used to - physical discomfort. I've become so used to being "out" as a bald woman, that I don't feel self-conscious anymore. I wore and still wear scarves, knit caps, and sunhats as needed for warmth or sun protection. But the moment I get warm, whatever is on my head comes off, the same way a coat or sweater would.

In August 2008, I created my first video about hair loss and uploaded it to YouTube, "Alternatives to Wearing a Wig." I demonstrated how I tie the scarves I wear, and also expressed my evolving preference for simply going out bald. I found that trying to help other women who are struggling with their hair loss has helped me deal with mine.

In 2010, I created an international support and awareness event called, *International Alopecia Day.* On *International Alopecia Day*, people all over the world take photos of themselves, send them to me, and I assemble a video slide show. In some locations, people have awareness events. In others, a social gathering. I encourage participants to hold a sign stating where they live. *International Alopecia Day* now takes place on the first Saturday in August every year. In 2014, there were over thirty-one countries represented. This was a big increase over previous years. My most recent alopecia undertaking is called, "The Bald Mannequin Project," where I encourage women (and men and children) to take photos of themselves at shops that have bald mannequins. In a world where fake bald women are the height of fashion in shops everywhere…where are all the REAL bald women? I haven't let my lack of hair stop me from doing the things I love. I play drums in a couple of bands and teach a weekly folk dance class. I go scuba diving, and being bald means that I can get into and out of wetsuits more easily, and I don't have wet hair to make me cold after a dive. At times, I've used my baldness to great effect: I dressed as the sexy bald character from the first Star Trek movie, "Lt. Ilia," when I attended San Diego Comic-Con in 2013 and 2014, and the costume was a big hit. Some people complimented me on my "commitment" to my character because they thought I'd shaved my head.

I firmly believe that public baldness is an issue of equal rights. Men who lose their hair aren't expected to wear a wig. They just shave their heads if they have any hair, and no one looks twice at them. Most women don't feel this is an option for them. I think the only way this situation is going to change is if we make it change. In other words, bald women won't become "accepted" and "normal" until there are more of us out there. I completely support women who prefer to wear wigs. I'm happy that they work for them. My goal is simply for women to feel free to go without a head covering too.

The most amazing thing of this whole journey is this: Today, I am MORE self-confident and LESS self-conscious than I was before I became bald. I had always been one of those women who worried excessively about what other people thought of me, particularly about my appearance. Today, not so much. My theory to explain the change is that when I made myself go out in public bald, I HAD to become less concerned about what people thought about me. It's as simple as that.

Mary is a retired attorney who first saw signs of alopecia areata in her late 40's, losing all of her hair at age 55. Discovering that she can't stand wigs, she embraced her new bald look and has become an advocate for people with alopecia, and an activist to raise awareness and provide support. In 2010, she created International Alopecia Day, an annual event celebrated worldwide and memorialized in a yearly video slide show. More recently, she started The Bald Mannequin Project, where people with alopecia pose for photos in shops with bald mannequins to show that real bald people are as attractive as the fake ones. Her interests include scuba diving and hiking, and she is a drummer and folk dance teacher.

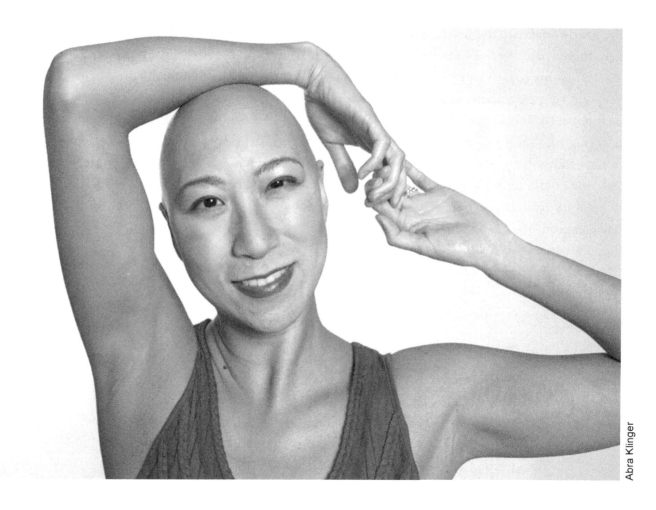

Abra Klinger

Carolyn
Becoming a Doctor

As far back as I can remember, I wanted to be a doctor. Perhaps it was just a standard answer to the question, "What do you want to be when you grow up?" or maybe it was because my dad is a doctor. Now, for many reasons, I think it was just the right profession for me, and maybe I subconsciously knew it all along. At that time, I'm not sure it was a choice connected to my alopecia, even though I have had alopecia areata since I was three years old. As time has passed though, it has become clear my experience with alopecia areata has been the driving force in my career.

Choosing to become a doctor means a lifelong commitment to learning and teaching. In fact, the word "doctor" is derived from the latin word "docēre" which means "to teach." There are many years of school and training to become a physician, but once we are practicing medicine, we continue to learn from other doctors. We teach our patients, and sometimes we also teach other doctors, and we definitely learn from our patients. As a result, it is a lot of talking! I typically see over a hundred patients a week and make phone calls to several more.

It is possible that if I knew precisely what it meant to be a doctor, that I would not have been so eager to become one. I was a shy and quiet child – my mother said I used to jump when a leaf would float my way. She put me in many activities to try and help me out of my shell. Piano lessons, tap dancing, swimming, Saturday enrichment classes in French and biology were some of the activities on my roster. I was quiet in these activities and made few friends. Some of this reticence may have been because of my alopecia, but having alopecia is what ultimately helped me overcome my shyness.

I don't remember when I first learned the term "alopecia," but it must have been early on since I often had to answer questions about it. Whether they are mean-spirited or well-meaning, these questions and comments are nearly always best met with a well-informed explanation. From a young age, I learned simple ways to explain my hair loss, and I learned firsthand that having a little knowledge can be empowering. This further drove my curiosity about this condition that I was living with.

This desire to understand alopecia areata has stayed with me. When I was in medical school studying the minute aspects of the human body and its functions, I kept wondering how they related to alopecia areata. Dermatology, the study of skin and skin-related appendages, including hair, was a natural specialty for me to choose. Now, I have a busy practice that includes many patients with hair loss due to alopecia areata and other causes. It is deeply satisfying to empower patients by teaching them about hair loss and to offer medical treatments when appropriate. I believe that I offer some degree of personal understanding of hair loss, which is comforting to patients. This is one reason I am a firm believer in support groups – they give people the opportunity to meet others with similar problems, learn more about their condition, and allow them to support others and gain support.

For me, the best treatment for my alopecia has been acceptance. At the age of eighteen, I chose to stop wearing a wig, a choice that was deeply liberating. This choice definitely pulled me out of my shell and forced me to face my alopecia and face the world honestly. Allowing the world to see I accept myself for who I am, helps the world accept me as well. It was a step that took a lot of courage at first but now is just natural and easy for me. I hope to provide support to others who are ready to reach that point of acceptance, whether they choose to continue wearing a wig or not, and whether or not they choose to keep treating the condition medically.

Ultimately, knowledge and acceptance have allowed me to live my life to the fullest because of, not despite, my alopecia. Life never turns out quite the way we think it will, but if we adjust our viewpoint, we just may think it turned out right in the end.

Carolyn continues her work as a Dermatologist in Los Angeles. She runs an alopecia support group that meets every two months, and is looking forward to the birth of her first child this summer.

Susan

Fourteen years ago, after returning from my morning run – I was taking a leisurely shower and washing my hair. I began to pull a comb through my hair and noticed large clumps of hair getting caught in the tines. When I ran my fingers through my hair, they were filled with massive amounts of loss. Just like that – No warning – No illness, just shedding, shedding, shedding. My initial trips to the doctors provided no answer to the mysterious hair loss. Only after seeing a third dermatologist did I receive the news that I had developed alopecia and would more than likely lose all of my hair. Alopecia? What a strange name for a disease. Never had I heard of it, nor had I ever known someone who had it. The doctor said, "No known cause and no known cure." Lovely! He also warned me that the hair loss might not stop at my head, and to be prepared to watch as my eyebrows and lashes fell out too. Unfortunately, his prediction came true, and in just five short months I was without so much as a strand of hair anywhere on my body. Wham! Life as I knew it came to a screeching halt.

No one (with hair) can truly understand how a drastic appearance change can affect one's life. The once active, confident, stylish, involved, and athletic woman I knew, soon became a self-conscious recluse in a desperate attempt to still be herself. The overall lack of understanding amongst my friends and family only served to increase the detachment I felt from my previous life.

Eventually, the shock subsided and reality set in as life as a bald woman. Seeking a way to feel feminine without hair, eyelashes, and eyebrows became extremely important. What to substitute my hair with was a hurdle I never wanted to encounter. Wigs? Sure – at first. Who doesn't try at least one wig when they first lose their hair, in a desperate attempt to hang onto the familiar definition of femininity? Wigs didn't cut it for me for many reasons. Wearing a wig actually made me feel more self-conscious. Although I was hiding baldness behind a wig, I came to believe that everyone could easily see my dirty little secret.

What next? Scarves? Sure, but where to go and how to find something feminine and fashionable? My first trip to a "cancer boutique" left me depressed and angry. I was determined to find something that did not scream, "Hey, I'm bald and sick!" No such luck. Determination is my middle name. If bald was to be in my future, then a fashionable solution was too. I dusted off my fashion design degree and got busy designing a fashionable solution that would work for me, and alas…the beaubeau scarf was born.

My hair loss issues did not end with a successful scarf business. Alopecia was to test me several more times. About five years after initially losing my hair, little hairs began to poke their way to the top of my head. I tried to ignore them, not wanting to be let down with a "hair tease." But these hairs were persistent. In about six months, I had a full head of hair. The hair was anything but normal, but it was hair. I enjoyed

a cute, short cropped hairstyle for about fifteen months, and then alopecia returned to my life. Once again, I went through the mourning of losing my hair. The second time was very difficult because just like I never knew anyone with alopecia on my initial hair loss ride, I was also not familiar with the re-growth process. I really had been thinking I was somehow miraculously "cured."

I wish this were the end of my alopecia story, but about two years later those persistent hairs began to re-appear. Just like the last time, I grew a full head of hair, only to lose it again after fifteen months. Only this time, it has left me with the alopecia patches which for me are harder to look at. I'd rather be smooth, clean, and bald. People understand bald (well sort of), but they really do not understand patches. My two regrowths left me vulnerable to unwanted questions. When I lost my hair, I spent so much time explaining the disease of alopecia, but when new hair regrew I found myself answering questions like, "Why do you have hair now?" With alopecia, there never seems to be a break in inquiring questions whether you have hair or not. My space is constantly invaded with the stares and unwanted questions.

In some ways, I hope my hair never grows back because at this point alopecia is who I am and I've accepted that. I love wearing my scarves. I don't like being mistaken for someone in treatment, but that seems to happen less and less. I've learned that although alopecia robbed me of many things, it has not robbed me of who I am, and I can stand confidently and say that in some ways it has made me a better and kinder person.

Susan is the President and CEO of www.4women.com, and developed alopecia fourteen years ago. Determined to find a fashionable alternative to wearing a wig, she created and designed the beaubeau scarf, a stylish, comfortable, and secure option for women without hair. The twice patented scarf has been giving bald women confidence and style for ten years. Her motto is, "Just because you have lost your hair, does not mean you have lost your sense of style."

Sheri Lossing

Pam

Over 2,500,000 women alive today in the United States will experience hair loss from alopecia at some point in their lives. Add that number to those women losing hair through chemo and radiation therapies, hormonal changes, disorders such as trichotillomania, chemical damage from hair products, tightly braided hair and a plethora of other reasons, and you've got a lot of women and children struggling with the emotional and social impacts of hair loss - just in the United States. Add those numbers to all women in the rest of the world, and you are looking at an astronomical number of women trying to cope with a condition that goes to the core of their feminine identity. Their families and communities are also impacted.

What is the meaning of a woman's hair? Her crowning glory…her visual certificate of health…her sex appeal- so much so that in some countries it is to be hidden away so as not to tempt a man. We associate bald women with sickness, rebellion, shame. The unsaid, but clearly spoken message is, "Stay away!"

I had no plans to spend the rest of my life bald. Nevertheless, now that I am, I'm incredibly grateful. I have alopecia universalis, the rarest and usually most permanent form of alopecia. There is no hair on my body anywhere. Now, believe it or not, there are some

pretty cool benefits to being hairless. No more bad hair days. No more need to shave armpits and legs. No more examining your chin for those unwanted coarse goat hairs that plague women from middle age on. No eyebrow tweazing. No clipping of nose hair.

Okay, losing my nose hair was awful. I never knew all the wonderful things nose hair does until it wasn't there anymore. Small bugs began to see my nasal passages as a tunnel to the great beyond – only to end up as unwanted protein snacks in the back of my throat. Nose hair gives you that much needed extra moment to fish out a tissue and blow your nose before it leaks all over. To those of you who have your humble nose hair, say a little prayer of gratitude. To those of you who don't – my heartfelt empathy. I feel you!

There's a lot to do when your hair falls out. First, you have to deal with the shock of picking it up from pillows and drains as it vacates your head. Next, you have to deal with the strange interloper looking at you from your own mirror. Of course, then there are other people. Your reaction to yourself is hard enough, but the deluge of comments and concern from family, friends, co-workers, and total strangers is embarrassing and frustrating when all you want to do is hole up and hide. You have to do all this while walking around in

184

a daze, grieving the loss of who you used to be. No wonder the first stop is the wig shop.

Wigs are hot and uncomfortable. At best, they are miserable. At worst, they look fake. To their credit, the really expensive wigs can fool the eye and provide external anonymity. You can be part of the herd of humanity again and save yourself the looks, comments, and questions. But not many of us can afford the price tag of the best wigs. The thought of having fake hair glued to my scalp is highly unappealing.

Aside from the physical discomfort, the worst part of wearing a wig is the constant awareness of wearing one. Is it okay? Is it on straight? Does it look good on me? Can I give this person in front of me a hug, or will it get caught on jewelry or glasses frames and get pulled off my head? Am I wind proof? Am I rain proof?

God help me if I forget I'm wearing the thing when I open the oven door to poke my roast for tenderness, and it ends up a melted frizzled unfixable mess. Will it stand up to a romp in the bedroom? What happens if it shifts, or worse, falls off?

Will the man in my life still love me if he finds out I'm bald? Who do I tell, and who do I hide my hair loss from? Will I remember to whom I told what? And on and on and on through as many scenarios as there are people who wear wigs.

How do I know? I tried it. I hated it. Really, really hated it. I was more angry over having to wear a stupid wig than I was over losing my hair. What I found when I pitched the wig, was personal freedom. I no longer worried about where and what my wig was doing on my head. I no longer had to ask myself what people would think if I walked boldly bald into the world. I no longer had to keep account of who knew from who didn't.

I was free. I was free to be the me I had morphed into. I could breathe again and hug again, and I found myself dancing a Snoopy happy dance every day.

Was it all sweetness and light? No, it wasn't. Suddenly, my boss decided I wasn't the right person for the job. Suddenly, my sister made me crocheted fedoras

because she couldn't handle the sight of my bald head. Suddenly, there were people looking at me, some with concern, some with pity, and some with disdain. There were a few deliberately bald men who looked at me with envy and asked how I got such a close smooth shave. They were the bright spots in my days.

But I was free. Free to respond, or not, to the various looks. Free to answer questions or ignore them. As time went by and people got used to seeing me, I frequently forgot I was bald. Truly forgot. I was just the me I was when I had hair – comfortably, solidly, happily me.

I found Alopeciaworld.com and connected with others all over the world who were dealing with hair loss – some newly diagnosed, some who'd lived with alopecia for many years – all seeking to help each other understand, accept, and move through the fear and grief alopecia brought into their lives, into a space of well-being, whether they chose to wear wigs or not.

I attended an annual conference put on by the National Alopecia Areata Foundation and witnessed the amazement on the faces of "people of hair" when the hotel was taken over by hundreds of "people of bald." It was a delight to meet so many of the people I knew from the website. The conference was interesting and fun. People went around without wigs – some for the first time – and experienced for themselves the freedom from self-awareness.

What I didn't know then was the life calling I would find in a grocery store one day.

A beautiful little girl, sitting in the child seat of her mother's grocery cart, stared at me for a moment. Her mouth drooped, and her sad blue eyes filled with tears. I had to know why.

Catching up with her cart, I asked why she looked so sad. She said, "Because you're going to die." Her mother intervened with profuse apology. Her daughter's best friend, she told me, had just died after a terrible losing battle with leukemia. All of her hair was gone when she died. For several moments, I spoke with the little girl, reassuring her I wasn't sick and explaining the cause of

Pam's Story Continues . . .

185

my baldness in kid friendly terms. I left her with a hug, and a sense of urgency I didn't understand.

I left that store with a new mission – to inform. To educate. To help women step out of the shadows of shame and embarrassment and into the light of self-acceptance and self-love. I wanted women to become so comfortable with their baldness they would not fear the reactions of others, and they would learn to advocate for themselves and their right to be comfortable within their own skins.

The result was: *Boldly Bald Women.* Suddenly, I was an international Amazon best selling author. Happily, I thought my work was done. One day, while walking my granddaughter to her kindergarten classroom, several children pointed at me and snickered. "Hey, lady. Do you know you're bald?"

"What a great title for a children's book!" I thought. Then I looked down at my granddaughter. Her face was grim and set. "What is it Jordyn?" I asked. "They are making fun of you, YiaYia." "It makes me mad and sad." What she didn't say was that it embarrassed her too. "Hmmmn," I said, "I'll bet there is something we can do about that. Let me think about it, and we'll talk about it when I pick you up this afternoon. Okay?" I stopped at the office on my way out of the school and told the principal I wanted to set up an assembly for all the children in the school to teach them about alopecia, and combine it with a lesson on bullying. She was quick to agree and schedule it. Everyone had a lot of fun during that assembly. After that, whenever I walked Jordyn to her classroom, the kids pointed, smiled and said, "We know you. You're Jordyn's Yia Yia!" I smiled back and said, "I know you too. You were in Jordyn's assembly!" Jordyn was happy because they all told her she has a really cool grandmother. The following spring when I brought Jordyn to her first grade class one day, a whole gaggle of children gathered around us and pointed and said, "We know you! You're Jordyn's Yia Yia!"

That was the humble beginning of my public career. Who'd have thought? Suddenly, I was expanding my reach to women all over the world! I met a new friend in China who found comfort and courage in the *Boldly Bald Women* book.

A lovely woman in Japan traveled two hours each way on the Japanese high speed trains each week to read and translate a chapter to a group of non-English speaking Japanese village women who had alopecia but knew nothing about it, or how other women coped with it. People are reading *Boldly Bald Women* all over the United States, in Canada, Europe, the Netherlands, Australia, Africa, and more.

Comments come back to me about how helpful the book has been, and how touching the shared stories are of the women who refused shame, and chose instead to reclaim their joy. And yet, there is more to do.

I have created a podcast called, *Boldly Bald Women: Surviving and Thriving in a Hair Obsessed World.* The podcast presents issues important to and for bald women in every walk of life. There are interviews of experts in their fields, providing information and insights about shaking off shame, reconnecting with courage, and reclaiming joy. They are full of stories, laughter, tears, and step by step how-to's of acceptance, understanding, and taking charge of change.

I am so blessed to have alopecia universalis. I've met many wonderful people and made dear friends I never would have come into contact with had I never lost my hair. I've found a new purpose in my life, and as a result of opening myself rather than closing off, and being seen rather than hiding, I have been the recipient of an abundance of unexpected love and joy. Yes, I'm a bald woman in a hair obsessed society, and I am so very grateful.

Pam continues to inform and educate women, encouraging them through her new podcast to embrace who they are. She is available for public speaking. Through small group and one on one life coaching, Pam offers women struggling with hair loss enhanced opportunities to dive deeper into the process of reclaiming joy. www.boldlybaldwomen.com

187

Kiah

Hi! My name is Kiah, and I am twelve years old. I have had alopecia areata since I was about three-and-a-half years old. I was really young when I got it, so I don't remember a whole lot from that time. I think I first started to notice that patches of hair were falling out of my head right before I began kindergarten. Alopecia has really changed my life in both negative and positive ways. While it's always a challenge, I feel like it's given me opportunities that I have been able to take advantage of.

Most times, I don't even think about my disease or how I look different than other kids. But once in a while, it can really bother me, and I get a weird feeling. One of the things about alopecia is that I can't really hide it. Even when I wear a hat, people can tell that I am still somewhat different. Yeah, I can cover my head, but I don't have eyebrows or eyelashes either. It's usually when I go out in public or am in a group of people who don't know me, that others will start to stare. Most times, I just ignore it…but sometimes it makes me feel bad. I've had people come up to me or my parents and say how sorry they are that I have cancer. But I don't have cancer, and I am glad about that. Usually, we will tell people I have alopecia, not cancer, and then people feel better. But you know what?… Alopecia isn't that great either! I don't want people to think that just because it's not life threatening, that alopecia is no big deal…because it is. It can be very life-altering.

I like to run and play, like any kid, but I can't run as fast as I would be able to if I had hair because I wear a hat. It will blow off if I don't hold it down. Every time I go swimming, I have to wear a waterproof cap, and I get worried that it could float off. It has come off my head while I was underwater, and let me tell you…that is not cool! I get looks and questions, and all I want to do is enjoy myself and be a normal kid. I also get stuff in my eyes all the time because I don't have eyebrows or eyelashes. Most people don't even realize how important they are!

Even though there are all these bad things I have to deal with, I think I have been able to handle my alopecia pretty well. I've had some really good experiences because of it too. For instance, I've been able to go to the National Alopecia Areata Foundation conference every year for the past seven years and visit cities all over the country. I've been to Louisville, Houston, Indianapolis, Los Angeles, Washington, D.C., St. Louis, and San Antonio. It has been amazing every time. I can still remember when I walked into my first conference when I was five. I felt so relieved to see all the other people like me. There were bald kids, teenagers, and adults, and everyone was so happy. Ever since then, the NAAF conference has been something I look forward to every year. It's almost like having a whole different family. Having alopecia also allowed me to do a lot of really fun things with my friends and family. When I was really little, I got to be in a magazine with NBA player Charlie Villanueva.

My sister, friend Alicia, and I all really love music and making movies. We really want to put our talents to good use. So, we take some very popular songs and change them a little bit. We change up some lyrics and make them have to do with alopecia. We took "California Girls," by Katy Perry and made it into, "Alopecia Girls." We took LMFAO's, "Party Rock Anthem," and made it into, "Alopecia Rock Anthem." Hopefully, the lyrics in these songs help people with alopecia to be more confident and to be more outgoing. I also get to spread awareness by going to different places and talking to different people about alopecia. For example, I helped MC a *Locks of Love* event at a High School called Divine Savior Holy Angels (DSHA), where my sister and I performed our songs, "Alopecia Girls" and "Alopecia Rock Anthem." Fifty girls donated their hair to make wigs for children who suffer from hair loss. After we were all finished doing our song, five more girls enjoyed our song so much that they wanted to donate some of their hair too.

Like I said before, helping out in the alopecia community really can make a difference. When my father, sister, Alicia, and I attended the NAAF Conference in St. Louis, we made another video. This one was just like the others, but in my opinion, BETTER. This one was called, "NAAF's Always a Good Time." It's a cover of Owl City and Carly Rae Jepsen's song, "Good Time." This one was different. Instead of performing this song at a mini talent show they have at the conference like we did with all the other songs, we created a music video for the song. At the closing ceremony, the NAAF staff let us show everyone (almost one thousand people) at the conference the video! It was so exciting! We were even given a standing ovation!

For the last three years, in September, my family, friends, and I have had a huge fundraiser for NAAF called, Milwaukee *Rock for Locks* and *Morgan's Ride for Alopecia*. Over the years of fundraising, we have raised about $70,000! It's quite the large number, don't you think? It's been great to find other Alopecians around the area and team up with them to raise money to fight for a cure. It feels good to help others out and teach them more about the disease. It's a bad feeling when you feel like you're the only person on earth dealing with something. When we first started, I thought I was the only kid in Wisconsin with alopecia. Now, there are over fifty different families who participate in our support group and fundraising events. That's why it's really awesome to be able to be here for other people with alopecia. I am so thankful that I have family and friends who are so concerned and keep giving me support. It makes me want to help others who may not have as much support as I do.

A couple years ago, I entered a contest held by Peggy Knight to be *America's Next Top Alopecia Model*. This gave people with alopecia the chance to win a wig and be a spokesperson for the company. My dad printed out business cards for me that said, "Vote For Kiah To Be America's Next Top Alopecia Model" and handed them out to friends, family, and strangers. I talked to people all over Facebook, and I shared my "Alopecia Rock Anthem" and "Alopecia Girls" videos. I shared these videos to lots of alopecia pages (even pages that are Spanish because I also speak Spanish), and I asked for them to also vote for me. I saw my video being shared all over the world, even in places like Japan, Australia, and the UK. Because of those cards and the videos, the votes for me went up fast. The day they announced I had won, I felt so happy. I was finally going to be able to see what it would feel and be like with hair. Life was for sure going to change for me. I just wasn't sure how...

Now that I have my wig, lots of things have changed. It was very different from my regular hats. It sure was something new to get used to. I decided I was going to start wearing the wig to school. Everyone in my grade was used to me wearing my usual pink hat, but when the school year started, some people started telling me about the school because they thought I was a new kid. It was so weird! Eventually, people started to get used to me with the wig, and so did I. Now, sometimes it feels weird when I put my head scarf on to wear to bed. I'm not as used to wearing hats and head scarfs now, even though I did it most of my life. My special wig just feels more normal than anything right now. Ever since I got my wig, I feel like I am able to fit in more. It doesn't make people think I have cancer anymore because it's not as noticeable that I don't have eyebrows and eyelashes when I wear a wig. Only a few people can tell I don't have them. This wig has changed my life so much, but with or without it, I am comfortable with who I am. I hope that other people can learn that their hair isn't what makes them who they are, too. My overall experience with alopecia areata is that it's made me very strong and more compassionate to others, especially those who are different.

Kiah and her team recently took on a Sara Bareilles song, "Brave." All the videos are on YouTube, so everyone can see them and hopefully be inspired; even if it is just for a little bit.

Mat

It was 1984, and I had a full beard. I was doing a lot of work with developing film and noticed a spot when I was touching my chin. It took about one and a half years until it was full-blown alopecia, and I started having steroid injections every other week. At the time, I was working two to three jobs, dealing with the break-up of my marriage, and a death in the family.

I started wearing "phony hair" for years, up until I got re-married in 1990. I felt the need to cover it up because I was tired of the looks. I'm the youngest of seven and although my family tried to be supportive, I sometimes wonder if it would have been easier to just tell me, "I don't know what to say." Instead, I heard comments like, "Mat forgot his hair. Should we tell him?" and the non-helpful ones like, "It's gonna be okay," "Don't worry dude," "Don't feel sorry for yourself," "Everyone loves a winner," and the best one yet from a co-worker, "As long as you still have hair on your nuts, you're alright!"

I had lost about three to six months of my life with all the stressors, and with counseling I found acceptance.

My first NAAF conference was in 1987, in New Orleans. I remember not wanting to leave my hotel room, but I needed to see someone else like me. I gave myself a pep talk, walked out, and saw over one-hundred people who understood. I thought, "People get it."

I feel like alopecia has contributed a lot to my growth and maturity. I understand others, and any racial bias I may have had is completely gone. Just as I look back on all that has happened, I do see all the support or attempts of support, giving me the opportunity to grow. I am, in many ways, thankful for the twists and turns alopecia has enriched me with. Would I wish it on anyone? No, but this is the card I was dealt, and I am going to play this game as long as I am able.

Every year, when I photograph the conference, I have two personal missions: To show what it is like to attend, and to tell the story through photos. To encourage even one individual out there who, like me way back, wanted to see and talk to another person just to know I was not alone. As we know, social media has done an excellent job of helping others reach out, but nothing beats the experience of personally attending a NAAF Conference. I always describe it as an intense group therapy session, but in a very good way. Parents and individuals could spend a lot of money on treatments, therapy… but I personally feel that by attending just one conference, they would leave with such a wealth of knowledge and confidence, along with personal growth. I pour every bit of energy into this, and every year I get back more than what I invest. You may hear me say, "I am tired," but I NEVER tire of the conference. I never really understood the phrase, "giving back" until I started contributing to this event. When I see the frightened expression of a person who arrives on Thursday, and the same person leaving with a bittersweet and beautiful smile on Sunday, I realize WE WON and have gained another family member.

For the past twenty-eight years, Mat has held the role as NAAF's official photographer. Over the years, he has captured images of thousands of people who have attended their first conference, along with moments when friends from past conferences reconnect. Everyone at NAAF knows and loves Mat, and appreciates all he does to promote alopecia awareness.

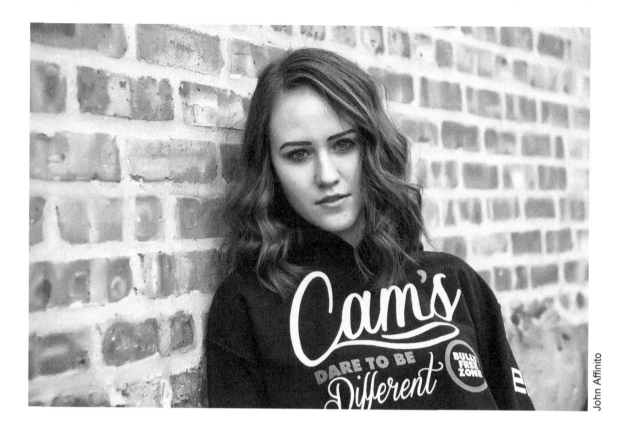

Camille

I am sixteen years old and was diagnosed with alopecia areata at the age of nine. My mother found my first spot on top of my head, the size of a dime, when she was doing my hair in the morning. At first, she thought I was cutting my hair. A few days later, she found more spots. In about a week's time, the hair at the crown of my head was gone, along with everything toward the back of my head at the bottom. My mom was confused, and I was upset.

My mother took me to several doctors. The first doctor told us my hair was falling out due to "stress." My mom asked, "Really, and what does a third grader have to be stressed about?" I was a happy girl, had lots of friends, and was a cheerleader. Stress was not it. The second doctor told my mom that I put too much hairspray in my hair. My mom quickly took me out of that office. I think I remember her saying something along the lines of "That doctor is a quack!" The third doctor finally diagnosed my alopecia. He

gave me steroid pills, but they just made me sick, and my hair did not grow back. He then gave me cream to rub on my head. That did not work either. Next, he said he wanted to do shots in my head, and I started to cry. I hate shots. I asked him if it would hurt and he said, "Yes it will, but do you want your hair to come back or not?" That did not sit well with my mother at all, and she asked him if he could guarantee my hair would not fall out again. He responded with, "Well no, but…" My mom returned with, "So, you're telling me that these shots will hurt, and her hair may or may not grow back?" I was crying at this point, and all I could think about was that needle. He looked at me and said, "Do you want her hair to come back or not?" Oh… he should not have said that because my mom looked at him and said, "You have no idea about alopecia, do you?" She took my hand and said, "You are NOT touching my daughter. Even if this would work, YOU will not be the one to touch her. You never speak to a child like that. My God. She is nine years old," and we walked out. I must say, I was very happy that I was not getting my shots. I looked at her and asked, "Mom, was he a quack?" I've never seen her laugh so hard.

My mom styled my hair a little different to try and hide the fact that I had no hair in the front. It really didn't bother me too much until the kids at school started to ask me about it. At first, they were nice. But when my friends got mad at me they would say things like, "At least I'm not a baldy!" That was really hard for me. I would come home from school crying, and my mom would tell me, "They just don't understand, honey." She would tell me to tell them those words hurt me. She also told me that God has plans for me, and that right now I may not know what it is, but when I was ready I would understand what He wants me to do.

Why me? Why does my hair have to fall out? I would think, as I looked at my sister's beautiful hair.

In the seventh grade, my eyebrows fell out, and that was devastating. I could hide my hair, but how in the world was I going to hide the fact that I had no eyebrows? My mom looked into having them tattooed, but that would require a needle, and that was out of the question for me.

I was bullied horribly due to my alopecia. I was called horrible names like "freak" and "hairless cat." I was told no boys would ever date me or like me because boys don't like freaks with no eyebrows. This put me into a very deep hole. I thought about suicide, stopped eating, and was self-harming. All I could think about was getting away from the pain I felt from my bullies who were once my friends. Why couldn't they understand I had no control over my alopecia? I started to believe the words… "Ugly." "No one likes a freak," and I became those words.

I endured so much pain in my life due to alopecia, but I know now that it is a part of me and will always be a part of me. I created an anti-bullying organization called, "Cam's Dare To Be Different." Now, I take all that pain and humiliation I've endured, and I speak to my peers about kind words. I empower, inspire, and educate. I feel that by sharing my own story, I reach kids on a different level. I feel blessed and honored for all of this. Did I figure out what God's plan was? Yes, I did. I am the voice for those who have no voice yet, and I am the voice of those who have lost their lives due to being bullied. I speak for them in hopes that others will think about what they say before they say it!

Having alopecia is what made me different, but it does not define who I am! I am Camille, and I have hopes and dreams just like every teen out there. Yes, I have only one eyebrow, and yes my hair falls out, but I love me, and I am strong! Without my family as my support system, I don't know where I would be today! I want to thank my Mom, dad, my sister Grace, and my brother Jack. Thank you for loving me for who I am!

Camille has spoken to many schools about bullying, competed in a platform based pageant and won the title of "Miss Teen Illinois International 2014." Her story is now in a first series comic book called "Bullying Is No Laughing Matter." She was featured on WGN, has been in several newspapers, and just received an award for being a hero in her community. More of her story can be read in the Woman's World Magazine, February 2, 2015 edition.

Carol Hector

Cheryl

In 1991, I noticed a small bald spot on the side of my head. Shortly afterwards, that bald spot quickly started spreading, and I was no longer able to cover it by strategically styling my remaining hair. I remember staring in the mirror and thinking, "This just has to stop!" I could not believe the bald image that was staring back at me. Eventually, all that was left were my bangs.

Watching what I thought was an essential aspect of my beauty literally go down the drain, I just could not bring myself to believe that any man could accept the "new" me.

I struggled with my "femininity" for the next five years - what it means to be a woman in today's society.

I no longer felt like a woman or that beauty salons and lingerie shops were acceptable places for me to be. I just really felt I did not belong in the "female" world anymore.

When I first ventured out while wearing only a scarf on my head, I thought I could only "pull it off" if I was in a tank top and cut off jeans. I truly struggled with how to be "feminine" and bald.

After years of struggling, I finally became aware of my need to make my own path. So I started experimenting. Could a bald woman look beautiful in a dress, heels, or polished nails?

I was starting to find "my way," and what I once thought was impossible was now becoming very

194

gratifying to me. I was beginning to appreciate what I saw in the mirror, and interestingly, so did others.

Although I learned to live with alopecia on my own, I still recognized that I held back when dating. When I wore wigs, I never knew when or if to tell my boyfriend. Even after I got to the point where I could tell him, I still couldn't bring myself to show him. I really wanted to experience true intimacy with a man, but I simply couldn't find it in myself to be vulnerable enough to experience it.

Being comfortable with my alopecia still didn't make me feel comfortable sharing it with somebody else. As long as I was single, I did not have to worry about a partner adjusting to my decisions regarding my alopecia.

For years, I had a good life, a good job, plenty of friends, and a large network of supportive Alopecians. However, I also remained single for thirteen years, which is a long time to look back at and see that I had not experienced the romantic love that remained important to me.

In 2007, I reached the conclusion that I had to do something different if I wanted something different. I opened my heart to what some call "appropriate vulnerability," and today find myself in love and married to an amazing man who I believe I met at just the right time in my life.

My husband, rj, encouraged me to extend my reach. Alopecia World was born, and it became that vehicle. Every morning, I wake up, look at the photos, blogs, and discussions on Alopecia World and see people from around the world sharing information, expanding limitations, and reaching new heights. People are visibly seeing that there are positive ways to live with alopecia. We all have to take and make our own path, but our possibilities are becoming endless.

So many Alopecians believe that once they have alopecia, they no longer have choices and that life will never be the same as they know it. This is part of the reason rj and I started Alopecia World. If there was one message I personally wanted to get across to people, it was that we have choices.

Wasted opportunities do not always come around again. I am now in my late 40's and count myself blessed to have finally learned this lesson. I have been given the opportunity to experience a fulfilling life, including true romantic intimacy, in addition to the love of my family and friends.

Alopecia World currently has thousands of registered members and provides resources and support throughout the world. A variety of support groups, including "Parents of Children with Alopecia," "Teens with Alopecia," "Newly Diagnosed with Alopecia," and many more can be found within the website. Alopecia World is the #1 social networking site for those with alopecia. www.alopeciaworld.com

Room to Grow

A recent diagnosis is just the beginning of a roller coaster ride with alopecia. Feelings of uncertainty and confusion lead to questions of how to react to new attention on us, how to find our way, how we should feel and why, and eventually how we can move forward and do something more valuable with our experience. These are all obstacles to negotiate in our own particular way.

Even after all these years, I think my story belongs right here. Although I find I am still most comfortable while wearing a scarf or hat in public, my ability to face the world as a bald woman is easier every time I give myself permission to completely be seen. Now, I refuse to get an awful tan line on my head because I won't remove my bandana. I am no longer embarrassed if my hat falls off, and I engage in conversation because I am not worried about what others are thinking of me.

Opportunities to grow in all aspects of my life have always been here, but by completing and sharing this book, I discovered I have become a new and improved version of myself. I am unsure what my life would be like without alopecia, but I am positive it has changed me for the better. I am thankful for it and can truly say I love who I am and how I look without hair.

Take one step, continue the climb, and keep running the race. When you get to the top, you will discover. . . there is always more room to grow.

"He is starting to understand that it's okay to be different . . ." - **Connor's Mum**

"This time, it is letting me lead because I needed to cross the finish line!" - **Glenda**

"Some days, it doesn't bother me, and other days I wish I had hair like everybody else." - **Nathan**

"I dig down deep for confidence and motivation to stay on course." - **Jauqui**

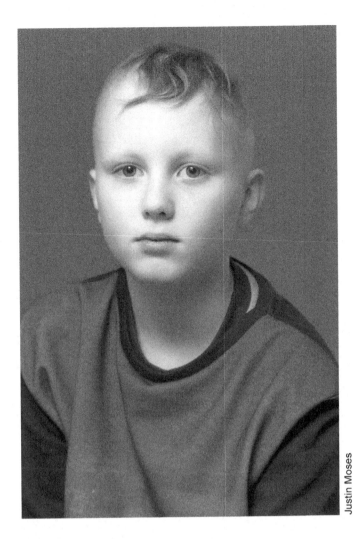

Justin Moses

Connor

I am ten years old. I got alopecia when I was about three, but I don't really remember having it then. I don't like having it because it's something people pick on me for, for having no hair. I don't know how my friends feel. I don't think it bothers them because they still play with me. The only good things are not getting nits (head lice) or having to brush it.

I don't like having it because I have been bullied a lot for having bald patches and then having no hair. It makes me feel very sad, unhappy, and different from everyone else.

There is another boy in school who has alopecia, but his isn't as bad as mine. He just has patches. My mom's friend, Susan, has it too. We went to an Alopecia UK picnic, and I met some older girls who had alopecia there. But there were no boys my age.

I'm not sure what I want to be when I'm older. Driving big trucks looks fun. I like to play on my Xbox, scooter around where I live, and play with my friends.

Connor lives in Greater Manchester, England, enjoys riding his bike and scooter, and has a number of interests including football club at school. He is starting to understand that it's okay to be different, and that being different doesn't make you less of a person. As his confidence continues to build, his mum looks forward to him seeing how much he can offer the world.

Jared Kotil

Glenda
Tears to Triumph

That voice you hear inside your head when you are sixteen and just beginning to drive, "Check the rearview mirror. Check the rearview mirror!" When I reached my fifties, there it was, that voice once again saying, "Check the rearview mirror!" "What?" I know how to drive. I've been in the driver's seat for thirty-nine years. I hear again, "Check the rearview mirror!"

Wow. Such persistence! To satisfy the voice, I think I will check. I glance quickly, and I see a reflection of myself. But the voice doesn't go away. "Check the rearview mirror!" I look close, as if I am searching the depths, the very soul of that rearview mirror, and that is when I see it.

I see myself celebrating my sixteenth birthday with family and friends. I'm smiling and laughing, and I don't have a care in the world. I even hear myself ask, "Could life get any better than this?" In an instant, as if someone simply changed the channel, I'm crying. I'm scared. I wonder what this could be? I discover a hairless, smooth patch at the nape of my neck just days after asking, "Could life get any better?" I see it all so very clear. Myself at my lowest point. I'm witnessing "the peeling of the onion," one layer at a time.

1. The initial diagnosis. Alopecia. A dark cloud appears. A sting is present. Tears are shed.

2. Fear of the unknown; when will it stop and what will it leave me with?

3. How will I cover the patches, and for how long will I have enough hair to cover and hide the affected areas. I now have several. I feel myself begin to fall…

4. If this doesn't stop, how will I ever be comfortable and confident again? How will I even like myself?

5. How do I go from my beautiful long, thick, straight black hair, to wearing a wig and facing my family and friends? How will I face anyone? I just want to crawl in a hole!

6. The Anger…Oh, the ANGER!!!

7. The Resentment…Oh, the Resentment!!! Why me?

8. Okay, now I HAVE to wear a wig! (In 1976-77 there was no choice. You wore a wig, and you hid your disease the best you could. You didn't talk about it, and you didn't draw attention to yourself.) How will I ever be accepted? Oh, where has Glenda gone?

9. Now I'm wearing a wig. A darker cloud appears. Will it stop…will it stop…will it stop??? Oh, PLEASE STOP!!! A stronger sting is present…a real burn begins. Tears flow and flow. I'm falling faster now. Like an avalanche, I am picking up speed as I go.

10. There goes my self-esteem! Alopecia totalis.

11. I pray to God, "Please don't take away my face…I will be okay, and I will get through this if you please spare my face!!!"

12. Oh, Dear God. My eyebrows are starting to disappear. My eyelashes are going now too! This is when the "peeling of the onion" does its final burn! I have reached the center core.

13. There goes the last of my self-esteem and what I believe to be "ME"! Alopecia universalis. The last ounce of my strength is pulled from me. I hate myself! Oh my God, "How will I survive this…?"

14. Oh, The ANGER…The RESENTMENT…The BURN!!! The cloud is at its darkest. The tears flow like a raging river.

15. WHY ME? The force of the landing is unbearable.

I close my eyes for what seems the blink of an eye. I open them and glance into the rearview mirror, and see once again a reflection of myself, a single tear still lingering on my cheek. I see a very strong woman in her fifties, compassionate, empathetic and passionate. A woman who is full of life and laughter, whose self-esteem is in check, and who is very happy with the woman she has become. A woman who counts her blessings. She is now asking herself, "Why the deep reflection into my young soul? How did I get from the peeling of the onion, to this point in my life?"

Looking deep into my self-reflection once again, there I am at the base of that mountain. I see myself as a young adult with alopecia universalis. I watch myself begin that climb back to the top, one step at a time. Once again feeling the sting, the burn, and the tears do flow, but this time it is because I am pushing myself harder than I ever thought possible. It is not an easy climb, but nothing worthwhile ever is. What is that I am picking up along the way? I pick up compassion, empathy, and the ability to be nonjudgmental. Each time I pick up an attribute, I see myself become stronger. I pick up more and more along the way. My character is rebuilding; my confidence is rebuilding.

Glenda's Story Continues . . .

I LIKE myself! I see "me" becoming stronger and becoming a better "me" with each step I climb. I can now see the top of that mountain. I'm almost there! Wow, this is remarkable to witness from the rearview mirror perspective! Oh, but wait Glenda. Why are you stopping? You are almost there, almost to the top. Don't stop, don't stop! I now appear to be aging, and time is passing while I wait just short of the top. "Glenda, you are not finished!" I shout. "How can you see that finish line and not cross it?"…What's that I hear? It is that voice again. The same one that told me to "Check the rearview mirror." Only this time, it is answering my question. "Glenda, you cannot honestly cross the finish line until you are completely honest about your alopecia with everyone, including yourself. You have to put it out there. Share your stories with others so they can gain strength from your experiences! Until then, you hang and you wait."

Blinking in an effort to get my thoughts in order, I glance again to the mirror, and my current reflection has returned. However, I am seriously upset with myself. I need to finish! I HAVE TO! I owe it to others with alopecia, and I owe it to myself. Suddenly, it is all so very clear. Me and my alopecia universalis. It walked by my side every day and allowed me to ignore it for thirty-nine years. Most days, I drug it behind me like I was taking out the trash. However, it became nearly invisible to my everyday lifestyle, as it should. I believe it was respectfully just hanging around waiting for our three children to be grown adults and on their way to starting their own lives. Waiting for me to have more time for the attention it longed for. Patiently waiting, and then asking me to dance center stage with it. Only this time in a very different fashion than when it first escorted me to center stage. This time, it is letting me lead because I needed to cross that finish line!

…And finish I have!! Just recently, because my heart was open and my vision was clear, I allowed a young girl named Sydney, an alopecia survivor herself, to reach down and give me that helping hand up. I am now perched high, and the views from here are splendiferous. I am shouting to the world! I found my voice. I want everyone to know the facts of alopecia and how we cope. Awareness plus education equals acceptance. I am shouting words of encouragement to other alopecia patients making that climb. If you are battling with alopecia, you do not want to miss the final reward. It is there for your taking. Waiting for you at the top of that mountain. You, want to be that hand reaching down to pull that someone up to the top!

I never, ever in a million years would have thought I would be giving credit to alopecia for making me a better person; for forcing me to experience such personal overwhelming adversities; for giving me the strength to stand tall and be proud of who I am, all in an effort to assist alopecia patients with their struggles. But you know what? I THANK alopecia! I feel extremely blessed to be able to stand here before you and say, "All will be ok during your climb, and it's extremely rewarding once you get to the top!" The question, "Why me?" has been answered.

In regard to the onion? I say, "Chop it. Cook it. Reduce it down and have it for lunch!" In regard to the rearview mirror? It truly is a force to be reckoned with. Take a moment from time to time to reflect in that mirror. You never know what it may allow you to see. I listened to that voice, looked in and saw deep into my soul. I opened my heart and found my purpose in living with alopecia universalis. Thirty-nine years of living silently. Let me tell you, this woman has a lot to say and is on one hell of a mission to spread the word to all.

Glenda's sprint for the finish line was worth every bit of effort. She continues to live by example and encourage those with alopecia to continue their climb to the top of their mountain.

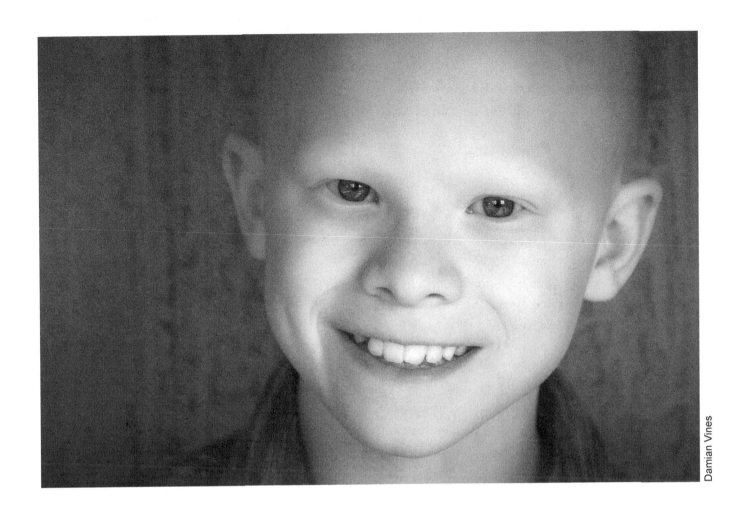

Damian Vines

Nathan

I'm ten years old, and I've had alopecia for two years. I don't really know how I feel about having alopecia. Some days, it doesn't bother me, and other days I wish I had hair like everybody else. I don't really know what my friends think about alopecia, but they don't seem to think it is a big deal. I don't know any kids my age who have it. I like not having hair when I am swimming, but looking different from other people sometimes is hard for me to deal with. I'm not sure what I want to be when I grow up, but I love to draw, work on art projects, design buildings, and going to computer game design camps.

Nathan was born on Christmas Day, 2004, with his twin brother, Henry, in Cincinnati, Ohio. For the first two years of their lives, they lived on a Navy base in Sicily, Italy. Nathan likes to play soccer and tennis, hiking with his family, and working with clay. He loves to be in the ocean whether it be riding waves or swimming, and oh yeah…he enjoys playing video games too.

A Mom's Perspective

A few weeks ago during Spring Break, my husband, Dave, and I relaxed in lawn chairs situated poolside at our Hawaiian resort. We were close enough to keep an eye on our twin ten-year-old boys, Henry and Nathan, as they shot down the water slide over and over again. Five years ago, we had stayed at a similar place, and back then, despite the boys being so comfortable in the water, we also kept tabs on them as they enjoyed the water slide. Overprotective? Yes, maybe a little. They had been preemies, and I'm a lawyer and Dave is an orthopedic surgeon. We are keenly aware that accidents happen.

Now at ten, even though they are still small for their age, they are great swimmers. So we don't need to worry so much about them in the water. Now, we stay near them for a different reason. While comfortably lounging in the sun with a great book in hand, I peer out from behind my sunglasses and watch for people's reactions when they see my beautiful, completely bald son bob by them.

Kids do double takes. Parents' eyes meet one another, often with worried looks, or they squint to inspect whether he has a scar. The big "C" word is always the assumption, I think, but Nathan has alopecia totalis. It has been over two years since all his hair has fallen out. Until then, I had never heard of this disease.

Nathan had minor surgery when he was in first grade, and shortly thereafter, Dave noticed a quarter-sized bald spot on Nathan's head during an evening bath. Having little in the way of medical knowledge, I didn't think much of it. Looking back, I realize now that Dave probably just kept his worries to himself. And Nathan's hair grew back.

A year later, however, we began to notice that his hair was thinning. At first it was just a tiny bit, but then it just fell out. The month beforehand, Nathan had visited the orthodontist, where he had been promised a mini-trophy of his thumb if he stopped sucking it.

He quit, cold turkey that day. Two months later, he was bald. His thumb trophy is still proudly displayed in our TV room.

The crazy part of this autoimmune disease is that no one knows what causes it, and there is no cure. For any parent, this is a tough pill to swallow, but for parents like Dave and me, who are both "fixers," this can cause even more extreme reactions and a delay of acceptance. I simply wasn't accepting the fact that there was no cure. As his mother, I felt like I had done this to him by forcing the thumb-sucking issue. It wasn't fair. And to make matters worse, he has a twin brother, his best friend, with lots of hair. This was so much for an eight-year-old to process.

We feel so fortunate that he was at a school that reacted so well and has allowed him to wear hats. One time in third grade, the boys came home from school and told me that a substitute teacher said he had to remove his hat during class. His class spoke up for him and corrected and explained to the teacher that he had alopecia.

We saw the best dermatologist at Seattle Children's Hospital. I researched, ad nauseam, articles on all sorts of autoimmune diseases, thinking I could come up with some new revelation that could lead to a cure. We tried steroids, topical ointments, and a skin irritant that only led to his head turning orange and our furniture stained. By that point, he no longer had eyelashes or eyebrows.

I changed his diet. We eliminated gluten, antibiotics, and went organic. Nothing worked. All it ever did was stress us out further, and the oral steroids made Nathan extremely angry and unhappy. We were all frustrated. I remember clearly the last appointment we had at Children's in Seattle. The doctor had run out of things for us to try. He asked if Nathan would be interested in going to a weeklong summer camp with other kids who had skin abnormalities. Tears

welled up in my eyes. I knew I had to be strong, but I was still unwilling to accept that there was nothing that could be done.

A year and a half after Nathan lost his hair, I quit my job practicing law, and I quit thinking about alopecia too. Nathan and Henry were nine. We spent the summer enjoying the sun and savoring real wheat bread and pasta. By the end of the summer, some hair had sprouted up on his head. His soccer teammates would even pet his blond, soft duckling hairs. On the field, he felt comfortable around his teammates without his hat on.

But then school started again, and the stress of fourth grade has led to not a single hair follicle. Seven months into the school year, and nothing has changed.

Do I blame stress as a cause of his condition? No. Do I think it is a trigger? Yes, but here again is the irony of this autoimmune disease; I cannot protect Nathan from stress. He has to learn to manage it himself, and I have had to learn to accept as a parent that I cannot fix all his problems. This is a pretty deep lesson for a ten-year-old to learn, but accepting who he is and what he looks like is an important one—he is simply getting a giant head start on it. As parents, we are learning some valuable lessons too.

On prior vacations while at a pool, on the sidelines of their soccer games, or at a ski lodge hot tub, I had always had a feeling of unease as I watched for reactions. I imagined that everyone was wondering, "Why is the cancer kid so happy?" and "Why do his parents look so okay with it?"

But sitting in my lawn chair this past vacation, I no longer felt that. Sure, I still watched to catch the double-takes, but inside I just felt different. I can't speak for Dave, but I do think we both have learned to accept that our son has a lifelong, life-altering but not life-threatening disease.

We are ready to help him through the tough years ahead. We want him to love how he looks. We want Nathan to love simply being Nathan.

Damian Vines

Kenny Johnson

Jauqui

In 2014, I trained and ran a 50K trail ultramarathon. I ran 31 miles in under 7 hours. I was never a natural or lifelong runner, so this was an incredible accomplishment. It took every ounce of mental and physical strength I had in me to finish that run. I had to dig way down deep in my reserves of motivation and confidence to believe I could run an ultramarathon. Although I doubted my ability to run that far, I continually fought to keep my doubts from taking over. I fought through tears, and I fought through pain to get to the elation and extreme high of crossing that finish line. On the scale of mentally challenging experiences in my life…running 31 miles still came in second to my journey of living with alopecia.

Sixteen years ago, I walked into the salon for a haircut and left with news that would change my life. There was a single round spot of hair missing on the back of my head… I had alopecia areata.

"Alopecia what? What is this? How did this happen? What does this mean? What is the treatment? Is there a cure?"

I was confident this had to be a temporary ailment, and so I made "the" visit to the dermatologist. There, I received confirmation that I did, indeed, have alopecia. I was prescribed topical creams and ointments that irritated my scalp, and I succumbed to painful cortisone injections, all with the goal of promoting hair growth and all with minimal success. My hair was falling out of my head…and I couldn't stop it.

Time went on, and the spots multiplied. I began to try out various alternative treatments. I sought out every naturopath, acupuncturist, energy healing professional and psychologist that I thought could cure me. I maintained strict diets and adhered to an ever-changing regimen of supplements and herbs. For the next eleven years, I lived with alopecia. I modified my hairstyle. I avoided swimming, wind, and rain. I wore headscarves or hats. I was open about my disease with friends and family, but fearful of its discovery by those beyond my inner circle. I cried…and cried…and cried. I pushed people away, afraid they wouldn't accept me…spotted. And I had a choke hold on the hope that as long as I ate healthy and continued to follow the advice of my healing professionals, I could continue to hide this disease…I could live with some spots.

All of that changed six years ago, when over the course of three months, I lost all my hair. What I feared most in this journey, happened… my condition progressed to alopecia universalis. Complete hair loss. I watched as the hair on my head…the hair on my body…my eyebrows… and the most upsetting, eyelashes, all washed down the drain. My disease got very real and very scary… and I started on the most challenging journey of my life.

After many months, it was obvious this condition wasn't going to change, not anytime soon. It was time to come to terms with what was happening to me… and OWN IT. If I didn't, and fast, this disease was going to own me. So, I shaved off the very last strands of hair on my head and walked out the door a very different person.

Those first few steps as a bald woman were terrifying. I felt naked in the world. It felt like everyone who looked at me could see right into my soul. But I couldn't let the fear pull me away from owning this disease. I had to keep going.

With the help of some friends, we organized a photo shoot… photographing me without hair for the very first time. To my surprise and amazement, it was a very liberating and transformative experience. It fed my confidence and proved that I could still walk out the door with my head held high. I felt beautiful again, and I was free from hiding this part of me. I shared my photos and educated my friends and family on

this disease. I talked to co-workers and asked them to support my new life as a bald woman in the professional world. Every single person I know stepped up and supported me in this journey. Their support was, in fact, overwhelming. I am incredibly grateful every day for my wonderful friends, family, and community. They helped me believe in myself.

A transformation had begun. I put on my face of confidence every morning, and eventually I was able to look in the mirror without crying. I slowly got used to going out in public. I slowly got used to the stares. I went through a variety of emotional phases and developed techniques on how to feel and react when strangers asked if I was a "survivor." I learned how to smile and wink at children who stopped and pointed, which usually made them smile back. I learned how to educate parents, that it's better to let their children ask why I'm bald, than to hush their questions. I went through the stages of grief over losing a part of me. I wondered if anyone would ever again see me as beautiful, appealing, attractive, sexy…whole? I wondered if I would ever see myself as whole. But eventually… I began to forget I was different.

Living as a bald woman is a lot like running an ultramarathon. I am constantly falling off balance, but I pull myself back up. I struggle to stay steady in my emotions but strive to always find my center. I arm myself with tools and training to help me get past the rocks and bumps, and hills in the road. I dig down deep for confidence and motivation to stay on course. I wake up every morning, look in the mirror and remind myself that this is exactly who I'm supposed to be, and this is exactly what I'm supposed to be doing.

I still wonder how others see me, but I know how I see myself, and it's much, much more than my disease. When the road seems too long…I take a long, deep breath, put one foot in front of the other and just keep moving. I remind myself that I'm in control of what I do and how I feel. I OWN who I am.

Jauqui has temporarily hung up her running shoes but still continues to push herself through yoga and living a holistic lifestyle. She is passionate about the Kansas City arts and music scene… and is an "around the house" guitar player, singer, and songwriter. She most enjoys spending quality time with friends, family, and her two adorable pups.

Photography Credits and Directory

When you are in need of a future photo shoot, please consider working with one of these photographers who selflessly gave their time to the project. You won't be disappointed.

Abby – Angela Lang Photography
San Francisco Bay Area, CA
www.angelalang.com

Alexis and Vangelis – Lydia Rawie
Zakynthos, Greece

Allison and Isabel – Sandra Burns
September Blue Photography - Long Island, NY
www.septemberbluephotography.com

André – Kimarie Martin Photography
Columbus, OH - www.kimariemartinphotography.com

Angelica – Cliff Gull, 2 point 8 Studios
Salt Lake City, UT - www.2point8studios.com
Makeup: Lisa Frehner

Anna – Stephen Tilley Photography
New Zealand - www.stephentilley.co.nz

Anthony – Leslie Hassler
New York, NY - www.lesliehassler.com

Bailey – Randy Wentzel Photography
Santa Rosa, CA - www.wentzelphoto.com

Caitlin – Jordan Jennings Photography
Lansing, Michigan
www.jordanjennings.smugmug.com

Camille – John Affinito, Flys Photography
Crystal Lake, IL - www.flysphotography.com

Carolyn – Abra Klinger Photography
Playa del Rey, CA - www.abraklinger.com

Cheryl – Carol Hector Photography
Southfield, MI - www.carolhector.com

Connor – Justin Moses, Moses, Inc.
Manchester, U.K.

Corrine – Emily Macauley
Pennsylvania

DK Wright – Reynoir Lewis, The Collective Vision
www.collectivevision.co

Dakota – Lisa Dean Photography
Indianapolis, IN

Dante – Frank White Photography
Rochester, NY

Dave – Dan Eden
www.danedenphotography.tumblr.com

Dean – John Morris

Deeann – Damian Vines Photography
(Story and About the Author Photo)
www.damianvinesphotography.com
Ashley Finch Photography (Back Cover)
Makeup Artist: Kat Aldridge

Deirdre – Maksimilian Dikarev
www.maksdikarev.com

Deryck – Aiste Ray, Bee Me Photo
Arlington, VA - www.beemephoto.com

Destiny – Renee Nicole Photography
Colorado Springs, CO
www.reneenicolephoto.com

Dino – Vanessa Alves, Imaginarium
Orlando, FL - www.imaginariumphoto.com

Diogo – Bruno Nabiça
Sintra, Lisboa, Portugal

Emma – Katrin Unge, Makeup Artist/Photographer
Stockholm, Sweden - www.katrinunge.com

Erin – Leigh Righton Photography
Vancouver, B.C. - www.leighrighton.com

Franchesca – Carmen Heller-Chariton
CHC-Photography, Inc.
Crown Point, IN - www.chc-photography.com

Georgia – Ksenia Koldeva
Los Angeles, CA - www.kseniaksenia.com

Glenda – Jared Kotil
Lincoln, NE

Heather – Whitney Allen
San Francisco, CA

Heather – SteelSwitch
Photographer: Ignacio Di Biaggio
Creative Director: Azuka Boutcher
Makeup Artist: Anastacia Jimenez
Washington, D.C./Maryland/Virginia

Jackson – Bill Weber

Jannica – Abra Klinger Photography
Playa del Rey, CA - www.abraklinger.com

Jauqui – Kenny Johnson Photography
Kansas City, MO
www.kennyjohnsonphotography.com

Joann – Clare Xinghui Che, ICameraU Photography
Toronto, Ontario - www.icamerau.com

Joyce – Celia Strickler
Bradenton, FL

Judy – Lina Hayes, Wild at Heart Photography
Sydney, NSW - www.wildatheartphotography.com.au
Henna - Helen Beasley, Rainbow Face and Body Art
Turning Heads Art Crown Project

Kaiya – Shayne Casto, Shayne Marie Photography
www.shaynemarie.com

Kevin – John Huewe, Convex Photography
Clovis, CA - www.convexphotography.com

Kiah – Mary Stephan Photography
Elkhorn, WI - www.marystephanphotography.com

Laura – Jennifer Curry Wingrove (Story Photo)
Wingrove Studios Photography
San Diego, CA
www.wingrovestudiosphotography.com
Meghan Meredith (Cover Photo)

Lucy – Brooke Kelly Photography
Nashville, TN - www.brookekellyphotography.com

Madison – Donn B. Jones Photography
Port St. Lucie, Florida

Marina – Natalia Kazakova
Moscow, Russia

Marlina – Sarah DeNeui, Buona Sarah Photography
Tulsa, OK - www.buonasarahphoto.com

Mary – Steve Gould, Steve Gould Photography
San Diego, CA - www.stevegouldphotography.com

Mat – Damian Vines Photography
www.damianvinesphotography.com

Maya – Rosie & Jamie, Captiva Photography
Ontario, Canada - www.photocaptiva.com

Megan – Jennifer Starcher,
Photography by JenniLee
Brocton, NY - www.jennileephotos.com

Melissa – Bill Hebert, BHPhotos
Philadelphia, PA

Mikaya – Darnell Wilburn
www.dwilburn.com

Nathan – Damian Vines Photography
www.damianvinesphotography.com

Pam – Sheri Lossing, mon Sheri Design
Grand Rapids, MI - www.monsheridesign.com

Paul – Brian Gonzalez
Boston, MA

Rachel – Randy Wentzel Photography
Santa Rosa, CA - www.wentzelphoto.com

Rebecca – Lucia Bisbee

Reuben – Dino De Luca Photography
www.dinodeluca.com
Artist - Kayleigh Dewar, Scotland

Rob – Damian Vines Photography
www.damianvinesphotography.com

Sammy C – Justin Mein, C&I Studios, Inc.
Los Angeles, CA - www.c-istudios.com

Sandra – Xavi Oribe
Barcelona, Spain

Sarah – Abra Klinger Photography
Playa del Rey, CA - www.abraklinger.com

Sarah – The Velvet Insides
www.thevelvetinsides.com

Sophia – Creative Photography
Hamburg, NY - www.thecreativephotography.com

Sophie – Aiste Ray, Bee Me Photo
Arlington, VA - www.beemephoto.com

Staciana – Naomi Calverd
www.naomicalverdphotography.com

Steph – Jessica DeLorenzo
DeLorenzo Photography
Bangor, PA - www.delorenzophoto.com

Sue – Anita Epstein
Berkhamsted, U.K.

Sydney – Carol Hofmann, Creative Images
Sutton, NE

Tanya – Machuca Photography
Vancouver, B.C. - www.machucaphotography.com

Front Cover (*Top to bottom, left to right*): Megan, Mikaya, Rachel and Bailey, André, Heather, Franchesca, Mat, Caitlin, Isabel, Laura, Destiny, Dino, Reuben

Back Cover (*Top to bottom*): Maya, Tanya, Deeann

Resources to Help You Along The Way

The resources listed below are helpful when looking for answers. Although both NAAF and CAP are two of the most informative and helpful communities available, access to social networking sites like Alopecia World and Facebook pages that focus specifically on alopecia areata are gaining momentum as avenues for help.

These stories are very specific to each person who wrote them, and you will find the common thread is community. You don't need to feel alone. We are in the age of information accessibility. Reach out to others who have alopecia. The support of friends and family are one thing, but finding a safety net made up of those who truly understand is extremely valuable.

NAAF

65 Mitchell Boulevard Ste. 200-B
San Rafael, CA 94903
415.472.3780
Email: info@naaf.org
www.naaf.org
NAAF supports research to find a cure or acceptable treatment for alopecia areata, supports those with the disease, and educates the public about alopecia areata.

CANAAF

Canadian Alopecia Areata Foundation
316 Kirkvalley Crescent
Aurora, Ontario
L4G 7S1
Email at info@canaaf.org
www.canaaf.org
CANAAF offers a support network that provides you and your family with the right environment to develop your own perspective and experience of alopecia.

CAP

906 Penn Avenue
Wyomissing, PA 19610
Phone (610) 468-1011
E-mail: info@childrensalopeciaproject.org
www.childrensalopeciaproject.org
Our focus is on building self-esteem in children living with alopecia, providing support for them and their families, and raising awareness about this life-altering disease.

Australia Alopecia Areata Foundation Inc.

PO Box 5029
Frankston South Vic 3119
Australia
www.aaaf.org.au
Our service philosophy is to give each person the best chance of managing their alopecia journey positively.

Alopecia UK

www.alopeciaonline.org.uk

Alopecia support in the U.K.

HeadzUp

www.headzup.org.uk

Alopecia UK's Page for Young People with Alopecia

ALOPECIA WORLD

Detroit, MI

United States

www.alopeciaworld.com

A unique, exciting, interactive and positively life-changing social networking site for Alopecians, their loved ones and friends.

BeBold Be You

www.bebold.org.uk/alopecia

Helping build confidence and self-esteem in children and adults who suffer from alopecia.

facebook

Many alopecia communities can be found on Facebook. Please note, most of these pages are "closed" to anyone who does not have alopecia. As with any social networking site, please use your best judgment while doing your research and reaching out to others.

Hair Donations

These are reputable names in the alopecia community who accept hair donations to make custom made wigs specifically for children with alopecia or any hair loss condition.

Hair We Share

www.hairweshare.org

Hair We Share is committed to changing lives.

Children with Hairloss

www.childrenwithhairloss.us

Covering young heads to heal young hearts.

Wigs for Kids

www.wigsforkids.org

Helping children look themselves & live their lives.

"What Motivates Us . . ."

What motivated you to start Mondo Baldo?

I looked at the "bald market," and I couldn't see ANYTHING positive being messaged or marketed to us. Whether by genetics (yours truly) or having a condition causing hair loss, no one was raising a flag and saying, "Where's my L'Oreal commercial?!" Being blessed with my father's male pattern baldness, I was bombarded with nothing but the ubiquitous products and infomercials telling me "It's a big PROBLEM! You must fix it, or you are not a man any longer! You are ugly! You must pay the price to get your self-esteem back! Order now and we'll..." I did buy in. I was so ashamed and extremely embarrassed. I had to wear a hat for a couple years to cover up the inevitable. My friends made fun of me.

Fast forward, and thanks to Michael Jordan, Bruce Willis and others, a booming niche of us men finally saying, "NO! to rugs, plugs, drugs and hair clubs," as I put it. I dubbed myself Baldylocks and branded myself. People couldn't forget the tag and the fact I could find pride in the outdated stigma. It always generated a smile. "Hmmm...,"my entrepreneurial wheels began spinning, as I was nearly having a heart attack at a desk in corporate America.

At the same time, my good friend, who had alopecia, and I shared a bond because of our baldness. It was awesome. "Good to see you, my bald brother from another mother!" It didn't matter that his arrival to bald was different than mine. The level of shame we both experienced was the same. He wasn't balder than I was, or vice versa. He experienced the very same, yet relative shame from our juvenile culture.

And by no coincidence, as I now see it, a friend's ten year old daughter was undergoing chemo at St. Judes. The images of them in the hospital, always with her head covered by a cute hat. Again, I saw that dirty word: "Shame." Only now, I saw it preying on this precious little girl with a life-threatening illness. Our hair-obsessed culture, relentless and indiscriminate in its clear objective: to make the Bald World feel bad about ourselves unless we cover or cure our heads. It angered me. It's only now that I'm able to laugh at the insanity of it!

So, this Bald World came to my mind, "Mondo Baldo" as it hit me in a dream (literally). "Mondo," world in Italian and "Baldo," a way to say Bald with a smile.

How to unite us? T-shirts of course! I trademarked uplifting phrases such as "Bald and Proud," "Bald Power," "Bald Pride Worldwide," and "Sorry to hear about your bad hair day," so that we could ALL come together and say; "You know what, I am beautiful BECAUSE I'm Bald." I wanted to capitalize the "B" and say the word "Bald" over and over and over to tear down the ancient condemnation, and in so doing, create community. Although the "shame machine" is still running, we're throwing a wrench in its gears, one shirt at a time. I believe they are the most powerful t-shirts in the world.

I felt fearless enough to risk it all in order to bring the idea to life. So I left the job, started designing shirts, and sought out partnerships with alopecia and cancer related organizations committed to research. Shortly after starting, I received a call from a large alopecia organization and was invited to join their list of approved vendors. "Would I be willing to bring shirts to offer at their annual conference in two weeks?" I managed to stutter, "Yes" and "Thank you so much!" and my journey with the alopecia community was underway.

When I arrived at the conference to set up with the other vendors, I looked around and was immediately petrified. They were all wig and hat companies. And here I was with a huge bag of t-shirts saying, "Take them off! You are awesome without them!" To my surprise and delight, Mondo Baldo was the hit of the party, so to speak. I couldn't believe how the message was resonating. While I completely understand and respect everyone's comfort level of exposing their heads, I was shocked at how many people said "Thank you." Talk about humbling.

I made emotional connections, and over the course of the past four years, I've made friendships unlike any I've known. They are people active in global alopecia communities, to the family living where there is no group support available. They all continue lifting me and Mondo Baldo up. Were it not for the alopecia community, I'm not sure where Mondo Baldo would be, quite honestly. Although it's having the same effect for Bald dudes like me, I will be forever grateful for the brave and beautiful people that simply want that phrase blasted from their chest.

I'm proud of this Mondo Baldo we're all creating. We are a community. We are "Bald and Proud," regardless of how we've arrived. But Mondo Baldo's alopecia "peeps" are a cornerstone. And it is my mission to provide these messages of power, pride, and levity. Folks with those pesky hairs? Johnson and Johnson loves 'em to death, but Mondo Baldo has something special: a true emotional connection with our community. It's brought me to tears more times than I can possibly count. In fact, I'm having them now as I see all the smiles passing through my mind and proudly displayed on the website. If I die today, I'll die the richest man in North America, and it's got nothing to do with my checking account, I assure you!

We only learn when we're challenged in life. But we can do it with a smile and determination. Mondo Baldo is screaming for you from the bleachers; "BALD and PROUD!!!"

- Andy "Baldylocks" Turpen
www.mondobaldo.com

"What Motivates Us . . ."

What motivated you to start CAP?

I have four daughters, with Maddie being the 2nd oldest. When she was in kindergarten, she started losing her hair. Like most parents, we searched for something that would help her regain the hair she lost, and after searching and putting her through things we really shouldn't put our kids through, we decided to just give her a hat and cover it up. We soon realized the hat wasn't the right thing to do because she never wanted to wear one. We hadn't given her a choice. As a five year old, she just decided to take it and wear it. She was in a play at school and didn't want to wear the hat because she had to put an American Indian headdress on her head. I went in and spoke with her kindergarten class. Soon after, she started wearing her hat less frequently, until she stopped wearing it altogether. After we got finished with all the medication and all the snake oil that was out there, we came to the realization that this was an autoimmune disease and internal. If anything topical worked, it was just going to fool the body. We decided we weren't going to waste any more time on this and concentrated on what was important, and that was her. We looked for support groups and attended a few that weren't really directed toward kids. When I couldn't find something specifically for children – I decided to start a local support group and look for other kids. I realized real quick that we were going to need resources to be able to do this, and not being in a financial position to do that, realized it was not going to happen. After I brought it up with my wife, we decided the best option for us would be to start a non-profit, and that's what we did. We started the process in 2003 and became a 501(c) 3 nonprofit in late 2004.

The philosophy has always been really simple. We want kids to do things with other kids who have alopecia. We want them to feel comfortable in that setting, so they can learn to become more comfortable with themselves in other settings. We realized self-esteem was the most important thing. Providing support for the child but more importantly, to the family. I always say if a child has alopecia, then the family has alopecia because your lives are consumed by it. Even though it's not life threatening and doesn't hurt, it's probably the best disease you want when it comes to a physical one. On the other hand, 85% of women with cancer polled in Redbook magazine, stated the thing they were afraid of most when diagnosed, was losing their hair. So on the other hand, it's a horrible disease. We wanted to make sure we changed the emphasis on growing hair, to growing self-esteem. That way, the kids could basically become stronger teens and productive adults.

I know I sound like a cliché, but everything I'm saying is exactly what I thought and what we did. It's been a progression when it comes to things we've done - support groups, camps, international camps, going to other states and countries, all the literature, support, and our Facebook page really took off because back in 2003 there was a need. There's still a need because our children are the most important asset that we have. It doesn't matter if they have a lot of hair or no hair. Their self-esteem is most important, and that's why CAP is CAP. I'm very glad I'm the guy who founded it and runs it. It's not a job or passion, it's truly my purpose. If Maddie grew her hair back tomorrow, I'd still be doing this because I know how I felt back in 2003, and helping others is important.

– Jeff Woytovich

A Special Thank You to ...

Stephanie - Who encouraged me by saying, "Let's make a pact. I'll work on developing my website, and you work on your book every day this summer." And we did (mostly). Thank you for your encouragement.

Deirdre - Who listened to the *Monsoon Wedding* soundtrack with me after hours in the paintball store while we each worked on our independent projects. We used any excuse we could find to escape the mundane tasks of diaper changes and laundry, and it's nice to see our efforts have paid off for each of us.

Mom & Dad - For instilling strength and perseverance in me, which are qualities I also encourage in your grandchildren. As a parent, I now know how difficult it is to navigate the waters of parenthood, and I can fully appreciate all the choices you made for me in such uncertain times. I love you and thank you.

Andrea - Who struggled with how unfair it was to have such thick and beautiful hair, when I had none. Who once excitedly called me after seeing an infomercial on television, stating "They can actually transplant hair!" For the many times you offered to make a wig for me from your excess hair. Your heart is filled with giving, and I'm so thankful to call you my friend and sister.

Kristan - Without you, this book would have taken many more months to publish. Thank you for your patience as I made the endless changes during final edits. The comma will always be the bane of our existence. I'm not sure if you know this, but you were the first person who talked to me about positive thinking. Before Oprah and vision boards, you came home from school one day, saw how distressed I was about my hair, and suggested making a collage board with words of encouragement and photos of the kind of hair I wanted…You were such a forward thinker. We have probably learned more about each other while working on this project than we have in our entire lives. Thank you for giving your time and expertise to this project. I appreciate you and your mad skills.

The Alopecia Posse - Alex, Caitlin, Marnie, Sara, Becky, Corrine, Sue, Allison, and Susan. Thank you for encouraging me to discover my true potential. You continue to inspire me to lead by example. You rock in every way!

A Special Thanks Continues . . .

213

Anne - For help with rewording, revamping and style and trying to convince me that less is more when trying to make an impact on readers. I appreciate your attention to detail.

Kyla - You were only seven years old when I told you that I had made a decision about not wearing my wig anymore. You simply said, "Okay." Just like that. You were completely fine with it, not caring what the world would think of you as long as it made me comfortable. I appreciate the way you view the world with such clarity, and I love you very much.

Lyric - Several years ago, when you kissed me on the head to say goodnight, you noticed a lone hair sticking off the side of my head. When you brought it to my attention, I reached up to pluck it out, and you grabbed my hand and said, "No, Mommy. Let it grow." You've never said you wanted me to have hair, but I know you think it would be pretty cool to actually SEE it grow. Thank you for reminding me to look at life in a more simple way. I love you so…much!

Cedar - You were a young man when we met. Knowing I was a diabetic who was potentially going to go bald didn't seem to affect you at all. You were responsible and mature with the way you approached loving me. I did lose all my hair, and you never missed a beat. You never felt or expressed that I was less than the woman you fell in love with, which is the way love is supposed to be. I don't need you to tell me I'm strong because I feel it in the way you understand and look at me. Thank you for all the nights you went to bed alone, allowing me to work uninterrupted. Thank you for not giving me too much grief when I came to bed and tried to snuggle up and nudge my frozen feet in between yours as you slept. I appreciate you taking responsibility for our family, running our business, doing all the extra loads of dishes and laundry, and feeding our kids when I said, "I need to work on the book today." You did it all with an understanding heart. You knew this was what I needed to do and supported me every step of the way. Thank you, Cedar, for being you.

About the Author

Damian Vines

Head-On, Stories of Alopecia is Deeann Callis Graham's; indie-published, non-fiction debut. Thirty years ago, she unwillingly exchanged the steady California sunshine for the perpetual liquid sunshine of Washington State, and is now happy to call Skagit Valley her home.

Deeann spends her time working with her husband, Cedar, in their salvage company, constantly reminding her children to pick up after themselves, and trying not to injure herself or her teammates while playing competitive volleyball with her slightly disorganized and aging team.

Her love of Hawaiian music and her strong desire to one day properly learn to hula dance are small ways she tries to connect with her Hawaiian heritage.

Her biggest accomplishments in life are becoming a published author, having her almost 10lb. daughter without an epidural, building her home piece by piece, dismantling and repurposing a 16,000 square foot horse arena, and the ability to stay married after doing all of these things together with her husband of 22 years.

Made in the USA
Middletown, DE
17 October 2020